A HISTORY OF
RUGBY

This new and revised edition first published in the UK in 2004
by Green Umbrella exclusively for
Sutton Publishing · Phoenix Mill · Thrupp · Stroud · Gloucestershire · GL5 2BU

First published in the UK in 2003

© Green Umbrella Publishing 2004

British Library Cataloguing in Publication Data
A catalogue record for this book is available from the British Library

Printed and bound in Hong Kong

ISBN 0 7509 3951 6

A HISTORY OF
RUGBY

The Origins of Rugby

A Split in the Ranks

The A – Z of Rugby

History of the Lions

The Southern Hemisphere Pt 1

The Southern Hemisphere Pt 2

The Greatest Ever XV

Record Breaking Players

A HISTORY OF
RUGBY

**History of the
Five / Six Nations**

**Amateur to
Professional**

**The
World Cup**

TABLE OF CONTENTS

Foreword by Rob Andrew 7

Chapter 1   The Origins of Rugby . . . . .9 - 18

Chapter 2   A Split in the Ranks . . . . .19 - 28

Chapter 3   The A – Z of Rugby . . . . .29 - 48

Chapter 4   History of the Lions . . . . .49 - 70

Chapter 5   History of the Five / Six Nations . . . . .71 - 96

Chapter 6   Amateur to Professional . . . . .97 - 110

Chapter 7   The Southern Hemisphere Pt 1 . . . .111 - 126

Chapter 8   The Southern Hemisphere Pt 2 . . . .127 - 138

Chapter 9   The Greatest Ever XV . . . . .139 - 156

Chapter 10   Record Breaking Players . . . . .157 - 168

Chapter 11   The World Cup . . . . .169 - 201

Index . . . . .202 - 207

ROB ANDREW

FOREWORD

Since the days when those young Rugby schoolboys famously picked up the ball and ran with it, the game of rugby union has undergone a transformation unmatched by any other sport in the world.

Rob Andrew

S *occer today is not too different from soccer in the mid-19th century, but if William Webb Ellis and his friends turned up at Twickenham today they wouldn't recognise the sport they helped to found more than 180 years ago.*

In this History of Rugby we've tried to do justice to the game's rich heritage, taking you on a fascinating journey that includes England's incredible World Cup triumph in Sydney, in 2003.

I played in both the amateur and professional era, so I speak from first-hand knowledge about the metamorphosis rugby has undergone since I made my England debut against Romania in 1985.

It was wonderful to flick through the chapters and, even for me, the memories came flooding back.

If we are to recognise the overwhelming appeal of our great game, it is important to delve into history, and appreciate the glory in the roots of rugby union. Names like Meads, Edwards, Lochore, Kyle and Blanco, and teams like the Lions, the Invincibles, the Originals and the Barbarians, all feature as we revisit the key stepping stones of rugby history.

The hardest part was fitting in every great player and great team, as this game of ours has produced legends by the score and sides that not only broke the mould but took rugby union on to greater heights.

So come with us on this journey, starting at Rugby School and the origins of the game, through the 20th century evolution of rugby right up to the first days of professionalism and England's 12th Grand Slam in 2003.

We take a look at some of the famous teams and individuals that have made rugby what it is today, and borrow the knowledge and authority of Rugby World magazine as we feature their greatest ever team (and before you ask, I didn't make it!).

Each of the major nations gets their own section and we also pay homage to some of rugby's finest institutions, like the Lions and the Home Nations (now Six Nations) Championship.

They say that if you want to know the future just study history... well, here's your chance.

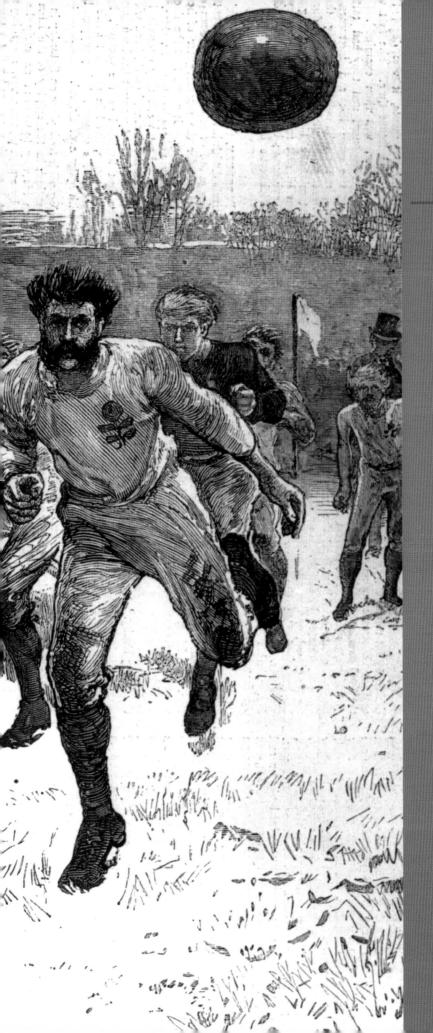

The Origins of Rugby

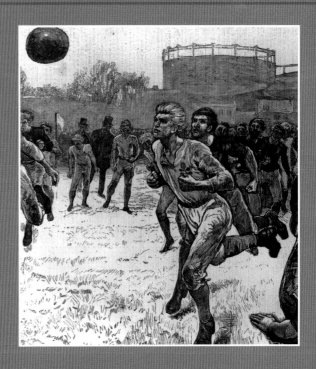

Chapter
ONE

• **Above**
Students playing at Rugby School.

• **Inset**
Rugby School Book of Football Rules.

Rugby School is the very soul of the game. First of all its pupils devised their own version of football (now known to the world as rugby football) and then, as former pupils, they helped to spread 'their' game throughout the world.

When we talk of 'football' being played at Rugby School, do not be misled and think of soccer. 'Football' is the term used for any game between two teams where a ball is kicked around or handled. Soccer (Association Football) is just one of these football games and rugby football is another.

All of the major public schools used to have their own unique version of football, developed by the pupils and descended from Medieval street football. These were incredibly rough and disorganised games that saw huge groups rampaging in pursuit of a ball throughout the Middle Ages. Not quite Wales against England at the Millennium Stadium!

Interestingly, soccer was the first major football game to remove handling of the ball for outfield players, and so it could be argued that soccer is the younger brother of rugby, which much more closely resembles Medieval football.

Football was being played at Rugby School from 1750 when the school purchased land for the boys to play on. From this point the game developed and changed as new rules and ideas came and went.

All of the senior boys had the opportunity to press for rules changes and in 1845 the boys wrote out their rules on paper for the first time. These were the first ever written football laws and they were an important factor in the growth of the rugby game. This allowed rugby, rather than the many other public school football games, to be spread easily to other schools and eventually around the rest of the country. The early rules of the game concluded that "if no decision is reached in five afternoons' play, a match will be declared drawn". Talk about player burn-out!

The old boys of Rugby School spread the word, as did Rugby School masters as they went to other schools and colleges.

In the early days matches were won by kicked goals, and one way to obtain a clear kick on goal was to cross the opponents' line. After he'd done so a player could 'try' and score a goal. So was coined the description of this touchdown.

Old boys of Rugby School arrived at Trinity College, Dublin to give the game its origins in

Ireland and again in Scotland, where Edinburgh staged the first games in 1858.

Edinburgh is the home of the oldest running fixture in the history of the game, Edinburgh Academy and Merchiston Castle first locking horns in 1858. Merchiston players were responsible for spreading the gospel of rugby to South Africa, when the civilians took on the military in 1862, and the Aussies came closely behind three years later, the Kiwis staging their first match in 1870.

Australia then established new ground as, after the Southern Union was established there in 1870, they became the first country to embark on a tour, to New Zealand in 1882. Their first club was Sydney University, which was formed in 1864.

Although the public schools dominated the game throughout the world, the one country where it quickly established working-class roots was Wales, where Neath lay claim to being the country's oldest club, kicking off in 1871.

Mirroring this the new sport also attracted working-class supporters in Yorkshire and Lancashire, a factor that was to become significant when the sport divided into two – union and league – in 1895.

International rugby arrived in 1871 but it bore absolutely no resemblance to England's victory over Scotland in March 2003, the 120th in the series. For one thing the sides in 1871 were 20-strong and not surprisingly the game was won, by the Scots, by the slim margin of a try and a goal to a try. England defence coach Phil Larder would have been in heaven with 20 defenders to deploy across the field.

Around 4,000 people watched that historic first International, at the Academy Ground, Raeburn Place, in Edinburgh. It was played over two periods of 50 minutes and a set of rules was varied to get the match staged, following a row that the Scots had narrowed the pitch to hamper the English backs.

• Above
An early England v Scotland international game.

• Below
Josh Lewsey scores a try for Engalnd during the 2003 Six Nations match against Scotland.

11

The English side weighed an average of just 12st 3lb. How times have changed! In 2003 the lightest Englishman in the pack when they beat Scotland 40-9 was Neil Back, who weighed in at 14st 9lb. Captain Martin Johnson was the heaviest and would tower over his 1871 counterparts at 18st 7lb.

Edinburgh Academicals was the dominant club, supplying six of the side, while for England there were four players each from both Blackheath and Manchester.

England had to wait until 1883 for their first victory on Scottish soil when almost 10,000 people saw them win in the first year of the International Championship, which was staged between England, Scotland, Ireland and Wales. England, with wins over the other three countries, completed the Triple Crown in that season and repeated the feat a year later.

That England v Scotland clash in 1871 was made possible by the formation of the Rugby Football Union (RFU) and their first job was to formulate a standard set of rules for the game to eliminate all of the variations being used.

The inaugural meeting of the RFU occurred just nine weeks prior to that match. Back in 1871, 21 clubs formed the Union. Today it has over 1,800 members.

Leonard Maton was given the task of drawing up a national set of rules for rugby (based almost exclusively on those employed at Rugby School) and he came up with 59, including the appointment of captains to resolve any disputes.

Until the RFU's 1871 rules it was possible to hack and hack-over in rugby. Hacking involved kicking an opponent's shins and hacking-over meant tripping them when they had the ball. I'm sure 130 years later Jonny Wilkinson and Jonah Lomu would have

been delighted with that first rules meeting! Nowadays, Rugby Union has 22 basic laws covering reams and reams of paper in the IRB handbook or on their website. Listing these laws would take up far too much space but to help our understanding of the game we'll take a look at some definitions:

Binding: grasping firmly another player's body from the shoulder to the hips with the whole arm from hand to shoulder.

Dead ball: when the ball is out of play. This happens when the ball has gone outside the playing area, or when the referee has blown the whistle to indicate a stoppage, or when a conversion kick has been taken.

Drop-kick: the ball is dropped from the hands to the ground and kicked as it rises from its first bounce.

Free-kick: a kick awarded to the non-offending team for an infringement by their opponents.

Front-row players: the three forwards who comprise the front row of the scrum, namely loosehead prop, hooker and tighthead prop.

Knock-on: when a player drops the ball in front

• *Opposite*
Neil Back during the 2003 Six Nations match between England and Scotland played at Twickenham.

• *Above*
The most capped front-row partnership ever – Australia's Phil Kearns, Anthony Daly and Ewen McKenzie.

• *Below*
An early England rugby match played at the Oval, 1872.

13

of him. A scrum to the opposition results.

Line of touch: an imaginary line at right angles to the touchline at the place where the ball is thrown in from touch.

Offside line: an imaginary line across the ground, from one touchline to the other, parallel to the goal-lines; the position of this line varies according to the facet of play.

Pass: a player throws the ball to another player backwards. If a player hands the ball to another player rather than throwing it, this is also a pass.

Penalty kick: a kick awarded to the non-offending team for an infringement by their opponents.

Possession: this occurs when a player or team is either carrying the ball or has it under their control; for example, on their side of a scrum or ruck.

Red card: this is shown by the referee to a player who has been sent off for an act of serious foul play.

Scrum: formerly named scrummage. This happens when (up to) eight players from each team bind together and push against the opposition to compete for the ball. The ball is thrown down the channel between the front rows and is hooked back.

Sin-bin: the designated area in which a temporarily suspended player must remain for 10 minutes.

Union: the controlling body under whose jurisdiction the match is played; for an international match it means the International Rugby Board (IRB) or a Committee of the Board.

Yellow card: this is shown by the referee to a player who has been cautioned and suspended for 10 minutes' playing time.

The first great reform in rugby was to change the size of the team as the sport began to develop into the game we see today in more than 100 countries across the globe.

The 20-a-side game became a casualty of history in the 1870s. Many clubs were having problems mustering 20 players for every match and some started to field 15 players in the 1873 season. They were perfectly entitled to do this since the laws did not specify the exact numbers required. In 1875 the first officially recorded 15-a-side match was staged, the Varsity Match between Oxford and Cambridge.

The unintended result was a faster and more skilful game than the rugby of the early days.

Another consequence of this change, once approved and set into the laws by the RFU, was that other teams further down the ladder found it easier to field sides.

A year later the international sides were also changed. When England ran out against Ireland in 1876 there were 30, instead of 40, players on the field.

With the rugby world settling on 15-a-side, the game began to form and positions were much more regimented. Another significant step arrived when more focus was put on the scrum. Today's fans wouldn't recognise the mess that passed for a scrum in the early 1870s. Fewer people on the field has made for a far more structured scrum and the ball gets out to the backs quicker, making for a more attractive game that has greater worldwide appeal.

The scrum was always the focus of rugby and before the sides were reduced to 15, each scrum could go on for five minutes at a time. Even Jason Leonard, who loves to scrummage, may have baulked at a five-minute scrum, although in those days there wasn't as much emphasis on physical

intensity as there is today.

In those early games there were no Jonah Lomu figures who picked up the ball and smashed their way through the opposition. In fact, it was perhaps closer to football because most of the time, when it wasn't in a scrum, the ball was kicked or even dribbled. Picking it up and running with the ball was a rare occurrence. Large groups of players used to put the ball in the middle of them and advance down the field in what must have been an astonishing, and probably terrifying, sight for the opposition. Players were seen in a gladiatorial light and passing backwards to a team-mate would be seen as a sign of weakness rather than tactical nous. They were encouraged to take the physical confrontation. Going through definitely made more sense to the Victorians than going round!

But once those five players from each side were removed it was harder to indulge in such tactics and, lo and behold, the players could see the ball for more of the game and actually make more use of it. Players were encouraged to get the ball out of those rucks and use it in a way they never had before.

The main aim of the reduction was to increase

• Above
'The Last Scrimmage', engraving by E Buckman, 1871.

15

• **Above**
In the early days
breakaway tries
were only awarded
one point.

the excitement of the game and this ethos was also the reason behind the many points changes. In soccer the scoring system is easy and will never need to change. One point, effectively, for a goal and that's that. But in rugby the points system has undergone massive changes since the game spread out from Rugby School in the 1840s, mainly because of the desire to empower or depower kicks and to place an emphasis – with more and more points for a try – on open, attractive play to please the crowds.

Many changes were made in the early days, as when rugby first emerged on the sporting scene no points were awarded. Each match was won by the number of goals (kicks through the posts) scored. In the event of a tie the number of tries scored was then calculated to determine the winner.

The first points system emerged in 1886 and awarded one point for a try, two for a conversion and three for a dropped goal or penalty goal.

Had that early scoring system remained rugby would have degenerated into farce with players queuing up to kick a drop goal and focusing their whole game plan on getting into position for the three-pointer!

The one-point try only survived until the 1890-91 season, when it was doubled to two, but it took 80 years to overtake the drop-goal in terms of points scored. The system went through many changes from the first game until in 1971 the value of a try was raised to four points. And 20 years after that we were given the current five-point try, two for a conversion, three for a penalty and three for a drop-goal.

Between 1891 and 1905 the drop-goal even moved up to four points and, in fact, none of the four current ways to score have maintained the same value since the start. Even the conversion spent two seasons in the 1890s worth three points.

Not all scoring methods have remained. Until 1977/8 players were allowed to score after making a mark and this was worth either three or four points. But from this season players were outlawed from calling for a mark outside their own 22 line. So until someone works out how to kick a drop-goal 80-odd metres from their own 22 it will stay outside the laws.

Kicking is still a crucial part of the game, but in the early days kicking was far more important than it is today. Before kicking the ball out on the full (without bouncing) from outside your own 22 was outlawed, it used to be a massive feature of the

game. Outside-halves who would kick their forwards downfield developed, but as with so many rule changes in so many games, revolution came after one particular and significant match. The days of the kicking fly-half were numbered when in 1963 Wales beat Scotland 6-0 in a match that featured more than 100 lineouts. Welsh scrum-half Clive Rowlands moved his forwards down the field and the Welsh won with two penalties. The Australians and New Zealanders had experimented just after the First World War with a law that meant you could not kick into touch unless you were behind the 25-yard line, and although it took the IRB 50 years to catch on to the idea from the south, catch on they did, in 1970. This new law not only changed the role of the outside-half but it proved a revolution for full-backs, who now had to develop a counter-attacking game. Full-backs of the 1970s and 1980s like JPR Williams and Serge Blanco thrived in this new era and the half-backs had to become more intelligent with their kicks outside the 25-yard line, having to make sure they bounced before going into touch.

• **Above**
JPR Williams kicks forward during the 1974 Lions tour match against South Africa.

• **Below**
Serge Blanco of France, one of the greatest full-backs of all time.

A Split in the Ranks

Chapter TWO

2

In the 21st century the rivalry between Rugby Union and Rugby League is intense. But if we look back at the history of the two sports this is not surprising considering the split that took place in the game of rugby in 1895 when one sport became two. There is no more significant date in the history of rugby.

The crux of the split, like the move to professionalism 100 years later, was money. In 1893 the Rugby Football Union received a proposal from members of the Yorkshire Union that clubs should be allowed to compensate players who lost wages from playing rugby. Mill and factory men still worked a six-day week and would have lost money by playing on a Saturday. Initially this proposal was rejected by the staunchly amateur membership of the RFU but that rejection was not accepted by certain clubs in Yorkshire and Lancashire – where the majority of their players were from working-class backgrounds and had more to lose, financially, from playing their sport.

The RFU refused to budge in two years of negotiations over the payment of players and eventually, before the start of the 1895-96 season, a handful of clubs from Yorkshire, Lancashire and Cheshire had had enough. They broke away to form the Northern Union, which was the inspiration for the formation of a completely new sport, Rugby League.

Ironically, many of the staunchest advocates of amateurism came from within these counties, notably officials of the Yorkshire Union and Lancashire clubs such as Manchester and Liverpool.

Initially 20 clubs resigned from the RFU and a new Northern League, which was the grandfather of the modern-day Super League, was formed for 22 clubs. More teams from the region would switch codes over the next few years.

Yorkshire were undoubtedly the strongest-playing county of the era: in 1889 12,000 people had attended a match at Halifax when Yorkshire took on the Rest of England, the England side winning by three goals to nil.

The two sports of union and league have lived in grudging acceptance of each other in Great Britain since the big split of 1895, one broadly regarded as a working-class pursuit (league) and the other as the property of the middle and upper classes (union).

Throughout those years, and until union went professional in 1995, the one source of friction was the way many of the great union players 'went north' and turned professional by moving to league. In return they were banned for life from union circles and, until 1995, were not allowed to retake the union field of play.

Once 1995 arrived the exodus changed direction and many union players who had gone to league, like Scott Gibbs, Scott Quinnell and Allan Bateman, returned to union. And as the next century dawned and the coffers of the union clubs expanded, they began signing some of the best league players, such as Jason Robinson, Henry Paul and Iestyn Harris.

Whereas Rugby League reverted to a 13-man game, Rugby Union has remained a 15-player game since that first 1875 Varsity match, although the formation of the XV was constantly evolving.

Moving into the 1880s most sides ran out with

• **Above**
Scott Quinnell of Wales powers his way forward during the 1997 Five Nations international against Ireland. Quinnell returned to Rugby Union from Rugby League after the game turned professional.

nine forwards and six backs as the game thrived on its forward-dominated roots.

Wales were pioneers in those times and became the first to use seven backs and eight forwards. Cardiff was the first club, under the influence of Frank Hancock, to use the extra back player. They started using this formation in 1884 but it was treated with suspicion in many quarters and it took some six or seven years to be universally adopted across the world.

Hancock's vision allowed the establishment of a scrum-half and outside-half who formed a partnership, as we see today, near the forwards. This concept was not adopted by the England team until Adrian Stoop (Harlequins) introduced it during the 1900s.

Forwards were also developing. In the early days the front row would be formed by the first two to arrive at the set-piece. So it seems it was better to arrive late and be in the back row than early and get stationed in the front row! It was inevitable that more rigid formations would take over and in the early part of the 20th century sides started defining forward play. The South Africans developed a formation that is still, with some minor modifications, in operation today. New Zealander Dave Gallaher was one of the first players to put huge emphasis on the wing-forward, or flanker. But the South African 3-4-1 scrum system, established in the 1920s, put even more emphasis on speed, releasing flankers on the side of the scrum. In the modern day it ensures players like Wallaby George Smith, England's Neil Back and France's Serge Betsen have a major influence on the outcome of matches. In 2004, with the tackle area now so important, these flankers can change the course of a game. And never was this better demonstrated than in the way Betsen ensured that France won the Grand Slam decider with England in 2002. The way he shackled Jonny Wilkinson in Paris was critical to France's victory and Betsen's influence owes much to the way Gallaher and the South Africans shaped the game after the First World War.

• **Above**
Jonny Wilkinson is stopped by Olivier Magne and Serge Betsen of France during the 2002 Six Nations Grand Slam decider between France and England at Stade de France, Paris.

• **Inset**
George Smith of the Wallabies during the Bledisloe Cup match between New Zealand and Australia in 2002.

• Above

The versatile Jason Leonard leads the England team out for his 100th Test, against France, in the 2003 Six Nations at Twickenham.

If Betsen, Back and Smith have the 1920 South Africans to thank for the way they play the game, then Jason Leonard, Sean Fitzpatrick, Ray McLoughlin and other front-row legends of the modern game should look to 1930s Lions Manager James Baxter. In the 1920s the New Zealanders had pioneered a new way of shaping the front row. The Kiwis went with two in the front, two behind and three in the back row. And you would see both those New Zealander front-rowers described as hookers rather than props. The idea of their system was to whip the ball out of the scrum quickly and into the arms of the backs.

But the New Zealanders hadn't bargained on Baxter and his 1930 Lions. When they arrived in the Land of the Long White Cloud, Baxter was enraged with the way the New Zealanders approached the front row.

Unfortunately for New Zealand, Baxter was a man of influence at the IRB and he soon got his way. They outlawed the Kiwi combination and changed the laws to ensure all front rows were made up of three players and so the modern-game scrum was formed.

A consequence was the emergence of props who could play on either the tighthead or loosehead of the scrum and Leonard, who became the first front-rower to win 100 international caps in 2003, is one of the few of his trade to be able to prop on either side.

Clearly, it took some time for the best formation of the XV to be finalised, but nothing like the time it took for a secure league structure to develop.

Twenty years after organised soccer arrived in England, the sides involved formed themselves into a league, but it took rugby union more than 116 years to establish the Courage Leagues for the English clubs. Friendlies and regional cup competitions prospered instead. Even the international game in the British Isles had been denied a league for the International Championship (now the Six Nations) and it was newspapers who drew up tables for this series of regular friendly matches.

The first proposal to have a league in England came in 1900 from Bristol, who felt it would help the development of the junior game. Rugby League had established a league system and Bristol, so soon after the split between the two codes, were worried that union would lose public interest and momentum if a league competition wasn't established. But it took until 1987 for the Courage Leagues to be formed. They resulted in a league pyramid that had around 1,160 clubs playing in 108 leagues, each with promotion and relegation.

Prior to the Courage Leagues, the John Player

Cup was introduced in England, in the 1971-72 season as a knockout competition for club sides. In the same year, Wales started the Schweppes Welsh Cup. North of the border the Club Championships began in Scotland in 1973-74.

A cup competition had started amongst the English counties in 1889 and before the advent of professionalism these counties and, above them, the English divisions represented the easiest way to be selected for the England team. Universities also played their part, indeed many of rugby union's roots lay deep in the British universities system, particularly at Oxbridge, where scores of internationals have been educated and groomed for our great game.

The BUSA Championship still prospers for the non-Oxbridge universities, but as we move further into the 21st century the student clash that generates the most publicity in the rugby world is the Varsity Match, between Oxford and Cambridge.

In 2003 the 122nd Varsity Match was drawn 11-11, the 14th tied game in the series. The game was remarkable in that despite being an amateur fixture in a professional era, it still attracted 42,000 people to Twickenham, the home of English rugby.

But the annual Varsity Match has changed since its early origins and in 2003 both Oxford and Cambridge forged links with the Australian RFU. It is envisaged that former professional players from Down Under,

after having stopped playing at the highest level, will take up postgraduate Oxbridge places.

The last 76 Varsity Matches have taken place at Twickenham, where Cambridge hold a 41-31 advantage. There have been four drawn games, in 1930, 1935, 1953 and 1965.

Former England full-back Alastair Hignell (Cambridge, 1975) and Ireland fly-half David Humphreys (Oxford, 1995) share the record for most individual points in a Varsity Match, with 19.

The oldest tournament in existence is a university competition, the United Hospitals Cup, which was won in 2004 by Imperial Medicals, a 20-0 victory over Guy's, King's and St Thomas' Hospitals. The University teams also have their role Down Under with Australia's Club Championship, the Sydney Premiership being won many times by Sydney

• **Above**
Oxford's Adam Slade is tackled by Charles Desmond of Cambridge during the 2003 Varsity Match.

• **Inset**
Mark Bailey of Wasps in action during an early John Player Cup match against Nottingham at The Park in Sudbury.

• **Above**
*Fabien Galthie, IRB
International player
of the year with his
trophy at the IRB's
Annual Awards on
January 26, 2003
held at the
Landmark Hotel in
London.*

University. Across the Tasman New Zealand's main tournaments are the National Provincial Championship and the Ranfurly Shield. The New Zealand province which wins the shield accepts challenges from other provinces. Auckland defended the title 26 times between 1960 and 1963 and Canterbury defended it 26 times between 1982 and 1985. In South Africa the main competition is the Currie Cup, an inter-provincial tournament which was first held in 1889. Western Province have been one of the most successful teams.

As of 1995 all three southern hemisphere countries competed in the Super 12 (a knockout competition involving the countries' best club sides) and the Tri-Nations (a series between the three national sides).

Having given organised rugby football to the world the RFU took a leading role in the early development of the game. Before the foundation of the various other national unions many of the early foreign clubs were members of the RFU – such as Dunedin (New Zealand), who were affiliated to the RFU from the 1870s until the NZRFU was founded in 1892.

Before the turn of the century arguments about the rules were commonplace and it is strange to think that it took until 1948 for the International Rugby Football Board (IRFB) to become a genuinely world-wide concern. England initially refused to join the organisation, which was set up by Ireland, Scotland and Wales in 1886. The others realised that the mother Union needed to be a part of the Board if it was to progress so England were tempted in, in 1890, with the offer of having six votes. The other three countries got two votes each, so without England's say-so nothing could be done.

Even though France started playing in the International Championship in 1910, they didn't get into the IRFB until 1958. The southern hemisphere giants of New Zealand, South Africa and Australia were admitted to the IRFB in 1948, but all three were only given one vote, compared to two each for the four Home Unions (England now falling in line with the other three home nations). The barriers were lowered further in 1987, when Argentina, Canada, Japan and Italy were admitted, but the original eight still receive two votes on international matters and the four newer members just one. The 12 nations themselves have grown immeasurably since they were founded. And today if you want to get anything done in the rugby world, you need the majority support of these 12 nations. They make every big decision, including where the Rugby World Cup is held (for detailed information on these 12 power brokers, see table overleaf).

Rugby is played in more than 100 countries and the IRB (the 'F' was dropped in the late 1990s) membership currently encompasses 94 national Unions and five Regional Associations. The historical membership has expanded enormously in recent times and encompasses all regions, races and peoples of the world.

The Executive Council of the IRB, which meets twice a year, has a membership of 21 with two seats held by each of the eight founding Unions, Scotland,

Ireland, Wales, England, Australia, New Zealand, South Africa and France. Argentina, Canada, Italy and Japan each have one seat on the Council as does FIRA-AER, the European Rugby Association. FIRA-AER has 35 members, ranging from Andorra to Yugoslavia. The full membership of the IRB meets at a General Meeting, currently convened every two years, and regional meetings are held at regular intervals. The day-to-day business of the IRB is carried out by a professional staff of over 30, who have been located in Dublin since September 1996.

The IRB organises and runs a growing number of global and regional events for both the 15-a-side and seven-a-side game. The Rugby World Cup, staged every four years, is the biggest of these events, making a huge global impact and providing a vital source of income for the development of the game worldwide.

The IRB Women's World Cup is the biggest event

in women's rugby. It takes place every four years and has been the catalyst for the tremendous growth of the women's game worldwide since the early 1990s. New Zealand (the Blacks Ferns) won the women's tournament in Barcelona's Olympic Stadium in 2002, beating England 19-9 in the final. The New Zealanders retained their title having won in Amsterdam in 1998.

The Rugby World Cup Sevens, also held every four years, is the biggest sevens event in the world. In addition, the IRB Sevens runs from around November to June every season and offers an enticing glimpse of many future stars of the sport in up to 12 venues across the globe.

The IRB also supports the development of young players, who are exposed to tournaments of an international stature in the form of the IRB Under-19 and Under-21 World Cups.

• Above
New Zealand women celebrate beating England in the 2002 IRB Women's World Cup Final match at the Olympic Stadium, Barcelona.

• **Above**
The All Blacks perform the 'haka' after victory against Fiji in the 2002 Commonwealth Games Men's Rugby 7's Final at the City of Manchester Stadium.

• **Inset**
Frantz Reichal, a member of the French Rugby team prepares for a throw in at a line-out during the 1900 Olympic Games in Paris.

• **Opposite**
Rugby's 12 Power Brokers who between them make every big decision in world rugby.

In addition to these global competitions, the IRB is committed to developing the game through regional events such as the European Nations Cup and the Pacific Tri-Nations.

Rugby is also a proud member of the family of world sports and of the International Olympic Committee (IOC). Full IOC status was confirmed in September 1997 for a non-participating sport. An application is under consideration for rugby's inclusion as a participating sport at the 2008 Olympics.

Rugby made its 15-a-side Olympic debut in 1900. The USA, gold medal winners in 1924, beating France 17-3, have been Olympic champions ever since. Rugby's emergence in the Games owed much to its popularity in America and it featured four times in total, in 1900, 1908, 1920 and 1924. But rugby was discontinued as an Olympic sport after 1924, due mostly to the lack of entrants. Only three countries, France, Germany and Great Britain, entered the first tournament in 1900. France were gold medallists that year but by the time Australia won the next gold medal, in 1908, they only had to play one match, against a British side represented by reigning county champions Cornwall.

Rugby, although of the seven-a-side variety, was a first-time medal sport at the 1998 Commonwealth Games in Kuala Lumpur, where New Zealand defeated Fiji in the final. This three-day event drew entries from 18 Commonwealth countries and a capacity crowd for the final day's play. The event proved equally popular at the 2002 Commonwealth Games in Manchester, where New Zealand again took gold.

The Asian Games also involves rugby tournaments, both 15 and seven-a-side. Winners of the sevens event at the 14th Asian Games in Busan, 2002, were Korea.

ARGENTINA - www.uar.com.ar

Unión Argentina De Rugby
Non-foundation Union - one vote on the IRB

Founded:	1899	Joined IRB:	1987
Full time staff:	8	Part time staff:	8
Rugby clubs:	317		

Male Players		Female Players	
Pre-teen:	10,000	Pre-teen:	0
Teenage:	15,000	Teenage:	80
Senior:	25,000	Senior:	80
Total male players:	50,000	Total female players:	160

No. registered players:	35,500	No. of referees:	355

AUSTRALIA - www.rugby.com.au

Unión Argentina De Rugby
Foundation Union - two votes on the IRB

Founded:	1948	Joined IRB:	1948
Full time staff:	116	Part time staff:	22
Rugby clubs:	752		

Male Players		Female Players	
Pre-teen:	15,114	Pre-teen:	0
Teenage:	65,821	Teenage:	0
Senior:	45,794	Senior:	1,572
Total male players:	126,729	Total female players:	1,572

No. registered players:	127,801	No. of referees:	?

CANADA - www.rugbycanada.ca

Rugby Canada
Non-foundation Union - one vote on the IRB

Founded:	1965	Joined IRB:	1987
Full time staff:	8	Part time staff:	2
Rugby clubs:	430		

Male Players		Female Players	
Pre-teen:	0	Pre-teen:	0
Teenage:	22,000	Teenage:	10,000
Senior:	12,000	Senior:	4,000
Total male players:	34,000	Total female players:	14,000

No. registered players:	16,500	No. of referees:	200

ENGLAND - www.rfu.com

The RFU
Foundation Union - two votes on the IRB

Founded:	1871	Joined IRB:	1890
Full time staff:	115	Part time staff:	45
Rugby clubs:	1,800		

Male Players		Female Players	
Pre-teen:	264,000	Pre-teen:	0
Teenage:	96,000	Teenage:	2,000
Senior:	174,000	Senior:	5,261
Total male players:	534,000	Total female players:	7,261

No. registered players:	634,460	No. of referees:	5,000

FRANCE - www.ffr.fr

The RFU
Foundation Union - two votes on the IRB

Founded:	1919	Joined IRB:	1948
Full time staff:	162	Part time staff:	82
Rugby clubs:	1,710		

Male Players		Female Players	
Pre-teen:	30,972	Pre-teen:	703
Teenage:	102,017	Teenage:	1,695
Senior:	93,470	Senior:	1,781
Total male players:	226,459	Total female players:	4,179

No. registered players:	252,638	No. of referees:	2,040

IRELAND - www.irishrugby.ie

Irish RFU
Foundation Union - two votes on the IRB

Founded:	1874	Joined IRB:	1886
Full time staff:	63	Part time staff:	2
Rugby clubs:	135		

Male Players		Female Players	
Pre-teen:	11,000	Pre-teen:	2,000
Teenage:	25,000	Teenage:	2,000
Senior:	11,500	Senior:	500
Total male players:	47,500	Total female players:	4,500

No. registered players:	47,500	No. of referees:	700

ITALY - www.federugby.it

Federazion Italiana Rugby
Non-foundation Union - one vote on the IRB

Founded:	1928	Joined IRB:	1987
Full time staff:	50	Part time staff:	114
Rugby clubs:	500		

Male Players		Female Players	
Pre-teen:	12,200	Pre-teen:	0
Teenage:	13,000	Teenage:	0
Senior:	9,000	Senior:	0
Total male players:	34,200	Total female players:	0

No. registered players:	39,856	No. of referees:	443

JAPAN - www.rugby-japan.or.jp

Japan RFU
Non-foundation Union - one vote on the IRB

Founded:	1926	Joined IRB:	1987
Full time staff:	20	Part time staff:	10
Rugby clubs:	4,050		

Male Players		Female Players	
Pre-teen:	21,632	Pre-teen:	0
Teenage:	42,638	Teenage:	0
Senior:	69,060	Senior:	500
Total male players:	133,330	Total female players:	0

No. registered players:	?	No. of referees:	?

NEW ZEALAND - www.nzrugby.co.nz

New Zealand RFU
Foundation Union - two votes on the IRB

Founded:	1892	Joined IRB:	1948
Full time staff:	50	Part time staff:	4
Rugby clubs:	520		

Male Players		Female Players	
Pre-teen:	36,183	Pre-teen:	1,840
Teenage:	23,892	Teenage:	2,932
Senior:	28,349	Senior:	2,022
Total male players:	88,424	Total female players:	6,794

No. registered players:	133,400	No. of referees:	2,384

SCOTLAND - www.sru.org.uk

Scotland RU
Foundation Union - two votes on the IRB

Founded:	1873	Joined IRB:	1886
Full time staff:	102	Part time staff:	29
Rugby clubs:	253		

Male Players		Female Players	
Pre-teen:	37,200	Pre-teen:	0
Teenage:	17,700	Teenage:	550
Senior:	10,500	Senior:	1,000
Total male players:	65,400	Total female players:	1,550

No. registered players:	33,593	No. of referees:	440

SOUTH AFRICA - www.sarugby.net

South Africa RFU
Foundation Union - two votes on the IRB

Founded:	1889	Joined IRB:	1948
Full time staff:	445	Part time staff:	850
Rugby clubs:	1,116		

Male Players		Female Players	
Pre-teen:	173,816	Pre-teen:	0
Teenage:	115,484	Teenage:	0
Senior:	145,000	Senior:	300
Total male players:	434,300	Total female players:	300

No. registered players:	361,302	No. of referees:	5,965

WALES - www.wru.co.uk

Welsh RU
Foundation Union - two votes on the IRB

Founded:	1881	Joined IRB:	1886
Full time staff:	85	Part time staff:	8
Rugby clubs:	372		

Male Players		Female Players	
Pre-teen:	5,500	Pre-teen:	600
Teenage:	32,000	Teenage:	500
Senior:	16,500	Senior:	500
Total male players:	54,000	Total female players:	1,600

No. registered players:	59,900	No. of referees:	522

The A - Z of Rugby

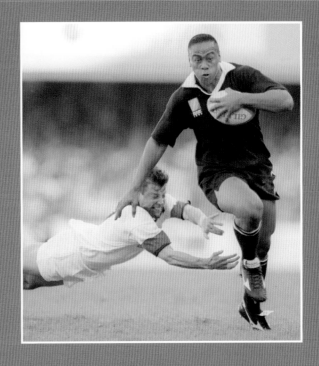

Chapter
THREE

3

A - Army rugby

The Army Rugby Union is unique in that it has a direct responsibility for its clubs wherever they serve in the world. Recently Brunei, Belize, Kosovo and Afghanistan have requested the mandatory RFU insurance.

The Guards and Cavalry played the earliest recorded game in the Army in a setting best known for the ill-fated Charge of the Light Brigade and the dedication of Florence Nightingale. The match was at Balaclava on 27 March 1855, in the middle of the Crimean War. *Three Men in a Boat* has its place in literature, but the Army Rugby Union owes its inception to three men in a railway carriage. Three Army officers, members of the Blackheath club, were returning from Scotland in the spring of 1906 when Lt 'Birdie' Partridge, later to play a Test for South Africa and have an England trial, proposed the forming of an Army Union. The War Office approved the suggestion and the Union opened for business on 31 December 1906. King George V, who became a regular supporter, honoured the Union with royal patronage and the use of the Royal Cypher as the Army's emblem.

An Army v Navy match had been played as early as 1878 at Kennington Oval. The Navy won by a goal and a try to a goal in that first match.

Wherever the Army served, the game was played, even in the heat of India on dried mud pitches. The Calcutta Club was an amalgam of the 3rd East Kent Regiment, the 62nd Wiltshire Regiment and a few local civilians. A free bar was one of the better traditions of the club but when this ceased for fiscal reasons, the membership drifted

away, the club folded and the rest is history.

Rugby was played throughout the two world wars and over the past century few Army teams have taken the field without a fair sprinkling of the 192 internationals to have worn the Army colours. Most recently Tim Rodber (England), and Scotland's Rob Wainwright and Mattie Stewart, have carried the flag, as did more briefly England pair Garath Archer and Josh Lewsey.

The ARU has struggled more than most to adapt to the full professional game. Players in the Premiership and national leagues expect financial rewards and conditions that the Army would not countenance. Nevertheless, the Army has a robust schedule culminating in May with the Army v Navy match at Twickenham. To quote The Daily Telegraph, the match is "a glorious anachronism which grows from year to year". More than 40,000 people attended the 2004 match, won by the Army 32-16.

The representative red shirt is now worn by the veterans, women, youth, under-21, sevens and tens teams. Some 200 regimental clubs play most weeks of the season, depending on the world situation. Seven challenge cups are at stake, including the Army Cup, which has been played for since 1907. The first winners were the Duke of Wellington's Regiment, which still turns out competitive teams.

The Army's most recent success was winning the Middlesex Sevens in 2001 and the Dubai club sevens in 2001 and 2002. Andy Dawling and Howard Graham have played sevens for England, Howard skippering the side in the IRB Sevens in Malaysia.

B - Barbarians

The Lions are Rugby Union's most famous team but running them a close second is a side that embodies flair, courage, spirit and passion – the United Nations of rugby, the Barbarians.

Winning and losing are never the most important things in a Barbarians match, as it is definitely a case of how you played the game.

They represent a glorious concept brought to life by the vision and enthusiasm of one man, William Percy Carpmael. Inspired by his playing experiences with both Blackheath and Cambridge University, his dream was to spread good fellowship amongst all

• **Above**
Tim Rodber passes the ball during a 1999 Five Nations match against Ireland at Lansdowne Road. He combined his early rugby career with his day job as an army officer serving with the Royal Green Howards.

rugby players. The dream became reality on 27 December 1890 at Friary Field, Hartlepool.

In Carpmael's vision this side had no ground, clubhouse or subscription, and membership was by invitation only, but that hasn't stopped the Barbarians becoming one of the most revered sporting institutions in the world.

They are a scratch side, with players from all over the world wearing the famous black-and-white hoops, black shorts and their own socks, to indicate the nations involved.

As a result of many scintillating performances, the Barbarians won respect worldwide and on 31 January 1948 they were invited to play the Australians in Cardiff in the final match of that tour. The battle captured the imagination of millions and drew a capacity crowd of 45,000. So successful was the fixture that it became traditional for Australia, New Zealand or South Africa – whichever was touring the UK – to tackle the Barbarians in 'The Final Challenge'.

Those great matches against touring sides hit a high point in 1973, when the Barbarians took on New Zealand at Cardiff's National Stadium, when Gareth Edwards finished off a length-of-the-field move to score arguably the most famous try in the history of the game.

Professionalism did threaten the existence of the Barbarians, and they have lost many of their traditional fixtures against club sides. But with great players like Jonah Lomu, Zinzan Brooke and Agustin Pichot backing the side, and the presence of its

spiritual leader and president Mickey Steele-Bodger never far away, they maintain a huge and respected presence in the world game.

Wilson Whineray described this great old club the best when he said: "Barbarian rugby is all about a feeling, spirit and essence to the game."

In 2004 the Barbarians embarked on another of their highly successful European tours, beating Scotland and England, but losing to Wales, as all three sides prepared for their summer tours.

C - Canada

British servicemen brought rugby to Canada, with the Royal Navy introducing the game at its bases in Halifax, Nova Scotia and Esquimalt, British Columbia in the 1860s.

Artillerymen in Montreal played the first recorded game in 1864 and concurrently Trinity College, Toronto, published the first set of Canadian rules for rugby. In 1868 the Montreal Football Club formed the first club, and in 1874 the first North American international game took place between McGill and Harvard Universities in Cambridge, Massachusetts.

The first documented game of rugby in Western Canada occurred on Vancouver Island in 1876 between the Royal Navy and an Army team. However, the British Columbia Rugby Union didn't form until 1889.

In the Maritimes, the game took hold with the formation of the Halifax Football Club in 1870 and, as other clubs appeared, the Maritime Provinces Rugby Union was established in 1890.

The famed North-West Mounted Police, made up of many expats and including Charles Dickens's son,

• **Above**
Barbarians' John Dawes makes a break against the All Blacks in that famous match at Cardiff Arms Park in 1973.

• **Below**
Ed Fairhurst of Canada in action during the 2002 Rugby Union tour match against Australia.

in 1965. In 1991 Canada joined the International Rugby Board and today Canadian rugby involves 100,000 people, with 220 men's clubs, 80 women's clubs and nearly 900 high-school teams across the Big Wheat Country.

D - Diego Dominguez

When Italy finally gained a place in the newly named Six Nations Championship in 2000, their entry owed much to the exploits of their Argentinian-born fly-half, Diego Dominguez. One of the greatest kickers the world has seen, Dominguez made his debut against France in 1991, and he completed his 13th season at the top level in 2003 as Italy's most capped back and second most capped player of all time.

He finished that 2003 Six Nations with 983 Test points, second in the all-time list to Neil Jenkins, who had scored 1,049.

Born in Cordoba in Argentina, Dominguez toured France with the Pumas in 1986, but after a move to France and then to Milan he decided to switch allegiance to Italy.

Having qualified for Italy through a grandmother, his debut came at centre but he was soon moved to outside-half, where he became Italy's greatest and most influential player.

But to regard him as a kicker alone would be to misunderstand the effect he's had on the Italian side. He controls and reads the game as well as the best in the business, and when you add in his kicking you have a world-class player.

His skills as a fly-half were evident when he played at No 10 during the 1991 World Cup, and he joined an elite band when he went on to feature in three World Cups.

At club level Dominguez has had a high-profile career as Stade Français' outside-half since 1997, and he was crucial when they lifted the French Championship a year later.

brought rugby to the prairies with the Manitoba, Alberta and Saskatchewan Unions forming in the early 1890s.

Because of its isolation behind the Rocky Mountains, British Columbia's (BC) teams competed with teams in the western United States and in 1906 when the New Zealand All Blacks were returning home through the USA, BC travelled to San Francisco to play them. Before that, Ireland toured eastern Canada in 1899, and in 1902 a Canadian team toured Britain, winning eight matches, losing 13 and drawing two.

After the First World War there was a marked increase in popularity as returning servicemen rejoined their old clubs. In 1919 a Canadian Services team played overseas matches against representatives from England, New Zealand, South Africa and Australia. In 1929 the Rugby Union of Canada formed, precipitating Canada's first official international tour to Japan in 1932, where they won five matches and lost two.

During World War Two, rugby participation waned, and after the conflict the game grew so slowly that by 1949 only three active provincial Unions remained.

Since then rugby has experienced a marked growth and the Rugby Union of Canada, which dissolved because of World War Two, reconstituted

• **Above**
Diego Dominguez (left) and Alessandro Troncon (right) of Italy celebrate victory after the 2003 Six Nations match against Wales held at the Stadio Flaminio, in Rome.

E - European Nations Cup

Tagged the second division of the Six Nations, the European Nations Cup has done a great job since its inception in 2000, supporting Europe's second-tier nations.

The Cup, European Nations Plate, Bowl and three regional divisions form a fully tiered 29 nations competition encompassing promotion and relegation through the various grades.

In 2003 the tournament was split over two years. Romania had won it in the inaugural year, 2000, and again in 2002. The rapidly improving Georgians took it in between.

Back in 2001, the tournament came down to a winner-takes-all clash between the Romanians and the Georgians. Romania had cantered to wins over Portugal (47-0), Spain (27-12), Holland (52-15) and Russia (42-13). Georgia, however, had to be at their sharpest in Russia and only some accurate kicking from fly-half Paliko Jimsheladze saw them scrape home 25-23.

In the decider against Romania, flanker Florin Corodeanu touched down in the 71st minute, and a late penalty sealed Georgia's 31-20 victory and the 2001 European Nations Cup.

But in 2002 Romania again took their place at the top of Europe's non-Six Nations sides as the Oaks, as Romania are known, took the honours thanks to a 31-23 win against Georgia on the last weekend of the tournament.

The game, played in Tbilisi, was the title decider and a crowd of 40,000 turned up to see if the Georgians could repeat their title triumph of 2001.

They failed, in part because Romania's fly-half Ionut Tofan was in fine form with the boot, kicking 16 points including a first-half drop-goal, but also because of the three Romanian tries scored by Cristian Sauan, Marius Tincu and Gabriel Brezoianu.

In 2004 the European Nations Cup had a new name on it when one of the emerging forces in European rugby, Portugal, claimed the crown.

This time the tournament was run over two years,

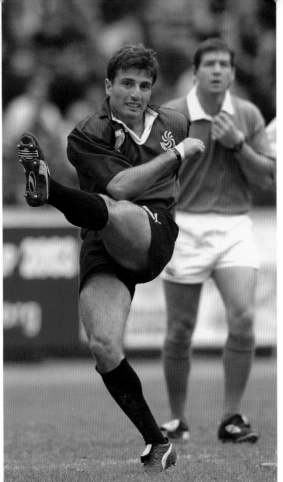

Portugal leading at halfway and then clinching the title with a 19-18 victory over Russia.

F - Fly-Half factory

Throughout the history of Welsh rugby, and even when the national side was losing, a factory producing great outside-halves never closed. From Percy Bush at the turn of the century to Cliff Jones in the 1930s to Cliff Morgan, who lit up the rugby world after the Second World War, through David Watkins, Barry John, Phil Bennett and Jonathan Davies, the Welsh nation has been blessed by players who wore the No 10 jersey.

The great Cliff Morgan, who made his debut for Wales in 1951, is accepted as one of the first who came off the production line, changing the very nature of the game in the post-war era.

One of Morgan's great rivals was the magnificent Irishman Jackie Kyle, who remembers him with affection: "Cliff was one of the great out-halves. He was brilliant on the Lions tour of South Africa in 1955, and they still talk about his performance on that tour there.

"The problem playing against Cliff was that I

● **Above left**
Georgia's Mako Urjunkashvili kicks a penalty during the 2003 Rugby World Cup qualifying match against Russia.

● **Above right**
Jonathan Davies of Wales during the 1987 Five Nations international against France. One of Wales' greatest ever players.

never knew what he would do next. That meant I was unable to concentrate on my own game as much when I played against him."

After Morgan Wales were blessed with two outside-halves in quick session as 'the Prince', Barry John, was followed in the side by Phil Bennett, both partnering Gareth Edwards at half-back.

Many felt John retired too early, playing his last game for Wales against France in 1972 aged just 27, before taking up a job with the Daily Express.

Wales No 8 Mervyn Davies said of him in Peter Jackson's *Lions of Wales*: "Barry was just about reaching his zenith. He should have stayed in rugby a damned sight longer than he did. The world never saw the best of Barry John.

"He was the first rugby superstar and he wanted to cash in on his fame."

John was the king of the pile when the Lions won that amazing series in New Zealand in 1971 and it was the turn of Bennett three years later, when the Lions won in South Africa.

Bennett's captain in 1974, Willie John McBride, said of him: "He was the best fly-half I've ever played with. You couldn't ask for a better team man."

Jonathan Davies followed these players into the Welsh team and achieved something they didn't – a fantastic career in rugby league.

He was arguably the greatest rugby union

convert to league, scoring 106 points in 12 Great Britain Tests and becoming the fastest man to 1,000 points in league history.

G - Grand Slams

The mythical Grand Slam trophy is awarded to the side that wins every match of a Five/Six Nations Championship. Throughout this book we have referred to a clean sweep of wins – especially in the championship – as a Grand Slam. But it is thought that the phrase wasn't coined until 1957, when England won every game and The Times and The Daily Telegraph used the phrase in their reports of the final game. Wales were the first side to take a Grand Slam in the Five Nations, in 1911, quickly followed by England, who won every game in both the 1913 and 1914 seasons. Wales were emphatic champions in that 1911 season, clinching the title with a 16-0 demolition of Ireland.

Except for Italy, every team has won at least one Five/Six Nations Grand Slam, Ireland's first (and only one) coming in 1948, Scotland's in 1925 and France's in 1968. England have won more Grand Slams than any other side, achieving their 12th in 2003. Wales (eight), France (eight), Scotland (three) and Ireland (one) follow England in the championship roll-call.

• Above
The French team celebrate their 2004 Grand Slam.

H - Heineken Cup

The arrival of professionalism demanded a pan-European competition fitting with the expansion of the game, and to compete with the status of the Super 12 in the southern hemisphere. So along came the Heineken Cup to give the Six Nations sides a second-tier competition that at times has been more intense than some of the international matches it aims to feed. At the beginning it was contested by club sides, except in the case of Ireland and Scotland, who entered districts or provinces.

The Heineken Cup started in 1996 and, reflecting the slow progress of the RFU in the professional era, it was in the early years dominated by French sides. Toulouse won the first competition, beating Cardiff 21-18 after extra time at the Welsh National Stadium. English teams failed to enter the first tournament and again in 1998-99, as politics took precedence over rugby. Brive were the second winners, 28-9 over Leicester in 1997, and in the third competition England produced its first winner, with Bath taking the trophy after three of the four semi-finalists came from France. Ulster prospered from the English boycott in 1999 to beat Colomiers 21-6 in the final and then began a period of English domination, reflecting the rise of the national side.

Northampton's 9-8 win over Munster in 2000 was followed by the incredible achievement of back-to-back wins by Leicester. In 2004 London Wasps became the fourth English side to lift the Heineken Cup, Rob Howley scoring a last-minute try as they beat Toulouse 27-20.

I - Andy Irvine

The greatest Scottish back of his generation and one of the greatest Scottish players of all time, Andy Irvine was his country's most-capped player when he retired in 1982, with 51 to his name. A counter-attacking full-back, in his 11-season international career Irvine, along with Wales' JPR Williams, changed the face of full-back play. Before Irvine and Williams most full-backs were concerned with defensive duties, but this duo turned the position into an attacking weapon.

After making his debut in 1972, Irvine scored a then world record 301 points, including ten tries for Scotland and one for the Lions. Irvine went on three Lions tours (1974, 1977 and 1980) and it was only the presence of Williams that stopped him racking up the Lions caps. His flexibility did ensure two caps for the legendary 1974 Lions, as he played on the wing in the last two Internationals, scoring a try in the 13-13 draw in the last Test.

• **Above left**
Wasps' hero Rob Howley with the 2004 Heineken Cup trophy.

• **Above right**
Andy Irvine in action during the 1974 Lions tour of South Africa.

J - Japan

Although the first recorded game of rugby in Japan took place on 24 February 1874, between two teams of British sailors on shore leave in Yokohama, it was another 16 years before the first game involving a Japanese side.

On 7 December 1901 a foreigners' team from the Yokohama Country and Athletic Club (YCAC) beat a side from Keio University 35-7 to set in motion events that would eventually see Japan have more clubs than other country in the world (4,050), and rank fourth in terms of the number of registered players (133,330).

Much of the credit for the sport's introduction lies with Ginnosuke Tanaka, a banker who attended the Leys School before graduating from Cambridge and Keio universities, and EB Clarke, an English professor at the Tokyo-based university (and Cambridge graduate), who set up the first Japanese rugby club at Keio.

Prior to the opening of Japan to the west in the 1870s, the only sports played in Japan had been 'Budo' or martial arts such as kendo (fencing), jujutsu (judo) and kyudo (archery), but new team sports such as rugby were quick to catch on.

In 1902 the YCAC took on their Kansai-based counterparts the Kobe Regatta and Athletic Club as part of the annual 'Interport' Sports Day, the YCAC winning 3-0. The two sides were instrumental in introducing the game to the increasingly westernized young men of Japan, and the fixture, like that between the YCAC and Keio, has been played nearly every year since then.

By 1907, Ota Junior High School in Gumma Prefecture had set up its own club and the game soon spread to the high schools and universities of Japan. The annual high school tournament played at Hanazono Stadium in Osaka is now in its 83rd year, while the first company championship and university championship were played in 1948 and 1964 respectively. The oldest sevens tournament is the YCAC invitational tournament, which this year celebrated its 45th anniversary.

The Japan Rugby Football Union was established in 1926 (with Tanaka as its first honorary president) and admitted into the IRB in 1987. The national team, known now as the Cherry Blossoms, played their first International in 1932 against Canada, winning 9-8.

In 2003 a new professional league – the Top League – was launched featuring the top 12 corporate sides in the country, and it is hoped that it will help rugby union cement itself as the fourth most popular sport in Japan behind baseball, sumo and soccer.

K - Jackie Kyle

The inspiration behind Ireland's Grand Slam win in 1948, Jackie Kyle OBE was a majestic outside-half and the dominant figure in Irish rugby from his debut in 1947 until his retirement after guiding Ireland to a

12-6 victory over Scotland in 1958. Those years were simply known as the 'Jackie Kyle era' in Irish rugby circles. An outside-half with vision and the ability to read any game, the diminutive Kyle hurt sides not only with his acceleration but also with outstanding tactical kicking.

A superb cricketer as well, Kyle is remembered in John Scally's book *The Giants of Irish Rugby* as one of the best to pull on the green jersey. Kyle is a modest man but he told Scally: "The famous poet Louis MacNiece was doing a radio broadcast here in Belfast one evening.

"He was asked if he could make one wish what would it be. His answer was that he would love to play rugby like Jack Kyle. That's the compliment that meant the most to me."

With Kyle in his pomp, Ireland not only won the Grand Slam in 1948 but the championship in both 1949 and 1951, only failing to complete the clean sweep in 1951 after a 3-3 draw with Wales in Cardiff.

Kyle played in all six Tests for the Lions on their first tour after the Second World War, when they travelled to New Zealand and Australia in 1950. He scored a try as the Lions drew the first Test 9-9 in Dunedin.

L - Leicester

One club side handled the move to professionalism in the northern hemisphere better than any other, reigning supreme in England and Europe in the years after the game went open – Leicester. Coached by Dean Richards and John Wells, in the late 1990s and at the start of the new century they left an indelible mark on English and European rugby. Before the game turned professional, Leicester battled for supremacy with Bath. But once the Tigers had won their first English title in the professional era in 1999, the season they were forced to abandon

their famous lettered shirts, they were unstoppable, completing four consecutive English championship victories and lifting back-to-back Heineken Cups in 2001 and 2002. In those four years of dominance in England, that ended in 2003, Leicester were, for the majority of that run, invincible at home and they went 57 matches undefeated in the Premiership at Welford Road between 30 December 1997 and 30 November 2002, when Northampton beat them. Their incredible run included 52 successive wins.

The Tigers, who were captained by Martin Johnson for all four of their titles, lost only 14 of the 92 Premiership matches they played over those four championship-winning seasons.

In claiming that last title in 2002, Leicester had it pretty much won by Christmas. They lost just four times in that season, scored more tries (72) than anyone, and conceded just 19, 17 less than the next best, Northampton.

Their relentless pursuit of those titles was the reason for their success. As soon as the fourth one was in the trophy cabinet, chief executive Peter Wheeler was already looking ahead. He said: "Nothing is taken for granted. There's a good work ethic here, a self-critical attitude too. Complacency isn't tolerated." In addition to their four successive titles, Leicester made the record books by winning three consecutive English Cups from 1979 to 1981.

• **Above**
Leicester's Martin Johnson raises the trophy after winning the 1999 Allied Dunbar Premiership. Leicester went on to win a further three Premiership titles.

M - Willie John McBride

Whenever you think of the most famous rugby team in the world, the British and Irish Lions, then one man springs to mind, their eternal spirit Willie John McBride.

The second-row from Toomebridge, County Antrim first played for the Lions on the 1962 tour, and he completed an incredible five-tour career for the best of British and Irish rugby on the 1974 tour to South Africa, where he was captain. He played a record 17 times for the Lions, giving them a resilience that helped ensure their historic series victory in South Africa in 1974.

Willie John McBride OBE played 63 times for Ireland, and by the end of the 2003 Six Nations he remained second in the all-time table of capped Irish players, behind Mike Gibson. And in 1973 he surpassed Hugh McLeod's (Scotland) record of 43 consecutive appearances in international rugby, finishing his career with an uninterrupted run of 52 Tests.

McBride was educated at Ballymena Academy and, after impressing with the Ballymena club, was

rewarded with a call-up to the Ulster side to face the touring Springboks in 1960.

His finest hour was on the 1974 Lions tour to South Africa when he led the side to a 3-0 series victory, with the final Test drawn.

South African provincial sides and the national team tried to intimidate the Lions but they hadn't considered the McBride effect and he pulled the squad together.

"It was the biggest challenge of my life," McBride recalls, "trying to get coal miners from Wales and solicitors from London to mix together. Those guys had a great attitude to life."

McBride coined the '99' call for use when a Lions player was in trouble on the field, which worked on the principle that if everyone joined in the referee couldn't send the whole team off.

It was clear how much regard these Lions, some of the most famous players the rugby world has seen, had for McBride. When the tour ended they presented him with a silver jug engraved: 'To Willie John. It was great to travel with you'.

In 1974 McBride captained Ireland to the Five Nations title, their first honours for 23 years, and he ended his career on a high note, scoring his only try for his country in his last home Test match, the 25-6 win over France in Dublin in 1975.

• **Above left**
Willie John McBride in action for Ireland against Wales in the 1968 Five Nations match at Lansdowne Road.

• **Above right**
Namibia's Johan Zaayman in action during the 1999 Rugby World Cup match against Fiji played at the Stade de la Mediterranee, Beziers, France.

N - Namibia

Namibia, which was formerly South West Africa, won the single direct qualifying place for African sides in the 2003 World Cup.

They also qualified for the 1999 World Cup, where they lost 67-8 to Fiji, 47-13 to France and 70-11 to Canada, and in 2003 they lay 20th in the Zurich World Rankings, just behind USA and Uruguay.

Rugby in Namibia started during World War One when South African troops arrived in Windhoek.

First structured as the Damaraland Rugby Union, most games tended to be between members of the services, but gradually railway workers and staff of commercial banks began to join in.

Before independence Namibia's players were available to play for South Africa and the region produced some Springbok legends, including Jan Ellis and Frik du Preez.

In 1954 the territory gained admission to South Africa's Currie Cup competition and it was also decided to change the name to the South West Africa Rugby Union.

South West Africa's first taste of international rugby came in 1955 when they met the touring British and Irish Lions at Mabel Vlok Park in Windhoek on July 5, only losing 9-0.

But since independence in 1990 rugby has tended to wane as many players sought greater opportunities in South Africa. On 19 February 1990, the Namibian Rugby Union was formed with Gert Muller, former president of the SWARU, as its first president. This development not only brought together fierce enemies but paved the way for Namibian rugby's participation on an international level.

The former South West Africa used to have the head of a zebra as their badge while the Namibian National Rugby Union used a depiction of an ancient and hardy desert plant, the welwitschia. Shortly after unity was achieved, both badges appeared on the dark blue national jersey, with red-and-white trim, before being replaced by Namibia's new national emblem – a fish eagle.

0 - 0-0 draws

In the modern era the IRB have changed many laws to increase the number of try-scoring opportunities and the prospect of seeing a 0-0 draw in international rugby gets more and more remote. But that wasn't always the case and in Test-match history 25 games have ended 0-0 at full-time, but only eight since the war.

The last major International to finish scoreless was at Murrayfield in 1964, when Scotland took on New Zealand. It was a significant draw in that it was the final match of the All Blacks tour and the scoreline denied the tourists the chance of being the first New Zealand team to defeat all four nations on tour, and claim a Grand Slam.

In the book *Men In Black*, the game is remembered along with the attempts, which included a number of drop-goals from both sides, to register at least one point: "As time moved on a hint of desperation crept into the play on both sides. Clarke [Don] attempted a further long-range penalty from nearly 60 yards but the kick passed just wide of the posts."

A year before the Scots and the Kiwis drew 0-0 came the last Five Nations match to end scoreless. Ireland and England drew 0-0 in 1963, preventing England from picking up a Grand Slam.

The first 0-0 draw was only the third Test in history, between Scotland and England at Hamilton Crescent, Glasgow on 3 March 1873. The last 0-0 Test match was Italy v Portugal in Padova on 20 February 1972.

• **Above**
Scotland draw 0-0 in New Zealand, the last major international to finish scoreless.

P - Francois Pienaar

When South Africa returned to international rugby in 1992, the apartheid regime crushed, they needed a sporting leader with the qualities of a statesman and they found one in Francois Pienaar.

On the field Pienaar emerged on to the international scene after leading Transvaal, for whom he played 100 times, to Currie Cup victories in 1993 and 1994 and then into the Super 10, where they beat Auckland in the 1993 final. He made his international debut in 1993 against France.

After the 1996 Tri-Nations, when the Springboks were hammered, Pienaar was replaced as captain and back-row forward by Gary Teichmann. Pienaar then moved to English club Saracens, where he won the Tetley's Bitter Cup in 1998 as a player before becoming the club's coach and chief executive. He returned to South Africa in 2002.

He won all of his 29 South African caps as

captain, and at the end of the 2003 season only Teichmann had captained the South Africans more times.

But it was at the 1995 World Cup where Pienaar gained legendary status, leading the Rainbow Nation to the Webb Ellis Trophy on their return to international rugby. South Africa president Nelson Mandela said of him: "Francois Pienaar's leadership extended way beyond the rugby field."

In his best-selling autobiography *Rainbow Warrior*, Pienaar said: "Can any rugby player ever have known a prouder moment? Can any Springbok ever have been so fortunate to be on that podium that day?

"I have since been surprised to read how many people, from other countries, recall the day as the fondest memory in their rugby lives. Somehow the emotion within the stadium and throughout the country went far beyond sport. It represented the unification, however brief, of a country once so cruelly divided."

Q - Queensland

The Australian state that has provided scores of Wallabies was crucial to the development of our game. Rugby was first played in Queensland (QRU)

in 1867 and in 1897 the All Blacks played two matches against the state as the game of Rugby Union took hold. But after the First World War many of the biggest players moved to Rugby League, and Queensland came under siege from the rival sport. Rugby Union almost disappeared altogether, only reviving in 1929. In that same year the QRU renewed annual matches with New South Wales (NSW) and when the Wallabies played New Zealand there were five Queenslanders in the side that beat the All Blacks 3-0.

Rugby in Queensland was in such a state after the First World War that their oldest club, Brothers, actually played league and when the Brisbane rugby competition resumed in 1930, the club went back to union. Since then Queensland, and lately the Queensland Reds Super 12 side, have greatly contributed to the strength of Australian rugby. As Jack Pollard explains in his book *Australian Rugby*: "Queensland's playing strength has steadily improved and many great players have worn the Queensland jumper, men like Mark Loane, Paul McLean, Jules Guerassimoff, Tony Shaw, Roger Gould and Brendan Moon." He adds that their performances against NSW "confirmed its claim to

be regarded as the strongest state in Australia".

Since the 1970s Queensland have recorded victories over the Lions and the All Blacks, and won the Super 10 twice, in 1994 and 1995. Queensland topped the Super 12 table in 1996 and 1999 and also qualified for the play-offs in 2001. But on each occasion they failed to make the final.

R - Romania

If there had been a World Cup in the early 1980s the Romanians would have been one of the favourites, such was their impact on the game before the Ceaucescu government led the country into chaos.

Throughout the 1970s and 1980s, Romania challenged, and often beat, the very best that Britain and Ireland could offer, yet they were never invited to take their place in the Five Nations.

The Romanians, increasingly beset by economic problems, suffered further under the nightmare Ceaucescu regime which eventually resulted in the bloody revolution of 1989. Sport almost ground to a halt, central government funding dried up and the necessities of life took precedence.

Their pedigree before the regime is exemplary. During a tour of New Zealand in 1975 they drew with the Junior All Blacks and in 1979 went down 13-12 in Cardiff to a virtually full-strength Wales XV. In 1980 they put in two of the finest performances seen by a touring side to the UK, beating Munster 32-9 at Thomond Park and destroying reigning John Player Cup holders Leicester 39-7 at Welford Road.

The same year they beat France 15-0 in Bucharest and in 1982 they repeated the exercise with a 13-9 triumph on home soil. In 1983 they outplayed Eddie Butler's Wales team to win 24-6 and a year later the Scots, fresh from a Grand Slam, were defeated 28-22. For ten years they remained unbeaten against Italy.

Even later in the 1980s they were still beating the best – Wales in Cardiff in 1988, France in Auch in 1990, Scotland in Bucharest in 1991.

But the World Cup came too late for them. Had it been staged in 1983 they were possible semi-final material but by 1987 they were enduring a frustrating dip in form. They started the Finals with a 21-20 win over Zimbabwe, but lost 55-12 to France and then 55-28 to Scotland, in the key game. Florica

• **Above**
Romania battling against a strong Australian team during the 1999 Rugby World Cup match played at Ravenhill Park in Belfast.

like Formula One does in motor racing, to all parts of the globe.

The Middlesex Sevens has an illustrious history but the World Series, launched by the IRB in 1999, has introduced the game into many new territories. Since its inception, the World Series has been played in 16 countries across five continents and no fewer than 46 countries have participated.

New Zealand dominated the World Series in its early years, winning the first three competitions, in 2000, 2001 and 2002.

Murariu scored two tries in that game but, tragically, was gunned down at a checkpoint two years later during the revolution. Former Romania captain Raducu Durbac also perished in the hostilities, as did many grass-roots players, supporters and coaches.

In 1995, Romania found themselves in an incredibly tough, physical group containing South Africa, Australia and Canada. Outclassed 34-3 against the Canadians in Port Elizabeth, they rallied to perform with superb courage against South Africa, the eventual champions, at Newlands.

South Africa could only manage a 21-8 win and Romania scored the try of the game through flanker Andrei Guransescu. They ran out of steam a little in the final game, losing 42-3 to Australia.

In 1999 the Romanians had the misfortune to be drawn in the same pool as the eventual winners, Australia, and Ireland, but they chalked up their second win at the World Cup Finals, beating USA 27-25 at Lansdowne Road. They will be back at the World Cup in Australia in 2003.

S - Sevens

The shortened version of the 15-a-side game has its roots in Scotland, inspired by a butcher from Melrose, Ned Haig, in 1883. After the First World War a sevens circuit grew up in the Scottish Borders and to this day most of them still thrive, sevens becoming a big part of the Scottish rugby culture. Since 1999 the International Rugby Board have harnessed the lure of sevens with an international event or World Series, that takes the game, rather

Perhaps the most famous sevens tournament in the world is the Hong Kong Sevens. This annual jamboree kicked off in 1976, and in the early years the title was confined to southern hemisphere sides, but England produced a hat trick of wins there between 2002 and 2004. The staging of the Five/Six Nations at the same time as the Hong Kong event has allowed the southern hemisphere their opportunity to dominate.

The Rugby World Cup arrived in 1987, but it took until 1993 for an equivalent tournament for sevens. The first event, fittingly, took place in Scotland and ended with a scratch England side beating Australia 21-17 in the final. Four years later there was a public holiday declared in Fiji when they lifted the World Cup in Hong Kong, beating South Africa 24-21 in the final.

And in 2001 New Zealand became the third different winner, taking the trophy with a 31-12 victory over Australia.

Rugby sevens made its debut at the 1998 Commonwealth Games in Kuala Lumpur, where New Zealand won gold. They repeated the feat in Manchester four years later, Fiji again picking up the silver medal.

At the 2002 Games in Manchester, the five sessions of sevens attracted 130,000 spectators, second only to the numbers watching the athletics.

The biggest sevens event in the world is the Rosslyn Park Schools tournament which annually attracts over 3,000 schoolchildren.

• **Above**
The England players celebrate their third consecutive Hong Kong Sevens Trophy after victory over Argentina in 2004.

T - Twickenham

The most famous rugby ground in the world started life as a cabbage patch before the RFU treasurer, William Cail, paid out £5,573 for it in 1910, after it was discovered by committee member Billy Williams.

Now that same cabbage patch – first used for an England rugby match in 1910 – is being transformed, starting in 2003, into a stadium with a wraparound roof, 82,000 seats, an in-house hotel, health club and leisure centre, ready (it is hoped) for the start of the 2004-05 season.

In the early days the RFU shared their home with Harlequins, so the first match staged there was not an International but a 14-10 win for the Quins over local rivals Richmond, in 1909. The first Test match came a year later when England beat Wales 11-6, in a season when they won the championship. Television cameras moved into Twickenham for the first time in 1938, and the great old stadium even survived being bombed in the Second World War. The ground staged the second Rugby World Cup final in 1991.

U - United States

Rugby's roots in the United States go back to the 1880s, when at times it looked like the USA would emerge to challenge the greatest nations. American rugby in the early 20th century thrived in California,

as universities like Stanford and California embraced the sport. An American Universities side toured New Zealand in 1910, with Australia and then the All Blacks returning the favour in 1912 and 1913 respectively. Stanford and California formed the nucleus of a powerful, athletic USA team that won gold at the 1920 and 1924 Olympics.

But while rugby was played before huge crowds into the 1920s, it was American Football that captured the independent spirit of the American sports fan. Banned from 1906 to 1914 for being too dangerous, gridiron re-emerged thanks to a professional league started in 1919. It was rugby's turn to be ignored, and it wasn't until the 1960s that rugby regained any following in the USA.

By then, rugby was a sport for the anti-establishment. The college teams were clubs, not varsity sports, and that freedom was refreshing. Encouraged by expats from rugby-playing nations, rugby spread to clubs in Boston, New York and Chicago.

• **Above**
A general view of Twickenham, host to the 2003 Six Nations match between England and France.

• **Inset**
USA Captain Dave Hodges battles with a Canadian defender during the 2003 Rugby World Cup qualifying match. Canada defeated the United States 36-13.

The 1965 University of California team under the great 'Doc' Hudson completed a successful southern hemisphere tour, drawing with Queensland. Coach Dennis Storer took a California Grizzlies team to New Zealand in 1972, losing narrowly to the Maoris and beating New Zealand Universities.

The USA Rugby Football Union was formed in 1975 and so started a sometimes rocky transition from counter-culture statement to a serious, professionally-run sport – a struggle that continues to this day. By the end of January 1976, the Storer-coached USA national team had played its first Test, a 24-12 loss to Australia. A year later there was a tour of England, and the first of what has now been 33 Tests against arch-rivals Canada.

One of those early Eagles was Jack Clark, whose career was shortened through injury and instead he took up the coaching reins of University of California, and then the USA national team. One of the most influential men in the sport, Clark returned California to the role of perennial champions and revitalised the national team into a self-funded programme with a regular Test schedule.

The women's game grew out of pockets in Florida, California, and the North-east, and stars like Jen Crawford, Krista McFarren and Patty Jervey led the USA to a World Cup title in 1991 and two more final appearances, in 1994 and 1998.

Throughout the world, American rugby has benefited from the talents of a few who have found rugby careers overseas. Current national team coach Tom Billups was among the first, while professionals Dan Lyle and David Hodges have gained reputations as dedicated and world-class rugby players.

Domestically Americans compete for 22 different national championships. The number of clubs continues to grow, topping 2,000 in 2002. The line between recreational and serious, professional rugby remains blurred but while youth-grade numbers are flat globally, under-19 rugby is still growing in the

United States, vying with college as the American athlete's first exposure to the sport.

V - Varsity Match

It is still one of the wonders of the modern rugby world. How on earth do the RFU manage to get more than 40,000 fans to Twickenham on a cold December afternoon every year to watch two university sides, Oxford and Cambridge, battle it out for the Varsity Match? The answer lies of course in rugby's great history and the number of former Oxbridge graduates working in London.

It's one of the oldest regular clashes in the game and is an annual pilgrimage to the home of English rugby for many people.

Cambridge University Rugby Union Football Club (CURUFC) was officially founded in 1872, three years later than Oxford University RFC. The first Varsity Match was played in 1872 and the Rugby School influence was still apparent, with eight out of the 20 players in the Cambridge team being Old Rugbeians.

The venue of the match changed in the early years and after the First World War, in 1919 and

• **Above**
Jason Wright of Cambridge charges upfield during the 2002 Varsity Match.

1920, it settled at the Queen's Club. But with this ground too small to accommodate the growing crowds, the fixture was switched to the new RFU ground at Twickenham, where the first Varsity Match was staged in 1921.

The Varsity Match was first sponsored by the Bowring Group in 1976, who provided financial support to secure the future of this historic fixture. The company merged with Marsh & McLennan companies in 1980.

In 2003 the match was drawn, 11-11.

W - Women's rugby

One of the fastest growing sports in the world, and the fastest in the UK behind women's soccer, women's rugby is gaining more and more attention every year. The number of women's and girls' clubs has climbed from 12 to a massive 450 in England in 20 years – that's around 8,000 trained players according to the Women's Rugby Football Union (RFUW).

The first women's International was France's 4-0 win over Holland in 1982 and in 1986 the RFUW staged a game between Great Britain and France, which the French won 14-8 at Richmond, giving the game in Europe the kick-start it needed.

The first World Cup was held in 1991, with USA toppling England 19-6 in the final.

The Scottish Rugby Union staged the 1994 event, after Holland withdrew, and this time England won, beating the United States in the final.

But in 1998, the tournament moved to a new level, with the arrival of both Australia and New Zealand into the competition. The Black Ferns, as the New Zealand side are known, won that tournament and finally gave the women's game a team to copy and admire.

They swept England aside 44-11 in the semi-final and beat USA 44-12 in the final, wing Vanessa Cootes scoring five tries.

The IRB backed the Women's World Cup in 1998, and in 2002 the biggest tournament to date was staged in Spain, with the final at Barcelona's Olympic Stadium, New Zealand retaining their title with a 19-9 win over England.

"I suppose the breakthrough for us came in 1996 when we competed in the Canada Cup tournament," said Darryl Suasua, who coached New Zealand to both their World Cup triumphs.

"Rob Fisher, then the NZRFU chairman, accompanied us and was so impressed it was decided that the whole might of the Union be thrown behind us."

In England the elite women players have benefited from funding through the national lottery. Carol Isherwood is one of the driving forces behind the women's game in that country. She was there as a player in the 1980s and in 2003 remained as the RFUW's performance director.

"Things have changed so much since those days when we started out," Isherwood said. "We were already doing well before the money because of the commitment and vision of a lot of people but clearly it's helped improve our game."

● **Above**
Sharon O'Kane of Australia is tackled by second row Teresa Andrews of England during their 2001 international. England won the game 41-19.

In Europe, England are far and away the dominant side, and they took the 2003 Grand Slam while conceding just one try, to Wales.

England's women made history in 2003 when they staged the first International at Twickenham, beating France 57-0 on their way to the Grand Slam. Saracens No 8 Clare Frost had the honour of becoming the first woman in an England shirt to score a try at Twickenham.

X - Cross-code moves

Once Rugby Union was fully professional, one of the big questions was: how do we treat those who went to Rugby League? With open arms was the answer as many of the players who had given up the union game earlier in their careers to be paid to play Rugby League made the return journey.

Wales outside-half Jonathan Davies was the first league player to return to union, in 1995, eight years after moving to rugby league.

After the union players came back, the union game began raiding league for some of their best players. In Britain players like Henry Paul (Gloucester), Iestyn Harris (Cardiff) and Jason Robinson (Sale) were the stars of the league code that switched to union.

Robinson was by far the most successful convert. England coach Phil Larder explains: "Jason is probably the most dynamic, exciting runner in the game. His great talent is his footwork. He can create

a hole from nothing. He is very dangerous close to the breakdown where he is attacking front-five forwards."

The same happened in Australia, with league players like Wendell Sailor and Mat Rogers turning their back on league for union and boosting the Wallaby ranks, similar to the way union had suffered from an exodus to league in previous decades.

Y - Youngest international

The youngest player to feature for one of the eight foundation nations of the IRB is, according to the International Rugby Yearbook, Jack Hartley. He was a mere slip of a lad at 17 years and 18 days when he played his one and only Test match for South Africa in 1891 against the British and Irish Lions. He played on the wing as the South Africans lost 4-0. Hartley beat Scotland's NJ Finlay to the title by 18 days, Finlay representing Scotland against England in 1875.

In the modern era two players broke the mould: Claude Dourthe set the French record when he played against Romania in 1966 aged 18 years and seven days; and the New Zealand mark is held by the great Jonah Lomu, who made his debut in 1995

• **Above left**
Jason Robinson scores England's third try against Australia in the 1995 Rugby League World Cup at Wembley.

• **Above right**
Jason Robinson during the 2003 Rugby Union Six Nations match against Scotland at Twickenham.

when he was just 19 years and 45 days old.

The book *Men In Black* commented: "The game had a crop of significant milestones...and it was the debut for an All Black of whom more later would be heard, a south Auckland Tongan-New Zealander by the name of Jonah Tali Lomu. At 19 years and 45 days, he became the youngest All Black to play a Test."

Lomu failed to score on that debut, as France won 22-8.

Z - Zurich Premiership

The most competitive domestic competition in the world is the Zurich Premiership. Its standard has taken a share of the credit for England 's victory in the 2003 World Cup. Leagues kicked off in England in 1987, with the establishment of the Courage Leagues.

The Courage Leagues were transformed when the title sponsorship was taken over by Allied Dunbar and at the end of the 1990s by Zurich, the Zurich Premiership.

At the start of the English league structure Bath and Leicester dominated proceedings and in the first ten years their monopoly was only broken twice, both times by Wasps.

Over the years the format of the league developed and today we see sides play every other side in the Zurich Premiership twice a season, away and home.

Bonus points are awarded for tries scored and for teams that lose by less than seven. The champions are decided by a play-off with the side finishing third in the Premiership playing the side that finishes second for the right to play the top side in a Grand Final, at Twickenham.

The first year of this play-off system was 2003, when Wasps emerged as champions of England, despite finishing second in the table, a feat they repeated a year later.

In 2004 they beat Bath in the final, after the west countrymen had won the regular season league by six points.

"For us, backing up successfully from the Toulouse European final only six days earlier was a pretty

• **Above**
Jonah Lomu brushing aside Rob Andrew on his way to destroying England in the 1995 World Cup semi-final.

• **Inset**
Wasps celebrate after their 10-6 win against Bath in the 2004 Zurich Premiership Final, Twickenham.

incredible feat," said Wasps coach Warren Gatland.

"We wanted to go out and play rugby, and I thought that we played some outstanding rugby in the second half."

But Gatland's tribute to the defeated West Countrymen was less enthusiastic, and the New Zealander put Bath's 10-6 defeat down to their dependence on a game-plan based on tight play and percentages.

"Bath played exactly as we expected them to – we knew they would be physical, but I thought that the best team deserved to win," he said.

"I feel that Bath need to play more expansive rugby if they are to go on from this."

Wasps captain Lawrence Dallaglio agreed, adding: "Bath demolished our line-out but they don't play with the kind of ambition you need if you're going to win trophies. They kicked everything and, with all due respect to them, you have to play with a bit more courage to win trophies and we've been doing that all season.

"Playing the way they do gets you so far, and they've won a lot of matches doing that this season.

"But we're very proud of what we've done and everyone at Wasps deserves a lot of credit.

"[The Heineken Cup] was the cake and this week was the icing on the cake. With the level of competition here and in Europe for us to do it is a big achievement, especially because we don't have the huge resources that other clubs have."

Leicester were England's first official champions, in 1988, beating Waterloo on the last day of the season.

Bath's 1989 title kicked off an incredible domination of the English game by the men from The Rec, who won six titles in the next eight years. Wasps stopped their total domination in 1990 and there was a title for Leicester in 1995.

From 1999 to 2002 Leicester were almost unbeatable in the top flight of English rugby. Those four years brought consecutive titles for Leicester, who were unbeaten at home for 57 Premiership matches between 30 December 1997 and 30 November 2002. Their amazing run included 52 successive wins.

The Tigers, who were captained by Martin Johnson and coached by Dean Richards and John Wells for all four of their titles, lost only 14 of the 92 Premiership matches they played over those four championship-winning seasons.

The four league titles weren't the first time Leicester had taken a stranglehold on a domestic competition. They won three consecutive English Cups from 1979 to 1981.

History of the Lions

Chapter
FOUR

The British and Irish Lions are without doubt rugby's most famous side and, as they now tour every four years, their trips to either South Africa, Australia or New Zealand have taken on legendary proportions in those countries. The World Cup arrived in our game in 1987 but it still hasn't overtaken a Lions tour in terms of importance. Every British and Irish player has the ambition of playing for the Lions and the side is guaranteed to play to a full house wherever it goes.

Without the initial backing of the Rugby Football Union and inspired by contemporary trips to Australia by cricket teams, Lions tours began in 1888. The 2001 Lions, with a team selected by the Four Home Unions Tours Committee, travelled first-class to Australia for a Test series they lost 2-1. But back in 1888, with accusations of professionalism dogging some of the side, the tour, which went to Australia and New Zealand under England's Bob Seddon, lasted from April to October and took in 35 matches, none of which were Tests. With the game still developing in the southern hemisphere, the 1891 Lions, who took 16 days to make it to Cape Town by boat, have a record that is unlikely to be beaten. Those Lions – the first to be backed by the RFU and

only featuring English and Scottish players – went to South Africa and won every match, conceding just one try.

The team today has players from England, Scotland, Ireland and Wales. But in the early days they took whichever players were available to them without ever trying to achieve an equal mix of nationalities. In the pre-professional days many of these amateur players would have had jobs to do as well as playing rugby. These were in essence the beginning of the Lions and, for ease of explanation, we have called them the Lions, well before they took that nickname as their own in 1924.

The first three tours didn't even have players from all four home unions and it was only in 1899, when Matthew Mullineux's Lions went to Australia, that they began to look like today's British and Irish Lions, with players from all four home nations.

In 1899 it wasn't the pinnacle of a player's career as it is today and only 14 of those 21 who made the journey Down Under had been capped by their relative countries. Today it is possible to have one 'non-capped' player in the touring party but to have seven would be unthinkable. Mullineux the skipper, or the Reverend Mullineux, to give the Englishman his full title, never played for his country before or after the tour, the only Lions skipper to have remained uncapped.

The Lions' first tour of the 20th century came in 1903 and at a time when the sides from Australia, New Zealand and South Africa were improving beyond all recognition.

This meant a far more difficult task for the former all-conquering Lions and they fell from a missionary status to a side competing on equal terms.

Mark Morrison's 1903 Lions ran into a South African side that proved the new century would also see a new force in the world game.

The South Africans hadn't won a Test on the 1891 Lions tour and just one in 1896, but in 1903 they won the three-Test series 1-0 with the first two matches, in Johannesburg (10-10) and Kimberley (0-0), being drawn. The series then hinged on the third Test where the infamous Cape Town weather created a mudbath and South Africa triumphed 8-0.

The 1903 Lions played 22 matches in all, winning 11 and they had their own stars, most notably Newport's Reg Skrimshire, who scored 59 points, including 10 tries on the trip.

Today the Lions only tour every four years but a British team travelled to Australia and New Zealand a year after Morrison's side, in 1904. To give you an idea of the make-up of those sides, only one player – the skipper of the latter tour, Dr Bedell-Sivright – made it in both 1903 and 1904, .

But despite the changes in personnel, Bedell-Sivright had some marvellous Welsh backs in his side and they went a long way to ensuring that this was the most successful British side ever to visit Australia. They won all of their 14 games in Australia and the most points they conceded in any one game was nine. Four of their opponents, including two of the Australian Test sides, failed to score against them.

The picture was slightly different in New Zealand for that 1904 side, as they lost the single Test in Wellington. They faced a side that a year later, under the magnificent Dave Gallaher, was to tour the UK with incredible success, newly christened as the All Blacks.

The potential of New Zealand as one of the hotbeds of the rugby world was demonstrated in the size of the crowd for the Wellington Test match. While 6,000 people came to Cape Town to see the 1903 Lions, 20,000 packed into Athletic Park a year

later to see Gallaher's side triumph 9-3.

Leading Lions historians, like the great Clem Thomas, accept that the first genuine Lions tour – with a team selected by the Four Home Unions Tours Committee – came in 1924, but one tour over which there can be no dispute is the 1908 trip to Australia and New Zealand. In 1908 AF Harding captained what was described as an Anglo-Welsh touring party Down Under. It was the first and last time such a side would leave British shores and only 11 of the 28-strong party had actually played international rugby. The side played 26 matches, winning 16, most of these victories coming against weaker opposition in Australia. Once in New Zealand they failed to win any of the three Tests, although they did draw the International in Wellington.

The last Lions before the First World War were also the first to wear a lion emblem on their jerseys, when they went to South Africa in 1910 under the captaincy of Tom Smythe.

Any thoughts that these Lions teams were now merely spreading the gospel of rugby had been

• Above
Dr Ronald Cove-Smith on deck with the captain en route to Cape Town with his 1924 Lions.

• Above
The 1924 Lions prepare for their tour to South Africa.

dispelled on the previous trips to New Zealand and now that was confirmed in South Africa.

The Lions had a record seven Newport players, we are told in Clem Thomas' definitive *History of the British and Irish Lions*, in their ranks for this trip, but it was still an Englishman who was the star of the show – loose forward CH 'Cherry' Pillman. He was revered by the Springboks, as the South Africans were now known, and set about developing a style of play that was followed by generations of rugby players to come.

Pillman was developing the roving flanker technique, acting almost as an extra half-back. He was switched to outside-half in the second Test, which the Lions won 8-3. Rugby fans gasped decades later when we saw two world-renowned back-row forwards, Zinzan Brooke and Neil Back, kick drop-goals, but Pillman's ability with the boot got there first as he scored 65 points on this trip, then the most by a Lion.

The 1910 Lions won 13 out of their 24 games, but lost the Test series 2-1. The crucial, final defeat came in Cape Town 21-5, after the Lions lost their full-back, Stanley Williams, early on and had to play

the majority of the game (before the days of substitutes) with 14 men.

Between the two world wars, the Lions only toured three times, in 1924, 1930 and 1938. Economic problems and the effects of the First World War ran through every facet of British life.

The 1924 side was the first to be formally known as the British Lions, although with players from southern Ireland involved they should always be referred to as the British and Irish Lions.

The 1924 Lions, missing some of their key stars like Wavell Wakefield, ran into a South African side which was on the verge of an incredible era for the game in that country. The British and Irish side were comprehensively beaten, winning only nine of their 21 games, and losing three of their four Tests with the other one drawn. It is the worst tour record of any Lions side. Dr Ronald Cove-Smith's 1924 team was also blighted by a number of injuries in a series where the Springboks gave the world their first view of their 3-4-1 scrum formation.

It certainly didn't get any easier for the next tourists, the 1930 Lions, who travelled to Australia and New Zealand. This side performed well in the

non-Test matches and they won 20 games on their 28-game tour. But it was the Tests that mattered and in spite of winning the first in Dunedin, the Lions were comprehensively beaten in the next three, including a crushing 22-8 defeat in the fourth Test in Wellington, to lose the series 3-1. To make matters worse, they also lost on their way home, 6-5 to Australia.

This tour was blighted by off-field problems and led to significant changes in the laws as manager Jim Baxter was incensed by some of New Zealand's interpretations. His complaints included the way they went off at half-time, instead of staying on the field and, particularly, their 2-3-2 scrum formation. This formation was later outlawed after Baxter's complaints, with sides forced to have three in the front row, as we see today.

But in 1930 that New Zealand formation allowed a 'rover' forward to play, something similar to an extra scrum-half, causing havoc in the Lions' ranks.

During 1936 a third and final Lions tour to Argentina took place. These Argentine tours were seen as being of far less importance since the Lions were infinitely stronger than their opposition and won every match played. In 1910, led by John Raphael, they conceded only two tries in six matches whilst the 1927 Lions of Scotland's David MacMyn played and won nine matches. The final tour to Argentina, under the captaincy of England's Bernard Gadney, fresh from masterminding the first England victory over New Zealand, saw another

demonstration of how the game should be played. All 10 matches were won and only one try was scored against them.

The 1938 Lions, captained by Sam Walker, finished their South Africa tour on a high note by winning the last Test in Cape Town 21-16, the first triumph in South Africa since 1910. But by then the series had been lost, as they'd been defeated in the first two matches. The victory did, however, confirm the Springboks as unofficial world champions, as they had beaten New Zealand and Australia earlier that year.

Commentators argue that this South African side, with legendary captain Danie Craven and Boy Louw, then the most-capped Springbok of all-time, was the greatest in their history. Certainly those in New Zealand regard it as the best side to visit their shores, explaining the monumental task the Lions had in winning on South African soil. To lose 2-1 was therefore an achievement.

The first tour after the Second World War saw Karl Mullen's 1950 Lions travel to New Zealand and Australia. Mullen had led Ireland to a Grand Slam in 1948 and the Triple Crown a year later. Only three Englishmen were selected and, as Grand Slam winners that season, Wales provided the bulk of the squad with 14 players.

To confirm the dawn of a new era, the 1950 Lions arrived Down Under with their new, now famous kit of red shirts, white shorts and blue socks with green tops, depicting all four home nations.

• **Above**
Three Lions' greats, Ronnie Cove-Smith (left) from the 1924 Lions, flying Welsh half-back Haydn Tanner (middle) who played in the 1938 side and Welsh winger Ken Jones (right) who represented the Lions in 1950.

and the series followed in Sydney, as the Lions ran out 24-6 victors.

After Australia the Lions made their one and only stop in Sri Lanka (then Ceylon), winning 44-6.

The second post-war trip took the 1955 Lions – the first to travel by aeroplane – back to South Africa, where, under the captaincy of Robin Thompson, they completed one of the most physical trips in their history, emerging with the respect of the Springboks and their supporters and a series drawn 2-2. In all they played 25 matches in South Africa, losing just five. They were the first side that century to return from South Africa with a drawn series.

In this party were some of the greatest players the game has seen, including Cliff Morgan, Jeff Butterfield and the prolific Irish wing Tony O'Reilly, who scorched through South Africa, scoring a record 16 tries.

The tour was staged under a political cloud and for many of these Lions it was their first taste of apartheid. The Lions were gracious to their hosts and many black supporters got behind the British and Irish side, lighting newspaper bonfires whenever they scored.

The first Test was a cracker and stands the test of time in terms of great matches. It was the first Test

This Lions team, the first to consist of just capped players, had some of the most feared backs in the northern hemisphere, such as Ken Jones, Jackie Kyle and Bleddyn Williams. But as if to stress the gap that was appearing between the hemispheres, they still failed to win one of the four Test matches, just managing a draw in the first, in Dunedin, 9-9.

New Zealand's abilities were perhaps best demonstrated by looking at the Lions' record on the same tour in Australia. There, they scored 150 points in six games, proving that this was indeed a strong Lions side. Lewis Jones, new on the scene, was the star of the Australian leg, scoring a try, two penalties, two conversions and an incredible 50-yard drop-goal as the Lions won the first Test 19-6. The second win

• Above
The legendary Cliff Morgan during a 1955 Test against the Springboks.

• Inset
Irishman Jack Kyle was a key member of the 1950 tour.

to see 45 points scored in South Africa, these great Lions winning 23-22, after Jack van der Schyff failed with a conversion, the last kick of the match.

After the difficult trip in 1950, the Lions of 1959, under Ronnie Dawson, must have headed back Down Under with some trepidation, although this time, they had the players to take on the All Blacks. O'Reilly was still there and five veterans of 1955 joined him, in Butterfield, Dickie Jeeps, Bryn Meredith, Hugh McLeod and Rhys Williams. The tour was the first for Lions legend Syd Millar. The All Blacks also had their legends on show. Colin Meads was recalled and the Lions got their first sighting of the awesome Kel Tremain.

However, it wasn't to be and although the 1959 Lions lost only six of their 33 games, winning both matches in Australia, three of those defeats came in Test matches against New Zealand. The boot of Don Clarke stole the first Test from the Lions in Dunedin, 18-17 and by the time they had also lost the second, 11-8 in Wellington, the series was beyond them. The All Blacks won the third Test 22-8, but it says a lot for Dawson's Lions that they came back to claim that fourth Test, by 9-6 in Auckland and record the first win by the Lions in New Zealand since the first tour in 1930.

The 1960s was a disappointing decade for the

Lions as both the New Zealanders and South Africans were in their pomp and the Lions failed to win any of the 12 Tests they played against the two nations.

Arthur Smith was the first man to lead the Lions in the 1960s when in 1962 he took on Avril Malan's mighty Springboks. They had come to the UK and Ireland in 1960 and 1961 and won every game, except the last match against the Barbarians.

To match them physically, the Lions chose a huge pack, which included the great Syd Millar and, for the first time, the man who was to play a huge part in the revival of the Lions fortunes, Willie John McBride.

But they struggled to match the Springboks in the loose and, although they performed well in the provincial matches, lost the last three Tests having drawn the first 3-3 in Johannesburg. They were only hammered once, 34-14 in the last Test, earning respect when losing the second 3-0 and the third 8-3, in Cape Town. The appeal of the Lions was such that they drew the biggest crowd in Newlands' history for that third Test. Thousands were locked out, yet almost 55,000 people saw Keith Oxlee grab the winning try with only a few minutes remaining.

The 1966 trip was another tale of two countries. By now the Lions were getting used to visiting

• Above left
Bryn Meredith, a Lions stalwart who played on the 1955 and 1959 tours.

• Above right
Hewitt diving over to score for the 1959 Lions in the third Test against New Zealand in Christchurch.

• Inset
Irishman Syd Millar, who first played for the Lions in 1955, went on to coach the famous '74 side.

55

Australia and winning there and it was no surprise to see them win both Tests against the Wallabies, the second in Brisbane by 31-0.

But, as it had been on previous tours, it was a different story when those Lions landed in New Zealand. This tour was a low point for the Lions as they lost the Test series 4-0, getting off to a terrible start in Dunedin, losing 20-3. Things failed to get any better and when they lost the last Test 24-11 in Auckland, they became the first Lions to suffer a Test-series whitewash. As if that wasn't enough, ignominy was to greet them in their stop-off in Canada on the way home, where they lost to British Columbia 8-3.

The 1966 Lions underwent an horrendously long tour, playing an astonishing 35 matches (the same number that elite players in England now are asked to play in a whole season) over five months and they left these shores amid controversy over the selection of the captain.

Alun Pask had led Wales to the Five Nations Championship in 1966 but the selectors controversially went for Mike Campbell-Lamerton as captain and during the course of the tour he agreed to be left out of the team due to a loss of form.

The All Blacks were becoming one of the greatest sides the world has seen and had a pack that contained legends of the game like Brian Lochore, Ken Gray and Waka Nathan, as well as the evergreen Colin Meads and Kel Tremain. And, if you

managed to overcome that lot, their backs were led, at scrum-half, by Chris Laidlaw.

The 1966 trip did teach the Lions one thing, that 35-match tours are too arduous and the next time they went on tour Down Under, in 1971, they played 26 times. The huge problem with the Lions, especially when they visit rugby-mad countries like New Zealand and South Africa, is that every fan, in every part of that country, wants to see them, hence the pressure to play as many matches as possible.

Just two years after the Lions returned from New Zealand, Australia and Canada, they were off again, under Tom Kiernan, for a trip to South Africa.

Things had gone badly in 1966 and in terms of Test victories little improved in 1968 as the Lions lost three Tests and drew one.

Every Lions tour needs to depart on the back of a good Five/Six Nations Championship. But in 1968 British rugby was in a parlous state and France were the Grand Slam champions.

It wasn't as bad as the 1966 trip – they came within five points of the Springboks in two of those Test-match defeats, though they were beaten 19-6 in the final match in Johannesburg to lose the series 3-0. As he left the field in that last Test, John O'Shea,

• **Above left**
New Zealand great Colin Meads took on the Lions in 1966, 11 years after he first played against them.

• **Above right**
New Zealand scrum-half Chris Laidlaw was instrumental in the 4-0 demolition of the 1966 touring Lions.

who was dismissed for throwing a punch after a general warning from the referee, became the first Lion to be sent off for foul play, as the Springboks managed a Test try count of eight to one in their favour.

But if the 1968 tour did nothing else, it gave a grounding in Lions rugby to two young men from Wales, Gareth Edwards and Barry John. Unknown on the world stage in 1968, they were to leave an indelible mark on the rugby world. John and Edwards started the first Test in Pretoria, but the Lions were forced to move Mike Gibson to outside-half for the rest of the series after John broke his collarbone and Edwards survived one more Test.

If the Lions had struggled to gain world supremacy in the 1960s, they certainly didn't in the 1970s, as some of the best players ever produced by Britain and Ireland journeyed to New Zealand, Australia and South Africa.

The 1971 side was the first to break the mould, bolstered by the greatest Welsh team in their history. The Lions won the Test series 2-1 with an epic 14-14 draw in the last match, but it isn't hard to see why they made an impact when you look at some of the members of their squad.

Coached by the great Carwyn James, these Lions had at their disposal legends like McBride, David Duckham, John Dawes (the captain), Ray McLoughlin, Fergus Slattery, JPR Williams, Gareth Edwards, Barry John, Mike Gibson and Gerald Davies. James was lucky to have an astute manager in Doug Smith, who had toured as a player with the 1950 side.

These 1971 Lions and those that followed in 1974, were crucial to British and Irish rugby as they

• **Above**
The 1971 Lions beat New Zealand by two Tests to one, the first Lions side of the century to defeat the All Blacks.

• **Below**
JPR Williams heads off on another surging run on that '71 tour.

57

destroyed the myth of invincibility that had grown up around the New Zealanders and South Africans. Up until that point no Lions side had won a major series abroad in the 20th century.

The 1971 Lions hit New Zealand hard on the counter-attack, with an attacking style that took the Kiwis by surprise and brought the Lions 15 straight wins, before their first loss of the trip, the second Test which ended 22-12.

Barry John – or the King as he was renamed in New Zealand – was the man of the moment, scoring 170 points on the tour. And as with all great series, it came down to the last match in Auckland, as the All Blacks tried to level it up at 2-2. It was an incredible game with JPR Williams' 40 yard drop-goal securing a draw for the Lions and the 2-1 series victory in the most dramatic fashion.

Carwyn James is always remembered fondly for his masterclass on the 1971 tour, but the trip to South Africa in 1974 will forever be recalled with Willie John McBride's name attached.

With apartheid protests wherever the Springboks played – the British government even ordered its embassy in South Africa to boycott the tourists – the squad bonded together more than any other Lions team had ever done. Legend has it that McBride called all the players together before they left London to say: "If you don't want to come, please leave now." And when no one spoke, McBride knew he had the men to stand toe-to-toe with the Springboks, adding: "Well, now we're all in it together."

The arguments about who were better, the 1971 Lions or their successors, still rage but in 1974 they topped the 1971 team on statistics alone, losing just one of their 22 games. They became the first side to beat the Springboks in a four-match series for 78 years and guaranteed their place in history.

To demonstrate what an attacking force they were, the Lions scored an incredible 729 points in 22 games, including 107 tries. In the Test series they outscored the Springboks 10 tries to one, ensuring that in South Africa rugby men like Edwards, JPR and McBride are still discussed in reverential tones 30 years later.

The 1974 Lions had to build their effort around their legendary pack, such was the physical presence of the Springboks and their provinces and during the tour McBride's men coined the '99' call. This was to be bellowed by McBride when a Lion was being attacked on the field and it was then a case of one in, all in, in the hope that the referee couldn't send

• Above
Gerald Davies was one of the great Welsh contingent who played in both the '71 and '74 Lions.

• Below
Lions captain Willie John McBride stands tall during the 1974 tour of South Africa.

everyone off or find the culprit.

The '99' call came in for a great deal of criticism, but it wasn't used as many times as legend suggests. It was, in fact, less about violence and more of a statement from the Lions that they weren't going to be pushed around on this trip by the South Africans who, in Test and provincial matches, tried but failed to intimidate these Lions.

McBride – on his fifth Lions tour – formed a great partnership in South Africa with coach Syd Millar and they ensured, along with manager Arthur Thomas, that the squad was as one for every match. Crucially, there was no division between the midweek side and the Test side, as there had been on previous trips and this helped mould them into one, very strong, unit.

Both McBride and Millar knew that players of this calibre didn't need coaching, only man-management and that extra piece of motivation to bring the very best out of them.

The second Test brought what South African rugby supremo Danie Craven called a "massacre" as the Lions won 28-9, inflicting the then biggest defeat on South Africa in their history. As if to confirm their superiority, the Lions then moved to Port Elizabeth for the third Test and won that one 26-9.

The last Test of the 1974 series ended in a 13-13 draw in Johannesburg, in front of an incredible 80,000 crowd, spoiling an otherwise perfect record. Indeed Slattery had a perfectly good try disallowed seconds before the final whistle blew.

The 1977 tourists had so much to live up to that it's not surprising they failed to match their expectations. They lost the series 3-1 in New Zealand, although they were only one point away from grabbing a 2-2 draw, as they were beaten 10-9 in the final Test in Auckland.

History will judge them as one of the unluckiest touring sides, losing just five of their 26 matches. The side had the Welsh team running through its

• Above
The great Gareth Edwards celebrates a try during that 1974 tour of South Africa.

• Above
The muddy 1977 Lions in a lineout against New Zealand Juniors.

• Inset
Captain Phil Bennett with the Lions mascot during the '77 tour.

backbone, 16 of them making the party, including the captain Phil Bennett, who later admitted that he should have turned the captaincy down.

Bennett and his backs struggled to get the upper hand and they had to rely on their forwards to take the battle to the All Blacks. It was a great pack and they almost did enough to take the series.

But with legends from the 1974 Lions like Gareth Edwards, JPR Williams and Gerald Davies unavailable to travel, they failed to gain the advantage in the backs that they'd had in '74. Bennett said: "By the end of the stay in New Zealand I had no desire to stay in that country, since I knew that all my weaknesses as a player and tourist were exposed in that short time.

"While I admit that I was a bad choice for the captaincy, there were others too who have cause to regret the events of 1977."

A Grant Batty interception try took the first Test, with a score from JPR Williams the foundation for a 13-9 Lions win in the second, to square the series.

But the second successive series victory for the Lions in New Zealand wasn't to be as they lost the final two Tests, in Dunedin they lost 19-7 and in Auckland, 10-9.

On their way home it went from bad to worse for these Lions as they'd agreed to play a one-off match against Fiji and they lost that 25-21. But the party did end on a high note because when they returned home, they beat the Barbarians, 23-14, in a match that raised £100,000 for the Queen's Trust Fund Appeal.

The problems of 1977 – the backs not matching the class of their forwards – surfaced again as Bill Beaumont's 1980 tourists lost 3-1 in South Africa.

Beaumont was riding high in 1980, after leading England to a Grand Slam in a championship where the tries flowed. Anti-apartheid demonstrations again disrupted the trip and it was the first of the shorter Lions tours as this party played just 18 matches in a 10-week trip, winning 15 and losing three. Unfortunately for them though, all three of those defeats came in Test matches.

But, as the Lions found in 2001 when they went to Australia, less is not more. Fewer games does not necessarily make for a fresher squad but it certainly makes for harder, more intense games, less 'warm-up' matches and, most importantly, less time for the coaching staff to arrive at their first XV.

Of course, every Lions coach steps on the plane with his Test side in his head, but the longer tours have allowed unexpected players to emerge, players who suit the Lions environment.

The back division in 1980 was unsettled throughout the tour and they even managed to use three different outside-halves in the Test series, Tony Ward, Ollie Campbell and Gareth Davies.

In the first Test the Lions had to rely on the boot of Ward as they lost the try count five to one and the match 26-22.

The second and third Tests went the same way and it wasn't until the final match of the series, in Pretoria, that the Lions got their victory, 17-13, which ensured they avoided becoming the first Lions side to be whitewashed in South Africa. The win also made them the first Lions to win a fourth Test in South Africa.

The fallout for British rugby from the 1983 tour to New Zealand was considerable and the whole structure of the Lions and the game in England, Ireland, Scotland and Wales was called into question by this 4-0 series defeat. They had a marginally better record than their 1966 counterparts, so just survived the tag of the worst Lions side to travel to New Zealand, but this was no consolation.

The gulf between the hemispheres was growing and one of the main consequences of the rout, in England at least, was the establishment of a league system – the Courage Leagues – for the domestic clubs.

The 1983 Lions never got close to achieving a victory in the Tests, losing the last by an embarrassing 38-6. In that game the Lions collapsed, conceding six tries and a hat-trick to Stu Wilson. They became only the second Lions in 100 years to be whitewashed 4-0.

The Lions played 18 games in ten weeks, far less than in the past and they won 12 times. Both manager Willie John McBride and coach Jim Telfer felt it simply wasn't enough time to mould a side from four different nations and their conclusions are never more relevant than at the start of the 21st century, when more and more pressure is put on to make Lions tours shorter and shorter. Shorter tours are a recipe for disaster on a number of fronts and although player burn-out is a serious concern, many commentators feel that in a Lions year British and

• Above
Lions' Clive Woodward pursued by Springboks during the 1980 second Test at Bloemfontein. South Africa won 26-19.

• **Above**
John O'Driscoll of the 1983 Lions during the fourth Test against New Zealand at Eden Park. The Lions were whitewashed in the series 4-0.

Irish clubs and provinces should be asked to play fewer games.

The ill-fated 1983 trip wasn't helped by controversy over the captain. Ireland's Ciaran Fitzgerald got the job, mainly on the back of a Triple Crown victory for Ireland, but many people thought his rivals for the position of hooker, Colin Deans and Peter Wheeler, were the better players.

20 years on Telfer admitted it had been the wrong choice, saying: "In hindsight it was probably a mistake. We were carried away with the euphoria of Ireland winning the Triple Crown and you have to be dispassionate when picking a Lions squad.

"Ciaran was a great captain for Ireland but captaining the Lions is different. You have to have a captain who is good enough to play in the first XV."

But neither Telfer nor anyone else would heap all the blame on that series defeat on Fitzgerald as they were facing a superb All Blacks side, captained by Andy Dalton, and the southern hemisphere was just starting to leave its northern counterpart behind.

The Lions were scheduled to travel to South Africa in 1986 but, under increasing pressure from the rest of the world to sustain a sporting boycott of the republic, the tour was called off and for only the second time in their history the Lions ran out on home soil.

A Lions team was selected to help celebrate the centenary of the International Rugby Board and they played a Rest of the World side at Cardiff Arms Park.

The Rest of the World won 15-7 and before the Lions could travel again there was a Rugby World Cup in 1987 to contend with.

Another consequence of the rise of southern hemisphere rugby and particularly its growth in Australia, saw the Lions make their first trip since 1899 to Australia alone, in 1989. And Finlay Calder's side enjoyed a glorious tour, losing just one match and taking the Test series 2-1.

As the 1986 trip had been called off, it meant the 1989 tourists were less experienced, in terms of Lions tours, than any of their predecessors. The Australians had proved their worth a few years before when Andrew Slack's 1984 side completed a Grand Slam of their own, beating all four home unions on their tour to Britain and Ireland and the

core of the side was to win the World Cup in 1991. On top of that only two former tourists, Donal Lenihan and Robert Norster, were in the tour party and it marked out a new chapter in Lions history. One of their number, Dai Young, was still there 12 years later when the Lions again returned to Australia. Basically, no-one thought the Lions could win and a first Test defeat seemed to bear this out. But, how wrong could they be?

A significant factor in their success in the Test series was the way the midweek or 'dirt-tracker' side performed. Nicknamed 'Donal's Doughnuts' after skipper Donal Lenihan, the side was unbeaten and helped create a winning mentality in the squad.

In a huge boost to the Test side, the midweekers were trailing 18-4 to ACT in the game before the second Test, yet roared back to emerge victorious, 41-25.

Lenihan made two Lions tours – without playing a Test – but his presence was vital to the party. He and his side gave the tour momentum and helped create an environment where they could go and win the Test series.

This 1989 tour had a violent undercurrent and the second Test was known as 'The Battle of Ballymore' as a brawl broke out following a clash between Robert Jones and Nick Farr-Jones. Later Young was lucky not to be sent off for standing on Steve

Cutler's head. The Australian media and Australia coach Bob Dwyer fanned the flames but the Lions took the second Test, significantly with Rob Andrew installed at outside-half.

Another Lions star was also born in that second Test as a fresh-faced young centre with one England cap to his name – Jeremy Guscott – announced his presence on the international stage with a try.

Before the deciding match Farr-Jones said: "I think the third Test could develop into open warfare. As far as I am concerned the Lions have set the rules and set the standards and, if the officials are going to do nothing about it, then we are going to have to do it ourselves. We won't sit back and cop it again."

But the game did not degenerate as was feared and will be long remembered for a blunder by Wallaby wing David Campese, who later took part in television adverts during the 2001 Lions tour, making fun of himself for the errant pass that decided the series in Sydney.

• Above
The official Team Photo of the 1989 Lions on Tour in Australia.

• Inset
Ieuan Evans charges into David Campese during the deciding third Test match in Sydney.

After England won Grand Slams in 1991 and 1992, they provided 17 players, assistant coach Dick Best and the manager, Geoff Cooke. England's contingent was the biggest ever on a Lions tour.

But despite England's domination of European rugby at that time, the captaincy was handed to Scotland's Gavin Hastings, ahead of England's Will Carling. Another Scot, Ian McGeechan, was the coach. Hastings certainly justified his place, breaking a number of Lions scoring records: most points in a match (18), most points in a Lions career (66), most penalties in a series (12) and most penalties in a match (six).

They lost the first Test 20-18 in Christchurch, but the second saw an awesome display from the Lions pack and at the heart of a heroic defensive display was the back row of Ben Clarke, Dean Richards and Peter Winterbottom, who tackled the Kiwis into submission.

In the third Test the Lions looked to be on the verge of history, going 10-0 up early on with a try from Scott Gibbs, but the All Blacks pulled clear to take the game 30-13.

In 1989 the midweek side had been crucial to the Lions' success in Australia and coach McGeechan highlighted the role of the 'dirt-trackers' when he analysed the trip. "The main weakness in our squad was the absence of a strong character who could captain the midweek side and give it purpose and focus," he said. "I would recommend future selection actually selects a player with this responsibility."

• Above
Tempers flared during the third Lions Test against Australia in 1989.

• Below
(From left to right) Rory Underwood, Dean Richards, Rob Andrew, Ieuan Evans and Brian Moore celebrate victory after that third Test. It was the Lions first series win since 1974.

Campese's attempt to find his full-back, Greg Martin, behind his own goal-line went horribly wrong and Ieuan Evans pounced to score a crucial try. Putting British and Irish rugby firmly back on the map, the Lions held out to win that deciding game 19-18, the first Lions series win for 15 years. They were also the first Lions to come from behind and win a series 2-1.

The last Lions tour before the game turned professional saw the best of British and Irish travel to New Zealand in 1993, but lose the Test series 2-1 after evening it up with a 20-7 win in Wellington. This was regarded as one of the better Lions squads but they still only won seven of their 13 matches.

McGeechan, who on that trip became the first man to coach the Lions for the second time, also dismissed any thoughts that the Lions would not have a place in the professional era. "The Lions must continue – the Test matches provided an arena which is completely different from any other experience the players get and the response in New Zealand is different from any national tour.

"As they kept reminding us, the Lions are the biggest thing which ever happens to New Zealand and South Africa for that matter. We must not underestimate the Lions' role and their significance on the world-rugby stage. Whatever we think nationally, we cannot provide what the Lions provide and, although there will be inherent difficulties in bringing four countries together, the advantages far outweigh any problems and British rugby will always benefit from the existence of the Lions."

For many people, most notably former England captain Will Carling, the start of rugby's professional era in 1995 was thought to sound the death knell of the Lions.

Carling and others believed that there was no space in the professional calendar for a representative side, playing in a four-year cycle, either side of the 'ultimate prize', the Rugby World Cup.

But not only did the Lions refuse to die in the professional era, they responded in a far more positive way than the individual unions of England, Ireland, Scotland and Wales. They produced a commercial plan and introduced sponsors that would ensure the funding of this great side for as long as rugby was played.

The mythical status of the Lions also helped their cause in the professional era, with the first two tours, to South Africa (1997) and Australia (2001), both massive successes on and off the field.

• Above
Rory Underwood charges down the wing to score a try during the second Test against New Zealand in 1993. The Lions won the match to square the series.

• Inset
Rob Andrew (centre left), Dean Richards (centre) and Martin Bayfield (right) trudge off the Auckland pitch having lost the third Test and the series to New Zealand.

• Below
Ian McGeechan, the Lions coach in '93, coached the Lions for three consecutive tours.

The arrival of the Lions brought commercial boosts to both host nations beyond the organisers' wildest dreams, with 20,000 supporters making the trip to Australia to follow the Lions. This was the biggest movement of fans from the UK to the southern hemisphere for any one sporting event and far more than went to the Sydney Olympics a year earlier. Those Lions fans injected an estimated Aus $100m [£38m] into the Australian economy.

The modern Lions are a guaranteed commercial success, even with the 1997 and 2001 Lions travelling first-class and getting paid, as Lions matches play to full houses wherever they go and the fans prop up local economies in every town and city they visit.

That first professional trip came two years after the game went open and saw the Lions emerge triumphant in that 1997 Test series in South Africa, 2-1.

Once again the midweek side provided the foundation for their Test series victory. After a tough start to the trip, the squad received a huge boost with key midweek wins, like the ones obtained in Gauteng (20-14) and Free State (52-30) shortly before the Lions clinched the Test series with an 18-15 victory in Durban.

It was crucial that the 1997 Lions were successful, both on and off the field as never did this famous

• Above
Jeremy Guscott celebrates kicking the winning drop goal against South Africa during the 1997 second Test at Kings Park, Durban.

• Below
Martin Johnson, the Lions captain, holds aloft the trophy after the 1997 third Test against South Africa at Ellis Park, Johannesburg.

team have so many enemies, all of whom were banished when Martin Johnson's side delivered the first series victory in South Africa for 23 years.

When the Lions arrived, tournaments like the Super 12 and Tri Nations had taken the southern hemisphere clear of their northern rivals, so the victory was far more unexpected than many that had come before.

The Tours Committee put confirmed Lions men in charge of this party. Fran Cotton was manager, Ian McGeechan coach for the third successive time and Jim Telfer his assistant coach.

They picked a captain, in Johnson, who at the time was inexperienced in leadership terms, but the decision proved inspirational and he was instrumental to their success.

Showing how rugby was developing, the party included six players – Dai Young, Scott Gibbs, Scott Quinnell, Alan Tait, John Bentley and Allan Bateman – who had returned to union from the professional ranks of rugby league.

The physical presence of Lions like Johnson and Gibbs was a big factor in their triumph, but it took a famous drop-goal from Jeremy Guscott to win the second Test and the series.

The 2001 Lions made the shortest tour in history, playing just 10 games. Seven victories were achieved and after going 1-0 up in the Test series, the Lions lost the next two to finish downhearted. They became the first Lions to lose a series in Australia but that probably reflected Australia's No 1 status in the rugby world at the time, rather than the weakness of the Lions party.

The Lions broke with tradition by appointing the first coach from outside the UK to lead the side. New Zealander Graham Henry, the Wales coach, took charge with Donal Lenihan as his manager.

As a professional team they were paid £15,000 a man, a sum that would have been increased to £22,000 had they won the Test series.

England were again dominating the Six Nations so 18 Englishmen were selected for the tour, along with ten Welshmen, six Irishmen and three Scots. It was one of the most unbalanced parties to leave the UK.

As history has shown, the best Lions squads are those that knit well and arguably a good balance of players from the four home nations would have made more sense, as opposed to one nation dominating in the way Henry allowed.

The Wallabies arrived at this Test series as World Cup holders and one of their greatest players, John Eales, was in his last season.

Six matches only leading up to the first Test and too little time to prepare the squad back in the UK, were two big factors in the defeat of these Lions, but

• Above
The 2001 Lions gather at Tylney Hall in Hampshire prior to the Australian tour.

• **Above**
Try-scorer Jonny Wilkinson is congratulated by team-mate Colin Charvis after scoring in the first Test against Australia in 2001.

notwithstanding that they did win the first Test.

The Lions kicked off with an incredible 116-0 win against Western Australia in Perth, but even in that rout the injury jinx that blighted their tour struck, with young Scotland back-rower Simon Taylor flying home with a knee injury. Those injuries surfaced in the last week with key players Richard Hill and Rob Howley ruled out of the last Test. Henry even reported that his third-Test side was unable to train as a unit once in the build-up week due to injuries within the team.

But this Lions tour must not be considered a failure. Mistakes in organisation were made but the players were capable of taking the series and only lost it to a 29-23 defeat in the final Test, in Sydney.

Manager Lenihan recommended: "In the professional era the whole tour structure needs to be looked at. If you are going to play a tour of this intensity at the end of the domestic season you will have to look at more time between matches.

"Players need more time to recover. It is a question of whether you can afford so many midweek matches."

The pressure on Lions tours has been growing

since the game turned professional in 1995 and many supporters of this great team believe it could be downgraded over the next few decades, or even disappear altogether.

But in an era when the 'brand' is all-important the two biggest brands in the rugby world are the Lions and the All Blacks.

In 2001, tour coach Graham Henry was already suggesting that trips should be shorter and more focused. Others believe that the domestic season in Britain and Ireland should be shortened in Lions years to ensure that they have enough time to prepare and that players get enough rest in this hectic age.

Henry said: "It may be that the way forward is to take a smaller group of players, 28 rather than 37 and play fewer games, perhaps three warm-up matches followed by three Tests."

Henry will be in a unique position in 2005 as the recently appointed New Zealand coach will become the first man to coach the Lions and coach a side who plays against them.

When the 2005 Lions arrive in New Zealand in June of 2005 they will be coached by Sir Clive Woodward, the man who won the World Cup in 2003.

Pressure on the Lions, though, has ensured that this tour will be the shortest on record to New Zealand and they will play just 10 matches, including three Tests against the All Blacks.

Lions Chairman and Tour Manager Bill Beaumont said: "The tour itself promises to challenge the 2005 Lions from start to finish with a series of difficult assignments but I am absolutely sure that we will rise to that challenge.

"The huge level of interest and enthusiasm

• **Above**
Brian O'Driscoll powers forward with the ball during the 2001 third and deciding Test against Australia played at Stadium Australia, in Sydney.

• **Inset**
Brian O'Driscoll with 2001 tour coach Graham Henry.

shown by the New Zealand public in the tour, even already, will be undoubtedly one of the highlights."

New Zealand head coach Henry thinks the tour will be much harder for the Lions than in 2001 when he was the Lions coach. He said "It's a lot tougher than the last tour of Australia and I think that's appropriate for the Lions, I think we had too many soft games in the last Lions tour.

"One of the problems of the tour was selection and in those games we were not really able to select players on their form and ability because the opposition was not strong enough. This is a lot more difficult tour and Bay of Plenty, Taranaki and Wellington etc, will bring the best out of the tourists and they will be able to know who their top team is.

"I think it's a more positive tour in that respect and probably a little harder but I think the guys who are playing professional rugby these days want a challenge rather than an exhibition."

LIONS 2005 FIXTURES
4 June: Bay of Plenty
8 June: Taranaki
11 June: NZ Maori
15 June: Wellington
18 June: Otago
21 June: Southland
25 June: 1st Test – Christchurch
28 June: Manawatu
2 July: 2nd Test – Wellington
9 July: 3rd Test – Auckland

History of the 5/6 Nations

Chapter
FIVE

5

The southern hemisphere has its Tri-Nations and since 1987 we've all had the World Cup. But since 1910 consistently the best show on earth has been the Five (and since 2000 the Six) Nations Championship.

This championship, now contested by England, France, Ireland, Scotland, Wales and Italy, embodies

everything great about the game of Rugby Union and ensures hundreds of thousands of people pack into European stadiums every spring.

This tournament, won by England in 2003 with a Grand Slam (five wins out of five), is more than a series of matches. For many fans it's a weekend when friendships are forged or renewed and the camaraderie of rugby comes to the fore. The games themselves are fiercely contested – it is, as England's Lawrence Dallaglio put it, the northern hemisphere's World Cup – yet up until 1995 there wasn't even a trophy for the winner to celebrate.

The first international rugby match was played in

1871 between England and Scotland. Matches between the two were then played annually and as Ireland and Wales took up the game over the following decade they also began to be granted fixtures against the others. It was not until 1884, however, that all four nations played against each other in one season for the first time.

The 'Championship' was never envisaged as such by anyone involved. It was actually the press who first started to create tables, champions and wooden spoon 'winners' from the annual series of friendly matches that the countries played. Since there was no way to officially decide tied championships many a season was shared or drawn between two or more teams.

It wasn't until the introduction of the Five Nations Championship trophy on the cusp of professionalism in the early 1990s that the competition was formally recognized by the participants for the first time.

At the start of the 1890s England and Scotland reigned supreme before Wales took their first championship in 1893 and a year later it was the turn of Ireland to go unbeaten in the competition, an achievement they managed again in 1899.

Wales' victory in 1893 owed much to their innovative tactics. They employed an extra back, a tactic that the English tried in the second half of their game but to no avail, as the Welsh ran out winners by two goals (one penalty) and two tries to England's one goal and three tries.

At that time the game in England was dominated by the arguments over amateurism and professionalism and in 1895 the great split between the RFU and some of their northern clubs occurred.

With the split in the rugby ranks affecting

• **Above pics**
The first ever international in 1871 took place between these English and Scottish teams.

• **Below**
Twickenham started life as a cabbage patch before RFU treasurer William Cail purchased the land.

England worst, the start of the new century was the first golden era in Welsh rugby, as the game caught hold in working-class areas.

Such was Wales' great run that they only lost five matches in ten seasons from 1900, taking the championship six times, sharing it twice with Scotland and Ireland and never being out of the top two in the table. It's a record that compares favourably with the legends of the 1970s.

Scotland were also having a good period in their history, beating that Welsh side three times, whereas England were suffering, only getting one point off the Welsh, with a draw in 1904.

As in 1970, the Welsh side was blessed with a glorious set of backs. At the turn of the century Wales had players like Gwyn Nicholls, Rhys Gabe, Willie Llewellyn and the majestic Jack Bancroft, whose career just moved into the 20th century.

In a fascinating comparison with modern rugby, when Bancroft retired in 1901, he had won 31 caps for Wales and The Daily Telegraph reported: 'He (Bancroft) has taken part in more international matches (33) than any other rugby player and his record may possibly never be surpassed.' I'm sure that Philippe Sella, who retired from international rugby in 1995 with 111 French caps, may beg to differ!

France started to play matches in 1906 and by 1910 they had fixtures against all four home unions for the first time thus creating the Five Nations Championship.

The French actually found it far harder to establish themselves in the Five Nations than Italy did in the Six Nations in 2000. While Italy grabbed wins in their first and fourth seasons, France only managed one victory, 16-15 against Scotland in 1911, in their first five seasons, before the First World War brought an end to the championship.

France's first game was a trip to Swansea to take on Wales, a difficult start considering Wales' domination in the decade before. But the French at least managed to get on the scoreboard, going down 49-14 having trailed by only seven points at half-time.

To prove that the only way was up for the French, they haven't conceded so many points in a championship game since. Their 37-0 defeat against England a year later, in 1911, still remains their biggest loss.

Wales' great start in 1910 didn't end in them taking the championship, as England had regrouped and won the deciding game 11-6 at their new home at Twickenham. Thus England, who drew 0-0 with Ireland, won the championship by one point.

• **Above**
This Welsh XV of 1906 tied the Five Nations Championship with Ireland.

The new Twickenham Stadium, which also housed home games of the Harlequins club, made its debut in 1909 when the Quins took on local rivals Richmond. Famously and to establish the new home of English rugby, RFU treasurer William Cail paid £5,573 for a market garden at Twickenham which had been discovered by a committee member, Billy Williams.

The English victory was their first over Wales since 1898, commencing with a try almost from the kick-off, inspired by a run from Adrian Stoop and scored by Frederick Chapman.

Wales bounced back from the defeat to complete the first ever Five Nations Grand Slam (five matches, five victories) a year later, scoring 78 points and conceding just 21 on their way to victory. The immediate pre-war years essentially belonged to

England, however, as they only lost one game in the championship during the next three years, taking a hat-trick of titles.

England players like Ronnie Poulton-Palmer (who was killed in the First World War), Cyril Lowe, Dave Davies and Cherry Pilman guaranteed their place in rugby history.

Lowe's English record of eight tries in the 1914 championship still stands today, as does his phenomenal record of 18 championship tries, from 1913-23. The prolific Rory Underwood equalled the record of 18 tries in his Five Nations career, which ran from 1984-96, two years longer than Lowe and not interrupted by war.

By the time England had won the 2003 Grand Slam no one had equalled Poulton-Palmer's English record of four tries in a championship match, achieved against France in 1914 in a 39-13 victory.

After staging that first ever International in 1871, Scotland spent much of the following period as the bridesmaids of European rugby. That changed in the 1920s as they claimed their first Grand Slam – but only after another overwhelmingly successful period

for English rugby.

Picking up where they left off before the First World War, England won four Grand Slams in the decade, in 1921, 1923, 1924 and 1928.

While France started to pick up wins, it was Scotland who challenged England's supremacy in the decade, winning the title twice and grabbing a share of it three times.

In 1925, as Murrayfield opened its turnstiles to the public for the first time, Scotland won their first Grand Slam and a year later they became the first Home Union side to defeat England at Twickenham.

More than 70,000 people had crowded into Murrayfield in 1925 and the victory was sealed with a drop-goal from Herbert Waddell. The Daily Telegraph reported that by the end of the game the English forwards 'could not get out of a walk' as they were 'done', although 'a few managed to trot' before Waddell struck with around ten minutes to go. Waddell may have claimed the glory in that game but Scotland owed much to the try-scoring exploits of wing Ian Smith, who scored eight in that Grand Slam season, a record he shares with England's Cyril Lowe. Smith continued in this vein

throughout his career, crossing the line 24 times in the championship, again a record that has stood the test of time. He was joined in one of the most exciting back-lines Scotland has ever seen by men of talent like Waddell, at outside-half, his half-back partner Jimmy Nelson and Dan Drysdale at full-back.

France claimed their first victory over England, in 1927 and it came by the slim margin of 3-0 at Stade Colombes, a try from Edmond Vellat ending their run of 15 successive championship defeats at the hands of the English.

Although there was harmony on the field for the French as they won two games in both 1930 and

• **Above**

Scotland v Wales from 1927. Scotland tied that year's Five Nations with Ireland.

• **Inset**

England's Grand Slam winning side of 1928.

1931, it was a different story off it and the championship soon returned to the Four Nations. France were excluded from the championship as a row blew up amid accusations of professionalism and ill-discipline within their club championship, and they didn't return to the tournament until after the Second World War, in 1946.

In January 1931 ten French clubs broke from the French Union and, after a few years of disquiet amongst the Home Unions, this rebellion gave them the chance to act. The French, though, did manage to go out on a high, beating England 14-13 in their last match in the championship for 16 years. They were welcomed back by the four Home Unions for the 1939-40 season, after receiving assurances about the French Championship, but the Second World War ensured their exile stretched into the new decade.

In the immediate pre-war years, England led the way as they had done in the 1920s, with three outright titles, which included two unbeaten seasons, in 1934 and 1937. For Scotland those years were either brilliant, with Triple Crowns in 1933 or 1938, or awful, with wooden spoons in 1930, 1932, 1935, 1936 and 1939.

Scotland's hold over England at Murrayfield was broken in 1937 when England won their first match at the magnificent stadium 6-3 after six successive defeats. The victory spurred England to an unbeaten season, Hal Sever scoring a breathtaking try in the 9-8 win over Ireland, sprinting 60 yards along the touchline to score.

In the 1930s, with the championship down to four sides, there was a rare success for Ireland as they took their first title of the century. A 3-3 draw between Wales and England, coupled with England's 10-7 loss at Murrayfield, allowed Ireland to win the 1935 championship, despite their 14-3 loss to England.

In the last championship before the Second World War, the title was shared by Wales, Ireland and England, after all three sides lost one match.

Although, like the rest of the nation, mourning the loss of many of its sons – Prince Obolensky being the most famous casualty – rugby started in earnest in the 1945-46 season with a series of 'Victory Internationals' that brought together England, Ireland, France, Wales and Scotland. But because the results also included matches against a New Zealand

army side, they were never constituted into a Five Nations table.

It was the Irish who started the post-war era the strongest, a decent 1947 season setting up their first ever Grand Slam in 1948. Some 32,000 people packed into Ravenhill to see Ireland clinch the Grand Slam with a 6-3 victory over Wales. Outside-half Jackie Kyle and hooker Karl Mullen were at the centre of so much of the brilliant Irish play and the side scored ten tries in their four games, more than they'd achieved for 20 years.

In Des O'Brien, Bill McKay and Jim McCarthy, Ireland had built a magnificent back row that nullified the threat of their greatest rivals for the Slam. Kyle, the genius at fly-half, would always deflect the credit on to this great trio. The Playfair Rugby Annual of that season concluded that Ireland snared the Grand Slam because of 'Kyle's clever tactics, both as kicker and passer, behind a steadily improving pack; Mullen's expert hooking and the dash and good hands of wings O'Hanlon and Mullan.'

• Above
Prince Obolensky was tragically killed in Suffolk whilst training to become an RAF fighter pilot.

As Mullen himself put it in Edmund Van Nesbeck's *Irish Rugby Scrapbook*: "I think the ability to remain error-free at crucial moments was a notable characteristic of the Irish side of that period. Then we had Kyle, in my view incomparable before and since.

"I know that many people think we had just one back of quality in Kyle, but I do not agree at all. Kyle was the genius and the inspiration, but in defensive terms I think our backs were first-class and our centres on that day [against Wales], Paddy Reid and Des McKee, were brilliant in defence. We had scoring power on the wings too." Incredibly, well over half a century later, this still remains their solitary Grand Slam.

France, who denied Ireland back-to-back Grand Slams the following season with a 16-9 victory, ended the decade with good wins in the three post-war championships, 1947-49 and started to hint at what was to come from the men in blue. Their threat to the old order was confirmed in 1948 when the French finally won in Wales, 11-8, at St Helen's, Swansea. On that breakthrough day for French rugby, Michel Pomathios, their try-scoring wing, was chaired off at the end to a hero's reception. He later, in 1951, became the first Frenchman to represent the

Barbarians, thereby starting a long association between the famous club and the French rugby community.

The French resurgence continued in the 50s, and although they didn't dominate the decade, it will be remembered as the time when France picked up their first outright title, in 1959, a good 49 (interrupted) years after their debut Five Nations season. So, as Italy still struggle for individual wins at the start of the new century, at least they have history and time on their side.

With legends like Lucien Mias and Jean Prat coming into their best form, the French were quick to make their impact, gaining their first triumph at Twickenham, 11-3 in 1951, flanker Prat scoring one of the tries. And Prat, or 'Monsieur Rugby' as he was known in England, stayed in great form for the 1952 championship as well, scoring a try, two conversions and a penalty as they won at Murrayfield for the first time, 13-11.

Prat was to play his last international season in 1955 and France came so close to delivering him the Grand Slam he deserved, falling at the final hurdle with a 16-11 defeat at home to Wales. By then the French had uncovered some other rugby jewels in players like Pierre Albaladejo, Andre Boniface and

• **Above**
The Welsh Grand Slam winning side of 1950.

77

Michel Celaya, but Jean Prat, though, had left his indelible mark on the Five Nations.

France took their first title (shared with Wales and England) in 1954, but 1959 heralded their biggest achievement to date with that first outright championship. The key victory, 11-3 in Stade Colombes, came against their great rivals, Wales. The Daily Telegraph reported that after clinching the title, they were "unmotivated" in the final game, against Ireland and they lost 9-5.

The French side of that period were innovators. With Mias at the helm (although Celaya was captain) they developed the rolling maul and came up with inventive ways to run tap-penalty routines. They were a spirited side, and those in the game with vision, who today would welcome victories for Italy in the Six Nations or one of the developing nations in the World Cup, welcomed the French progress. Men like Welsh back Carwyn James, later coach of the Lions, who, having witnessed his team lose 16-6 to the French in 1958, said: "It was a bad day for Wales but a great day for rugby football."

But the 1959 triumph nearly didn't happen as they came close to being thrown out of the championship again in the 1950s, the problems with the French Championship and the amateur / professional debate still unresolved.

It was Rene Crabos, a former international, who was credited with the diplomatic skills to keep

France in the championship. He brokered a compromise whereby the French clubs pledged to abide by amateur regulations and in return the national side stayed in the Five Nations.

The Welsh were also moving into a dominant period in their history, winning Grand Slams in 1950 and 1952, while only finishing out of the first two in the championship once in the 1950s. They had players like Rex Willis at scrum-half and the legendary Ken Jones on the wing, a sprinter who will never be forgotten by his nation for scoring 17 tries in his international career. The 1952 side contained the latest player to roll out of the famous Welsh fly-half factory, a certain Cliff Morgan.

England were not without their successes in the 1950s, taking their own Grand Slam in 1957 with a team that included England greats like Dickie Jeeps, Eric Evans (the captain, a hooker from Sale, who started his international career at prop), Jeff Butterfield, Peter Jackson – who scored three of England's six tries in the Slam – and John Currie.

A 16-3 victory over Scotland delivered the 1957 clean sweep and 72,000 people, including the Queen and Prince Philip, came to Twickenham to watch them take their first Grand Slam since 1928. Skipper Evans took three scrums against the head in a game which was a triumph for the incredible English pack.

• **Above left**
The Queen and Prince Phillip arrive at Twickenham to watch England secure the 1957 Grand Slam against Scotland.

• **Above right**
Eric Evans, captain of that 1957 side.

It was an entirely different story north of the border, as Scotland became the ones to suffer the most from the French success, finishing with the wooden spoon five times in the 1950s. Scotland went three seasons, from 1952-54, without winning a single game in the championship, crashing 26-8 at Twickenham to England in 1953. That run of 17 consecutive championship defeats ended in 1955 with a 14-8 victory over Wales.

Scotland did achieve one notable feat in the 1950s, when more than 80,000 people came to Murrayfield, then a world record for a rugby match, to watch the Scots hammer Wales 19-0 in 1951. To show that some things never change, there were 25,000 Welshmen in the ground! A year earlier the Welsh hordes had played their part in breaking the old attendance record, when 75,532 were at Twickenham to see the visitors beat England 11-5.

The 1960s will ultimately be remembered as the decade when South Africa and New Zealand moved ahead of the rest on the world stage, but in the Five Nations France continued the good work they had started in the 1950s and Wales prepared Europe for what was to come from them in the 1970s. The two teams dominated the championship, with seven outright wins between them.

France kicked off the decade at the top, sharing the title in 1960 and winning it outright in 1961 and 1962 to complete four years of winning rugby. In 1961 they finished a championship season unbeaten for the first time, though the Grand Slam eluded them due to a 5-5 draw at Twickenham, Michel Crauste levelling the scores with a second-half try to complete the third successive draw between the sides. Their 1962 success included a new record for flanker Crauste when he became the first forward to score a hat-trick of tries as the French beat England 13-0 in Paris.

But their greatest day was still to come when in 1968, a year after winning the championship again, they finally completed their first Grand Slam, 58 years after joining the tournament.

It all started pretty badly for the defending champions in the vital last game in Cardiff as they slumped to a 9-3 half-time deficit. But they roared back in the second period to claim a 14-9 win and the Grand Slam, under the captaincy of Christian Carrere.

• *Above*
England beat France 6-5 on their way to winning the 1963 Five Nations Championship.

79

• **Above**
The French team prepare to play Ireland in 1968, the year they won the Grand Slam.

The 1968 Slam was tinged with tragedy though as two French internationals, Guy Boniface and Jean-Michel Capendeguy, were killed in separate road accidents.

Wales took until the middle of the decade to show their potential, winning the title outright in 1965 and 1966. They followed this up with the Triple Crown and the championship in 1969, the Grand Slam eluding them after an 8-8 draw with France. The season included a 30-9 hammering of the English in Cardiff with winger Maurice Richards equalling the Welsh record of four tries in a match. Richards' six tries in that season was still a Welsh record by the end of the 2003 Six Nations, although Keith Jarrett's then record of 31 points in one championship season was later overtaken. Jarrett had made a spectacular start to his Wales career when, aged just 18, he scored 19 points as Wales trounced England 34-21 in 1967.

The decade is also memorable for the arrival of a new Welsh captain who, when taking over from Norman Gale to face Scotland in 1966, became their youngest ever. This Cardiff College of Education student went by the name of Gareth Edwards.

England, like the French, kicked off the decade in style by remaining unbeaten in 1960, but their 3-3 draw with France stopped either side picking up a Grand Slam, and they shared the championship.

The same fate befell the 1963 English side when they won the championship by three clear points, the Grand Slam fading away in atrocious weather during a 0-0 draw in Ireland.

Ireland saw their opportunity of a second Grand Slam, in 1969, disappear in a 24-11 defeat in Cardiff, which was their only defeat that season. They finished second with a fine team that included Tom Kiernan and a strong pack.

Scotland's poor run of form in the 1950s continued into the 1960s as they finished in the table's bottom two five times. But they did share the title in 1964 (the first time they had done so for 26 years) and along the way beat England 15-6 at Murrayfield, winning the Calcutta Cup for the first time in 14 years. In that season Wales had the distinction of participating in two draws, 11-11 with France and 6-6 with England, as well as two victories, so were unbeaten but still had to settle for a share of the title with the Scots.

The Scots also managed to break new ground in 1969, when scrum-half Ian McCrae took over from Gordon Connell to become the championship's first replacement. In today's rugby, players go on and off

the pitch at regular intervals, summed up by the Grand Slam match between England and Ireland in 2003 when Matt Dawson and Graham Rowntree each went off twice during the game. But back in 1969 when Connell left the field he only did so after a doctor made the decision that he was unfit to carry on.

By the 1970s the Five Nations had become the incredible tournament we see today, with most matches becoming all-ticket affairs. The competition gained huge popularity and a large television audience, helped to no uncertain extent by a remarkable Welsh team.

From 1969 to 1979, Wales again came to power and this period will be remembered as the golden era of Welsh rugby. Winning three Grand Slams, two outright championships (sharing two others) and six Triple Crowns, the Welsh side was absolutely unstoppable. Only an outstanding French side prevented them from adding to the three Grand Slams they achieved.

They were thwarted in their attempt to kick off the decade with a Grand Slam by the Irish, who won

14-0 in Dublin, with captain Tom Kiernan winning his 47th cap to overtake Jackie Kyle's record. But the championship couldn't hold the Welsh side back for longer than one year and in 1971, under the captaincy of John Dawes, they swept the board, scoring 73 points as they clinched their first Grand

• **Above**
John Dawes, the Welsh captain, during Wales' 23-9 defeat of Ireland in 1971.

• **Below**
Gareth Edwards with his 'shadow', Mervyn Davies, in 1978. Gareth was the lynchpin around which the Welsh side revolved.

81

• **Above**
Barry John kicks forward during Wales' 1972 game against France at Cardiff Arms Park.

• **Below**
Peter Wheeler loses the ball and England lose the opening match at the 1976 Five Nations 21-9 to Wales at Twickenham.

Slam for 19 years with their first win in France, 9-5, since 1957. Their run to the title included one of the most thrilling games in championship history as flanker John Taylor kicked a touchline conversion, following a try from Gerald Davies, in the dying moments to deliver a 19-18 win over Scotland at Murrayfield, after the lead had changed hands five times during the game.

David Hands, in his *Five Nations Story*, remarked that one newspaper had described Taylor's kick as "the greatest conversion since St Paul".

Barry John was in his pomp in this great season for the Welsh as was Gareth Edwards who said: "It was truly a wonderful feeling to reach the end of the 1971 Five Nations campaign as both champions and Grand Slam winners for the first time since 1952. I played in two more Grand Slam seasons, in 1976 and 1978, but that first one stands out in my memory, for so many of us were starry-eyed and in our rugby infancy."

By the time the second Grand Slam arrived for the Welsh in 1976, John had departed but he had been replaced by another legend of the No 10 jersey, Phil Bennett. Bennett was skipper of the 1978 side and he led them to the Grand Slam in his and Gareth Edwards' last International, a 16-7 defeat of France. But in 1976 Wales really did sweep all before them. Their lowest score was 19 points, no side scored more than 13 points against them, and their total of 102 points was a championship record. They crushed Ireland, Scotland and England and the crucial match came against France in Cardiff, a game that Wales won 19-13 inspired by a magnificent 50-yard penalty from giant Aberavon lock Allan Martin.

The Irish, too, had some glory to remember the 1970s by, as they won the championship outright in 1974, with the Scots runners-up. They had Mike Gibson, who scored two tries against England, casting his spell in the back-line and a certain Willie John McBride stoking things up in the boiler room. For McBride 1974 was also a momentous year as he won his 56th cap (then a world record) and led Ireland to their third successive win over England.

In 1975 McBride scored his first try for Ireland, in his 62nd and penultimate Test, as France were beaten 25-6 at Lansdowne Road, ending French hopes of the title. But it wasn't all good news for the Irish that season as they were turned over 32-4 in Cardiff, to suffer their biggest Five Nations defeat for 68 years.

France themselves lifted the Grand Slam in 1977 and such was their domination that they became the first side to take the clean sweep since 1913 without conceding a try. In the same year, Wales' 18-9 victory over Scotland made them the first country to win a Triple Crown but not the championship title.

France have always been known for their flair but it was their huge pack that came to the fore in 1977. Marshalled by one of rugby's greatest ever props Robert Paparemborde and with a back-row unit of

• Above
Phil Bennett is congratulated by Derek Quinnell and JJ Williams having scored against France in 1978 to clinch Wales' third Grand Slam of the decade.

• Inset
Team photograph of the 1978 Grand Slam-winning Welsh team.

the mighty Jean-Pierre Rives, Jean-Claude Skrela (who later coached the national side) and Jean-Pierre Bastiat, this was some side. The Slam was secured with a 15-6 victory over Ireland, but the key game was the titanic struggle against England at Twickenham which the French eventually won 4-3. The seeds for that French Grand Slam had been sown in 1976 when they hammered England 30-9, 'Le Petit General', Jacques Fouroux, at 5ft 5in, in terrific form.

For their part, Scotland failed to win a championship outright during the 1970s, but they did partake in one world record, as 104,000 people flooded into Murrayfield on St David's Day to see them beat Wales 12-10 in 1975.

Moving on to the 1980s and one of the most endearing pictures in rugby history shows Bill Beaumont being chaired off the pitch at Murrayfield after England had clinched their first Grand Slam for 23 years. The victories in 1980 were built on an incredible England pack that not only delivered the Grand Slam but a prized victory in the Parc des Princes 17-13, their first in Paris for 16 years. Crucially, England now had a dependable goal-kicker in Dusty Hare.

It wasn't a vintage England team, and most people acknowledge that they played poorly against Wales in their penultimate game before scraping through 9-8, but the victory kept them on course for the Grand Slam. In that Welsh match violence surfaced and Wales flanker Paul Ringer was sent off, allowing England the chance to triumph against 14 men, the boot of Dusty Hare doing the damage. However, England proved in that final game against Scotland that they could also play with flair, John Carleton scoring a hat-trick of tries in the 30-18 victory.

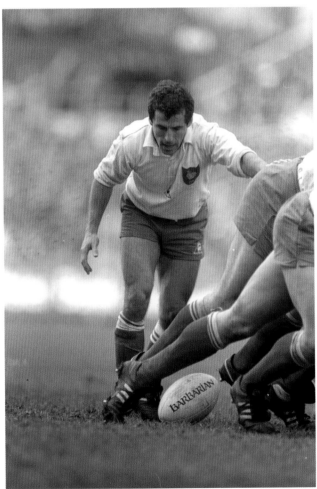

Yet this was an isolated success for England and it was France who took over as the outstanding team of the decade, winning the title outright three times, including two Grand Slams, and sharing it on a further three occasions.

France's first Grand Slam of the 80s came in 1981, the back-row combination of Jean-Pierre Rives, Pierre Lacans and Jean-Luc Joinel to the fore as they hung on 16-12 at Twickenham (having led 16-0) to clinch their prize.

They had to wait six years for their next Grand Slam, but it was well worth waiting for as they staged a series of thrilling matches with their widest margin of victory only seven points. In the deciding game of 1987, against Ireland in Dublin, they were again behind, but with players of the calibre of Serge Blanco, Philippe Sella and Eric Champ, they roared back to secure a 19-13 victory and with it their fourth Grand Slam.

In between France's two Grand Slams, Scotland conjured up one of their own. They certainly didn't go into the 1984 championship as favourites, having won just one game the season before. But the other four nations knew they had a foe to contend with after Scotland won the 100th clash with England (who had just beaten New Zealand) 18-6 at Murrayfield on the second weekend of the championship.

• **Above**
Bill Beaumont is chaired from the pitch after England beat Scotland to win the 1980 Grand Slam at Murrayfield.

• **Below**
Pierre Berbezier in action against Ireland in 1987. France won the game 19-13 to secure the Grand Slam.

Gala prop Jim Aitken was the Scotland captain and he was lucky to have one of the most potent half-back pairings in Scottish history, Roy Laidlaw and John Rutherford, to call upon. Coached by Jim Telfer, the side also had a formidable pack in Colin Deans, Iain Milne, Alistair Campbell, Bill Cuthbertson, Iain Paxton, David Leslie, Jim Calder and Alan Tomes.

The final game in 1984 was the Grand Slam decider with both Scotland and France still unbeaten. Scotland, without the injured Laidlaw, triumphed 21-12 after falling 9-3 behind. Peter Dods kicked the penalties to finish the championship with 50 points, then a record.

Scotland had the ultimate prize in 1984, but Ireland also did pretty well in the battle with the French, taking the title in 1982 and 1985. In 1982 only France, in Paris, stopped an Irish side inspired by fly-half Ollie Campbell from taking the Grand Slam. Campbell scored all 21 points in their 10-point victory over Scotland, but those points only told half the story of what was a truly inspirational performance.

• **Above**
Scotland captain Jim Aitken celebrates with some Scottish fans after clinching the 1984 Grand Slam by beating France 21-12 at Murrayfield.

• **Below**
David Leslie being tackled by Phillippe Sella in that 1984 Grand Slam match.

their glories of the 1970s, never really threatening to take a championship, let alone a Triple Crown. They showed flashes of brilliance, such as the 25-21 victory at Murrayfield in 1985, but with the team being constantly changed and coaches coming and going, they were never able to live up to their predecessors. A championship did arrive in 1988, though shared with France, as well as their first Triple Crown since 1979, thanks to the reliable Paul Thorburn, who kicked a late penalty to ensure a 12-9 win over Ireland. But a year later they were bottom again, winning just one match.

Wales also played their part in the 'Battle of Cardiff' in 1987, when Wales and England seemed more intent on staging a boxing match. There was a series of punches, kicks and off-the-ball incidents and four England players, Wade Dooley, who had broken Phil Davies's jaw, Richard Hill, Gareth Chilcott and Graham Dawe were dropped for the following game.

Three years later, the Irish came closer still to the Five Nations' ultimate prize, this time thwarted by an ill-tempered, bruising 15-15 draw with the French in Dublin, but they still ended the season one point clear at the top. Again the Irish looked to the boot, but this time it belonged to Michael Kiernan, who slotted five penalties from seven attempts, while the French scored two tries. Ireland secured the Triple Crown and the championship in a 13-10 Dublin win over England and again it was Kiernan who proved the hero, dropping a vital injury-time drop-goal.

Wales came down to earth with a bump after

• **Above**
Brendan Mullin crashes through Rob Andrew's tackle as Ireland clinch the 1985 Triple Crown by beating England 13-10 in Dublin.

• **Below**
John Orwin of England and Ciaran Fitzgerald of Ireland run for the loose ball in the same match.

• Above
Paul Ackford jumps to win the line out during the 1991 Five Nations match against France at Twickenham. England won the match to win their first Grand Slam since 1980.

• Inset
Rory Underwood takes the ball past Ieuan Evans of Wales during the 1992 Five Nations match played at Twickenham.

As Wales had done in the 1970s, so England started the 1990s in total domination winning the Grand Slam three times, and taking the Triple Crown six times in eight seasons. They did it under one captain, Will Carling, who had been appointed to the role in 1988 while still only 22, a year after completing his studies at Durham University.

England had some great backs in that period, notably Rory Underwood (49 tries in 85 appearances) and the mercurial Jeremy Guscott, but it was in their pack where their real strength lay.

Carling's first Five Nations Slam came at an opportune time, in 1991, as his side were starting their preparations for the forthcoming World Cup, which was being held in the British Isles and France for the first time.

The 1991 triumph was achieved after a crucial 21-19 victory over France at Twickenham, a match which saw the visitors score two magnificent tries. One, scored by Philippe Saint-André, covered the length of the field and began when an England penalty attempt went wide of the posts and France caught their hosts napping by attacking from behind their own goal-line. But England would not be denied and the pack allowed goal-kicker Simon Hodgkinson to grab 14 precious points and their first Grand Slam for 11 years. England went through that season unchanged, only the second time they had ever managed to do so.

Before the 1992 championship season, Carling led his side to the World Cup final, beating France and Scotland along the way. So, with only the newly retired Paul Ackford missing from the team, England went into the 1992 Five Nations as overwhelming favourites. They did not disappoint their supporters and flew through the other four nations, scoring a championship record 118 points (35 more than in 1991) against just 29, scoring 15 tries on their way to the Grand Slam.

It was the first time since 1924 that a side had won back-to-back Grand Slams and one game stood out, perhaps for the wrong reasons. England won 31-13 in Paris in a game which saw both prop Gregoire Lascube and hooker Vincent Moscato sent off as the English pack set about winding up their hosts to good effect. It was in the days when the French Achilles heel was their indiscipline and England were the best at exploiting this weakness.

The following year brought two wins for Carling's team, but they had to wait until 1995 for their final Grand Slam of the decade, and their last until Martin Johnson's side in 2003.

Carling's 1995 vintage missed out on the 100-point mark by just one conversion, but they ruled the roost all the same, with no side coming within 12 points of them.

Scotland, runners-up in 1995, pushed them hardest and it was left to the power of the English pack to deliver the 24-12 win, courtesy of seven Rob Andrew penalties and a drop-goal. Both sides had gone into the final game unbeaten.

England's 1995 win over France was their eighth in succession against the Bleus, but this time the 31-10 victory, with two tries from Tony Underwood and one from Jeremy Guscott, was their biggest against them since the First World War.

England followed their 1995 Grand Slam with a 1996 championship, the first of the professional era, after they finished level on six points with Scotland. England's only defeat came in Paris, 15-12, but the Five Nations almost became four that year after England were thrown out. England were expelled for signing their own television deal with BSkyB, but after some hasty negotiations they were allowed back in before the championship began, although it took them many years to recover the trust of the other nations.

The reality of England's exclusion was summed up by Scotland's Director of Rugby Jim Telfer, who said: "To be honest Wales, Scotland and Ireland need England more than they need us. They are the country everybody wants to beat."

England may have dominated the middle period of the decade but they didn't get the start to the 1990s they wanted, Scotland winning the Grand Slam in 1990, again with a winner-takes-all showdown against England on the final day of the championship. The Scots set the tone for one of the greatest days in their history when captain David Sole led out the side on his famous slow walk, instead of the traditional charge out of the tunnel. The walk was designed to unnerve Carling's men and it seemed to do the trick. Tony Stanger delivered the

• **Above**
The 1990 Scottish team pose for a photograph before the Five Nations Grand Slam decider against England at Murrayfield.

crucial try for the Scots and they were also indebted to goal-kicker Craig Chalmers as they won 13-7.

There was not much more to shout about until the end of the decade, although in 1995 when they were runners-up to England in what was the legendary Gavin Hastings's last season, Scotland won their first ever match in the Parc des Princes and their first in Paris since 1969. In this game Hastings became not only Scotland's most-capped player but also the first player to score more than 600 championship points.

Scotland ended the decade on top, clinching the 1999 Five Nations with a last weekend victory over the French in Paris, though they still needed England to slip up 24 hours later against Wales at Wembley. Incredibly the Scots had their vital game all but won by half-time, as they ran up a 33-22 lead. It was a remarkable turnaround for a team who had conceded 120 points in 1998 and yet a year later had now scored the same number to claim the last Five Nations title.

Wales had limped through the 1980s but worse was to come in 1990 when they suffered their first whitewash in the Five Nations. The nearest they got to a victory was the 13-9 defeat at home by Grand Slam winners Scotland. A year later only a 21-21 draw at home to Ireland prevented the ignominy of back-to-back whitewashes.

But under the captaincy of Ieuan Evans, they did buck the trend once, in 1994, when they were Five Nations champions, losing one game on their way to winning the championship on points difference over England. Wales, who introduced a future great in Scott Quinnell that season, arrived at Twickenham with the Grand Slam on the table, but they never looked like clinching it, eventually losing 15-8. It left the strange situation of skipper Evans having to go up and collect the trophy on a losing day.

But anyone who underestimates the Welsh nation does so at their peril and with the new millennium beckoning, they still had one trick up their sleeve and it arrived at Wembley at the end of the 1999 championship.

With the National Stadium in Cardiff being redeveloped, Wales had decamped to Wembley for their home games and it was Clive Woodward's England, captained by Lawrence Dallaglio, who arrived to secure what appeared to be a certain Grand Slam to end the decade. All looked to be going to plan for the English, despite the fact that prolific goal-kicker Neil Jenkins had kept the Welsh in touch throughout the game. But then, in the dying minutes, England gave away a needless penalty and, from the resulting lineout, Chris Wyatt found Quinnell and he pulled off a rehearsed move that brought Scott Gibbs into the line for one of the most famous runs in rugby history. Gibbs scythed through the English defence to score and when Jenkins kicked the conversion Wales had won, incredibly, 32-31 thereby handing the trophy to the Scots.

Meanwhile, France struggled to maintain their incredible form of the 80s, although they did manage to take the 1993 championship, the first in which points difference was introduced to separate the teams, with three wins out of four. France's 26-10 win over Wales in Paris set it up and then England's shock 17-3 hammering by Ireland in Dublin delivered them the title.

They had to wait until the end of the decade though before reasserting their supremacy on the Five Nations, taking back-to-back Grand Slams in 1997 and 1998.

In 1997 the records tumbled as the sides shared 53 tries – the best total since 1911, when France were on the end of some fierce hammerings – and scored an incredible 511 points in ten matches, smashing the previous best of 363 six years before. England scored a record 141 points (12 more than France) but they couldn't hold the French at Twickenham. Despite going 20-6 behind in the first hour, France rallied for a dramatic 23-20 victory, with Christophe Lamaison the inspiration. They went on to steamroller Scotland 47-20 to confirm their fifth Grand Slam, the first they had clinched on their own soil. Coach Pierre Villepreaux said: "Today they played modern rugby. They ran with the ball and when they were stopped, they kept it and ran again."

France repeated the Grand Slam in 1998, in a championship which saw the arrival of Sunday play and this time the French were in a new stadium, an 80,000 all-seater in Paris called Stade de France,

• **Opposite**
Gavin Hastings of Scotland clears his lines during the 1995 Five Nations match against England at Twickenham. It was the Scottish legend's last ever international.

• **Above**
Scott Gibbs charges forward on his way to scoring that famous try against England in the 1999 Five Nations match at Wembley.

• **Above**
Stuart Grimes of Scotland is tackled by Giovanelli and Dominguez of Italy during the 2000 Six Nations game played at the Flaminio stadium in Rome. Italy won the game 34-20.

• **Below**
Alessandro Troncon, captain of Italy, celebrates the victory over Scotland in what was their first ever Six Nations match.

which was to host the 1998 Football World Cup final.

They celebrated their new home with a record number of points in the championship (144), in a season that yielded 55 tries, a feat that equalled the 1911 total. The France team was in free-flowing mood in 1998, scoring 18 tries, but more importantly their defence was on top form, conceding just 49 points.

In the 1980s Romania would have made an excellent addition to the Five Nations, but in the 1990s the clamour to make the five become six was too great for the Home Unions and France to ignore. But it was not the Romanians who were invited to the top table but the Italians, who in 1998 had beaten Ireland and Scotland in non-championship matches.

It made so much more sense to have six nations rather than five, if only to make sure that every side played at the same time. With five competitors, one side had always sat out one weekend of the tournament.

Italy offered the Five Nations committee a proven club championship, good competition for their national sides and a venue, Rome, that supporters were dying to visit. They kicked off the Six Nations in 2000 and did so in dramatic style, beating Scotland 34-20.

But it was clear that the team was ageing, losing some of the players that had brought them great success in 1998, and they proceeded to struggle, though not as much as the French had done when they arrived on the scene at the start of the 20th century.

The Italians lost 14 consecutive games in the Six Nations after that win over Scotland, finishing with the wooden spoon in 2000, 2001 and 2002. But their fortunes took an upward turn with their best championship performance in 2003. After the arrival of Kiwi coach John Kirwan, the Italians beat Wales 30-22 at the start of this tournament and with the Welsh failing to register a win, Italy finished fifth in the table, scoring a very respectable 100 points in their five games.

But 2003 was England's year as Clive Woodward's men ended four years of near misses by finally winning a Grand Slam. It was clinched in a pulsating last match against Ireland in Dublin.

Woodward took over the England team in 1997 but his love-hate relationship with this great tournament began in 1999, when his side was unbeaten until that game against Wales at Wembley.

A year later it had been the Scots' turn to rob England of the Grand Slam on the final day. This time England swept all before them in the first four games, their toughest test coming at home to France, but even they were comfortably beaten 21-10.

They arrived at Murrayfield as 1-15 favourites but they were badly prepared for the Scots and, when the heavens opened to bring a deluge on Edinburgh, England's hopes of a Grand Slam were washed away. They still managed to score first, through a Lawrence Dallaglio try, but with injured talisman Martin Johnson sitting in the stands, they failed to have a plan B, with plan A clearly failing, and lost the match 19-13.

The defeat prompted former England captain Will Carling to question whether Clive Woodward was the man to coach England. Carling said: "There has to remain a huge question mark over Woodward's ability to make England a true force in world rugby. My position on Woodward remains sceptical.

"He has produced a team that can play awesome rugby, especially against the weaker sides, but his England simply aren't winning the crunch games."

By the time England arrived at the 2001 tournament they were hot favourites again and would probably have taken the Slam had it not been for the foot-and-mouth crisis, which ensured two of Ireland's games were postponed. The second of

• **Above**
At last! England Coach, Clive Woodward, holds the 2003 Six Nations Trophy at Twickenham after England completed the Grand Slam.

these was against England in October which Ireland took 20-14. Although England still won the championship, they were left disconsolate by failing yet again to win the Grand Slam.

In 2002 France were the pre-eminent team in the competition, beating England 20-15 in the crucial third round decider and scoring 156 points in total as they marched to the Grand Slam. England scored more points in the 2002 championship than the French (184) and, of the other nations, only Wales got close to toppling Bernard Laporte's France, losing 37-33 at the Millennium Stadium.

But those bad memories for the English team were banished to the history books in 2003, when both Ireland and England arrived at the last game in Dublin unbeaten for a winner-takes-all Grand Slam showdown.

It was the first time since 1995 (when England beat Scotland) that the Grand Slam could have been won by either team playing in the last match. As on that

occasion, England held their nerve, this time to triumph 42-6, Will Greenwood scoring two tries. England scored 29 unanswered second-half points to complete their 11th successive Test-match victory, equalling their record set in 2000 and 2001.

"The ramifications of losing would have been huge, but I think that we have got a big-match team and the preparation was excellent this week," Woodward said. "If we had lost today, then it would have been a very tough year for us all. I am delighted with the way everyone responded."

England came into the 2004 RBS Six Nations as overwhelming favourites after their victory at the World Cup. However, England, suffering from the loss to retirement of captain Martin Johnson and to injury of Jonny Wilkinson endured their worst Championship in the professional era.

Ireland became the first side to win at Twickenham in the championship since 1997 and when England lost the

last game of the championship, 24-21, in Paris , France owned the Grand Slam and England were left third.

The defeat of the world champions earned France their eighth Grand Slam and centre Yannick Jauzion believed it could signal the start of a new era for the French.

"We showed the English that they had to stop being arrogant, and thinking that they can always win," said Jauzion.

"They have to show us respect."

"This was a dream night with a French crowd that had a great time from the start to the end," added French rugby union president Bernard Lapasset.

"We were expecting a lot of English fans but they were beaten as well.

"We still think about it (the World Cup semi-final) and we still feel a twinge of sadness when we mention it.

"This match won at the Stade de France gives us some regrets about the World Cup but we know we can beat the English and we should not miss out when we meet them again."

Celebrations went on in Dublin as Ireland picked up their first Triple Crown (wins over the other home nations, England, Wales and Scotland) since 1985.

Ireland coach Eddie O'Sullivan claimed that runners-up spot in 2004 should give them the platform for further progress.

"It's very good for Irish rugby to finish second two years in a row. We've won 10 out of our last 13 Tests, which is a tremendous record," O'Sullivan said.

"In last year's Six Nations, we lost to England in the Grand Slam decider. This year we had away games against France and England, but still won four matches, so I think we're knocking on the door.

"We're putting ourselves in position to win something bigger than a Triple Crown, but that's easier said than done. The last two years have been an excellent stepping stone for us."

Ireland centre Gordon D'Arcy was been rewarded for his sparkling form in the RBS Six Nations by being named player of the championship. D'Arcy received half the 12,000 votes cast – four times as many as team-mate Paul O'Connell who finished in second place – in a poll run by the BBC Sport website.

England winger Ben Cohen finished third in the vote, Gareth Thomas of Wales fourth and France's powerhouse flanker Serge Betsen was fifth.

• Above
Gordon D'Arcy was Ireland's hero in their 24-21 defeat of England at Twickenham, 2004.

Amateur to Professional

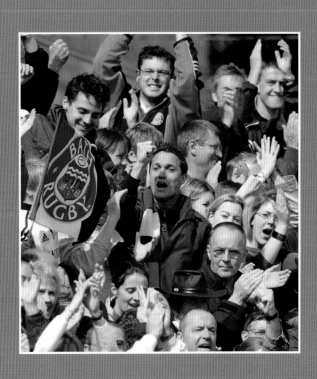

Chapter
SIX

The road from Richmond to Twickenham – the A316 – is travelled more often by rugby fans than perhaps any other in the world, as it leads to the home of English rugby.

This short stretch of dual carriageway is a microcosm of the effect professionalism has had on Rugby Union in Britain. In the spring of 1995, while Rugby Union was still an amateur sport, there were some of the biggest clubs in England along that stretch of road. Richmond, London Welsh, London Scottish and Harlequins were all local residents and, just a little further on, there was also London Irish.

Rugby Union was the last major sport to turn professional and the effect it had on the game was as great as the split between league and union in 1895.

Travelling along that stretch of road today it is a different scene, the consequence of the sport's move to professionalism and the way the game handled that move. Outside the Richmond Athletic Ground, which is shared by Richmond and London Scottish, is a huge billboard listing the next game to be staged at this famous rugby union venue. From 1995-97, with both Richmond and London Scottish in England's top two divisions, the opponents on that board would have included the likes of Leicester,

Northampton and Saracens. But today those illustrious names have been replaced by junior clubs such as Staines, Barnes and Old Hamptonians, and the tale of how this occurred sums up the strife that has afflicted English professional rugby.

In 1995, when the game turned professional, in the southern hemisphere the players were contracted to the individual Unions. But in the north, with the RFU sitting on their hands, some clubs were left at the mercy of the people with the biggest bank account.

The dilemma was never about whether the players should be paid or not – as they had been paid covertly for years – but about who would control their contracts. That is where the southern hemisphere moved streets ahead of its northern counterpart in the years after 1995.

The clubs on the A316 suffered badly. London Irish outgrew their welcoming and passionate home in Sunbury, and decamped to a new home in Reading, while London Welsh settled for life in England's National League One (England's second tier), which they may be stuck with for the foreseeable future.

But at least these two clubs stayed in with the elite. When both Richmond and London Scottish's

backers left the game, these two grand old clubs were forced into administration and in 1999 were thrown out of the English league. Not relegated a division or two but told that if they wanted to play league rugby again it would have to be in the bottom division of the whole league pyramid.

"It was an unpleasant situation," admitted Tom Walkinshaw, the owner of Gloucester and the man who headed up English First Division Rugby (EFDR), the organisation that represented the English elite.

"But sometimes unpleasant things have to be done to protect the overall entity you are charged with looking after. One or two clubs in the league raised the possibility of going into administration because of financial problems, and each time they were told they would lose their league membership if they did."

Both clubs were obviously furious at the way they were treated by their fellow top-flight clubs, as they thought they should have received help and been given enough time to put a rescue package together.

One of their players, former England back-rower Ben Clarke, said: "Rugby is about people and building friendships, about a respect for each other and each other's clubs. And when you get people like EFDR ripping all this away, it sums up the state of the sport."

Luckily both clubs had supporters who were committed to the cause and both started life right at the bottom of that league pyramid in England, gaining a series of promotions in the following seasons.

No club in England was exempt from the fallout. Even in the town of Rugby, where the sport was invented, the game almost disappeared. The 120-year-old Rugby club had debts of around £400,000, most the result of building a new clubhouse. The RFU were forced to bail them out as they were not going to allow the town of Rugby to disappear from the map.

Clubs like Saracens (Nigel Wray) and Northampton (Keith Barwell) were lucky as they were bought by people who not only loved rugby but had an almost endless supply of cash to prop up the professional game in England.

Sir John Hall was the English owner who opened the floodgates, buying Newcastle Gosforth, to add to his controlling interest in Newcastle United FC, and signing Rob Andrew as his director of rugby, for a reputed salary of £150,000 a year.

The Unions in the northern hemisphere were so slow out of the blocks when professionalism began that it looked as though they were running backwards. For many years before 1995 there was a lack of realism amongst the Home Unions about the developments in the rest of the world, and they were

• **Above**
Rob Andrew repaid Sir John Hall's faith in him by winning the Allied Dunbar Premiership for Newcastle Falcons in 1998, at the first time of asking.

• **Inset**
Gloucester rugby club owner Tom Walkinshaw.

ill-prepared when the big announcement arrived. They felt it was their way (amateurism) or the highway, but what they failed to realise was that the rest of the game, and their own players, were already travelling down the highway!

Through the 20th century union fought hard to stay amateur. But as early as 1990 the walls began to tumble when the IRB allowed earnings from ancillary activities, including advertisements and endorsements that were not rugby-related.

It was clear that in most countries these 'amateur' players had been paid to play the game for many years but in 1995, when the game finally went open, the RFU declared a moratorium on professionalism, saying that it would start 12 months after the rest of the world.

This led the Celtic Unions to blame the RFU for the mess British rugby became in the five years after the sport went open. The moratorium did nothing but create a vacuum which was quickly filled by entrepreneurs who took over several clubs. The RFU's inability to grasp the nettle of professionalism meant that instead of mounting a campaign to

contract the players directly to the Union, and setting up a provincial or divisional structure as happened in the southern hemisphere, the clubs contracted the players.

The reality was that, in the days immediately after professionalism arrived, nothing happened. When English rugby should have been investing in its major clubs, it was instead portraying them as trouble-makers.

The RFU have always claimed that the decision as to whether to contract the players was taken out of their hands. And what followed was a series of damaging political battles with the clubs.

Brian Baister, who was RFU chairman from 1998 to 2001, said: "The criticism that we did not centrally contract the leading players has been misguided. We were not in a position to do so then because we had an overdraft of £10m.

"It is a question of entering into a partnership with the clubs to ensure that the disputes of recent years, which harmed the game, never happen again, but we must not overload the players. There has to be a sensible number of fixtures."

Before Baister, and a number of other officials, tried to repair the RFU's reputation in 1996, England were also thrown out of the Five Nations Championship for going it alone on a crucial TV deal, only to be readmitted at the last moment.

As the loan payments for the new stand at Twickenham began to bite and pressure came in from the clubs, the RFU, without consulting the other sides in the Five Nations, signed an £87m deal with satellite television station BSkyB to cover all their matches at Twickenham. But the RFU didn't seem to appreciate that to play a match you need opposition, and their opponents – Wales, Scotland and Ireland – quite rightly demanded a slice of the action.

"This is selfishness gone mad," said the late Vernon Pugh, chairman of the Welsh Rugby Union and Home Unions TV committee. "What infuriates the other Unions is that the deal has been done in a deceitful way. The RFU, in taking this decision, have done it in the knowledge that the other countries will no longer play them."

Rumours of England forsaking the Five Nations and joining the Tri-Nations came and went, as did the clubs' threats to break away and start their own league without the RFU.

This again was in contrast to the southern hemisphere as the three major nations of New Zealand, Australia and South Africa worked together, signing a 330m TV deal in 1995.

Unfortunately for the RFU, the way they handled the TV issue was typical of the way they blundered through the first years of professionalism.

It was in England where the traditional club base remained the dominant competition. And what followed were years of battles between the clubs and the RFU for control of the game.

Due to the inactivity of the Union, rugby's history should regard the millionaires who lost a reported £150m getting professional rugby going in England as saviours. They were often painted as greedy and out for control of the Union, but without them how would the game in England have survived?

Geoff Cooke, the former England coach who took charge of Bedford, explained what a thankless task it was to try and run a big club in England after professionalism.

"For an investor at this level it must be like standing in a cold shower tearing up £20 notes," Cooke said. "Most investors have found the actual costs are way beyond those they envisaged when they set out on this voyage of discovery. But there is no alternative other than to get out."

Critics who attack the top clubs forget it was not they who voted for professionalism but it was they

• *Above*
Geoff Cooke took Bedford from the bottom of the second division and into the Premiership at the start of the professional era.

• Above
Damian Hopley,
Chief Executive of
the Professional
Rugby Players'
Association.

who were left to deal with professionalism. Having had it thrust upon them, the Premiership clubs initially stuck together in a partnership called the English Professional Rugby Union Clubs (EPRUC).

Their relationship with the RFU deteriorated, and in 1996 and 1997 the clubs threatened to pull their players out of their national squads following disagreements with the RFU and its chairman Cliff Brittle.

Some players and their Unions felt that the only thing that would change in 1995 was that they would get paid to play. Those who made that mistake went backwards.

In England, it was only the eventual intervention of the leading players that finally knocked heads together, and got both the Union and the clubs around the table, to hammer out an agreement that benefited both sides. The turning point in England came in March 2001 with the creation of Premier Rugby Partnership, an alliance of the Premiership clubs and more than 370 players, which in itself forced the RFU into signing an agreement. It meant

that the players were siding with the big English clubs.

Damian Hopley, chief executive of the Professional Rugby Players' Association, explained: "I think the RFU saw the writing on the wall then. The message of the players was clear: club rugby was on the verge of disintegrating because owners had reached the point where they were prepared to walk out unless they were able to run their clubs on proper business lines. The agreement reached largely reflects the proposals put to the RFU earlier which were then rejected out of hand.

"It was only when the players took sides that the Union was forced to reconsider its position, and the result is a deal which will allow the English game to make considerable strides. When you consider what has been achieved in the last five years in terms of playing standards, the future looks incredibly bright.

"From the perspective of the players, what the agreement means is that we will be able to put into operation welfare programmes which will help them come to terms with life when they retire."

Howard Thomas, chief executive of Premier Rugby Partnership, added: "I am being constantly asked why it took five years to find a common-sense solution. There are times when you have to get to the brink before something happens. Despite all that was said before, both sides recognised that they needed each other, that each on its own would be immeasurably weaker."

To complete England's five-year move to professionalism other policies such as a salary cap were introduced to boost the chances of an 'open' game being a success.

For decades before the move to professionalism came, administrators around the world had fought the change and rather like King Canute eventually the waves lapped over their feet and they were forced to admit defeat.

When it did come it came in bizarre circumstances and the overnight move from an amateur to a professional game led to many of the problems that beset rugby union – especially in the northern hemisphere – in the years that followed.

On 27 August 1995 IRB chairman Vernon Pugh told his colleagues that unless they declared the game professional, it would be taken away from them by commercial interests. He had the vision to see this and in hindsight he was undoubtedly right.

"I don't think we had an alternative," said Pugh, "and we do have a very strong belief we can properly control the game for the future."

Bill Bishop, then president of the RFU, said: "It's a momentous day in the history of the sport, but it's a sad day at the same time. The game will never be the same again. Hopefully we can hold on to what is good about it."

If the game hadn't gone professional at that time it is likely that the top players from around the world would have signed for an outside organisation and broken away from their Union and the IRB.

Pugh, though, had his reservations as he knew it would ensure the rich Unions would get richer and the poor Unions may just get poorer.

Before the announcement, Pugh said: "They [the smaller Unions] believe if it becomes pay for play it may well be impossible for Unions and the International Rugby Board to retain control. It's only New Zealand who are pressing for a position where players are paid to play. The others favour, and New Zealand are happy to accept, a position where they continue to operate through their developing trust funds."

But this halfway house was never going to suffice. The speed at which the rules were altered reflected

the inevitability of the change, and many in the years before the move not only predicted it would happen but also indicated the salaries players and coaches would be earning.

Australian officials declared in April 1995 that the game was no longer amateur. Especially in that country, if the best players weren't being paid they would have been spirited off to rugby league.

The move to professionalism was, in the end, unavoidable. The 1996 Five Nations Championship arrived and as David Hands explains in his book *The Five Nations Story*, a payment structure was quickly

• Above
Robert Howley and his Welsh team were celebrating a reputed £25,000 salary for their six games in the 1996 season.

• Below
The late Vernon Pugh was Chairman of the IRB, overseeing the move to professionalism.

agreed for the players.

"In 1996 England's players received a retainer of £24,000, with a match fee of £2,000, the French a very similar sum save they also incorporated a win bonus.

"Ireland (£7,500) and Scotland (£5,000) had much smaller retainers with match fees of £3,000, though the Scots had a substantial win bonus of £5,500. Wales players were able to earn around £25,000 from involvement in six games though, true to form, details of their retainers were a dark secret as the championship began."

In 2003, when England won a long-awaited Grand Slam, the players were each paid a reported £65,000 for their eight matches over the season. The players were paid a flat fee of £6,000 per International, win or lose. They won all eight matches – against New Zealand, Australia and South Africa in the autumn, and then the five matches in the Six Nations Championship to deliver the Grand Slam.

That gave them £48,000 each, and the squad also picked up a £350,000 bonus for winning the Grand Slam. So the likes of Martin Johnson, Jonny Wilkinson and Lawrence Dallaglio received a bonus of £17,000 each.

In the early years of professionalism, while the southern hemisphere continued a largely harmonious relationship with their players, it seemed the English players and the RFU grew further and further part on financial issues.

The players wanted less of their fees to be governed by performance-based win bonuses and more control over their intellectual property rights. And after failing to reach agreement the England players threatened to initiate rugby's first strike, to hit one of professional rugby's low points.

In November 2000 the England players downed boots and said they would not play in the coming week's International against Argentina. Jonny Wilkinson, in his book *Lions and Falcons*, explains

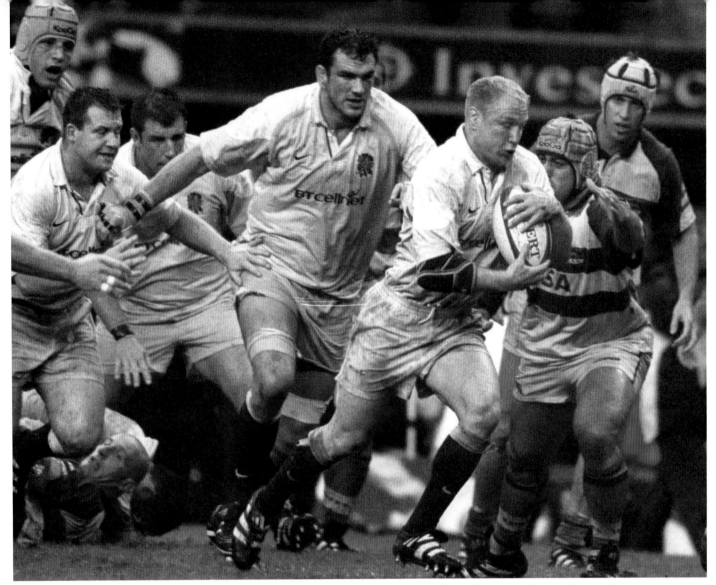

that the secret ballot vote was unanimous.

"We had come to the end of our tether," said Wilkinson, "and the England squad was withdrawing its labour for the Argentina game. We could not agree our contracts with the RFU so we decided to take the last and most drastic course of action left to us.

"It was the culmination of more than a year's stalled negotiations that had frustrated the players and threatened to distract them from the business of playing rugby."

The RFU did eventually settle the dispute and a full-strength England side beat Argentina. But it was yet another example of the poor way the RFU had handled professionalism and it was another unnecessary episode that damaged the image of the game in England.

As soon as the IRB announced a Rugby World Cup in 1987, it was a question of when and not if the game went professional, as the tournament, and increased tours, brought more and more demands on players – anything less than paying them would simply have been unfair.

The move to professionalism was never about the greed of the players and those who opposed it often misunderstood the game, saying that it was a middle-class game, played and watched by people who could afford it.

This view, and with it the notion that the game could have stayed amateur, is attacked in Stephen Jones's *Midnight Rugby*.

He says: "The real rugby people, the people who played it and loved it, were always elsewhere. In fact, they were everywhere, unrestricted. High-calling servicemen, Tigers' family outings to Welford Road, unemployed steelworkers at Stradey Park, woodsmen in the Forest of Dean, Cornishmen at Hell Fire Corner, raging Tucumanos in Tucuman, pullovered punters shivering in Carisbrook, Dunedin or Hawick, Scottish Borders or Thomond Park,

• **Above**
Neil Back of England leads his team on a charge during the International match between England and Argentina at Twickenham in 2000.

• **Above**
Van Der Westhuizen
of South Africa
clears the ball under
pressure from Lee
Stensness of New
Zealand during the
2002 Tri-Nations
match at Ellis Park in
Johannesburg.

• **Below**
John O'Neill of the
Australian Rugby
Union talks to the
media during the
2001 Super 12
launch.

Limerick; Stade Toulousain striped hordes in the South of France; Northampton Saints roaring on their cosmopolitan men; millionaires sprung up from working-class families, investing in rugby clubs; redneck farmers in Potchefstroom.

"The labels were applied by others and did not represent rugby, only small parts of it. The reality was always far different."

As the 1995 World Cup was being staged, the three southern hemisphere superpowers, Australia, New Zealand and South Africa, were battling for the future of the game, trying to ensure they had a head start on the countries in the north.

As other organisations began to fight for control of the players the three SANZAR unions fought off the challenges. Following a £370m, 10-year television deal with Rupert Murdoch's News Corporation, the three unions had the financial muscle to keep their players. In fact if the International Rugby Board hadn't sanctioned the move from amateur to professionalism, it was clear from this deal with Murdoch that the southern hemisphere unions would have done it themselves.

Australian chief executive John O'Neill accepted: "They are professional players now. But we are aware of the fine balancing act that needs to be made, and the dangers of burn-out. We don't want to overload the players. But by the same token, television money pays their salaries and television wants product."

The first television deal that unified Europe's leading nations came in 2002, when the BBC, crucially for rugby's profile a free-to-air channel, paid £65m to cover the Six Nations Championship and a

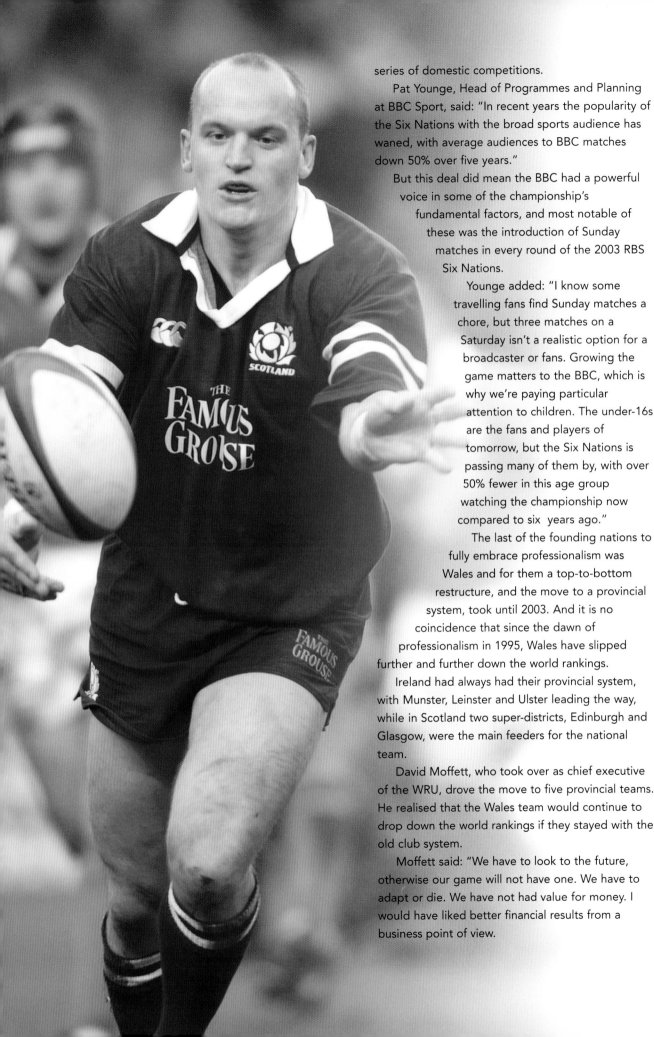

series of domestic competitions.

Pat Younge, Head of Programmes and Planning at BBC Sport, said: "In recent years the popularity of the Six Nations with the broad sports audience has waned, with average audiences to BBC matches down 50% over five years."

But this deal did mean the BBC had a powerful voice in some of the championship's fundamental factors, and most notable of these was the introduction of Sunday matches in every round of the 2003 RBS Six Nations.

Younge added: "I know some travelling fans find Sunday matches a chore, but three matches on a Saturday isn't a realistic option for a broadcaster or fans. Growing the game matters to the BBC, which is why we're paying particular attention to children. The under-16s are the fans and players of tomorrow, but the Six Nations is passing many of them by, with over 50% fewer in this age group watching the championship now compared to six years ago."

The last of the founding nations to fully embrace professionalism was Wales and for them a top-to-bottom restructure, and the move to a provincial system, took until 2003. And it is no coincidence that since the dawn of professionalism in 1995, Wales have slipped further and further down the world rankings.

Ireland had always had their provincial system, with Munster, Leinster and Ulster leading the way, while in Scotland two super-districts, Edinburgh and Glasgow, were the main feeders for the national team.

David Moffett, who took over as chief executive of the WRU, drove the move to five provincial teams. He realised that the Wales team would continue to drop down the world rankings if they stayed with the old club system.

Moffett said: "We have to look to the future, otherwise our game will not have one. We have to adapt or die. We have not had value for money. I would have liked better financial results from a business point of view.

• Above
Gregor Townsend of Scotland passes the ball during the match between Scotland and Ireland at Murrayfield, the first Sunday game of the 2003 Six Nations. For the first time Sunday games featured in every round.

• **Above**

Wales fans celebrate during the 2001 Six Nations match against France played at the Stade de France. Wales won the match 43-35.

"The only good thing Welsh rugby had going for it was its fans. They still travel the world to support their team. In fact, I'd go as far as to say that they are the best rugby fans in the world, considering the lack of success they've had to endure. The bottom line is that since the game turned professional, the sport in Wales has seen no success at either international or club level."

Having been instrumental in the creation of the Super 12 series in the southern hemisphere, Moffett believed that only by reducing the number of clubs and professional players in Wales, as had happened in New Zealand, could the game move on.

"The problem was that the northern hemisphere followed a flawed machine that is football," he said. "Now all the problems this approach created are hitting the game. Don't just think it's been bad for Welsh rugby. I can assure you that it's hardly a bed of roses in the English country garden right now. They have 12 top teams, and they all have too many foreign players in them and over-the-top wages. It was the same in Wales, with nine clubs and hordes of journeymen foreigners playing." We only have to look at the plights of Bristol and Bath who finished last and second last in the 2003 Zurich Premiership to see what Moffett means.

In 2002 Scotland also expanded their two districts, with the establishment of a third, Borders.

"The new professional Borders team is the missing piece in the jigsaw for Scottish rugby," explained Scotland coach Ian McGeechan. "Scotland had four regional teams when the game went professional, but for financial reasons Edinburgh merged with the Borders and Glasgow merged with Caledonia – and four became two. That was a huge mistake which we've been trying to redress ever since.

"Scotland needs a wide playing base. A country of our size can't produce 200 professional players, but we should be able to get 100 to 120. When we went down to two teams – Glasgow and Edinburgh – it wasn't just players that were lost but the structure behind it."

The advent of professionalism has certainly helped raise the profile of rugby union across the globe and according to recent surveys it is now the UK's second most popular sport after football.

• Above
Despair for Bristol as defeat in the final game of the 2003 Zurich Premiership season against London Irish spelt relegation.

• Below
Jubilation for Bath fans as their 2003 final game victory over Newcastle Falcons assured their survival in rugby's top flight.

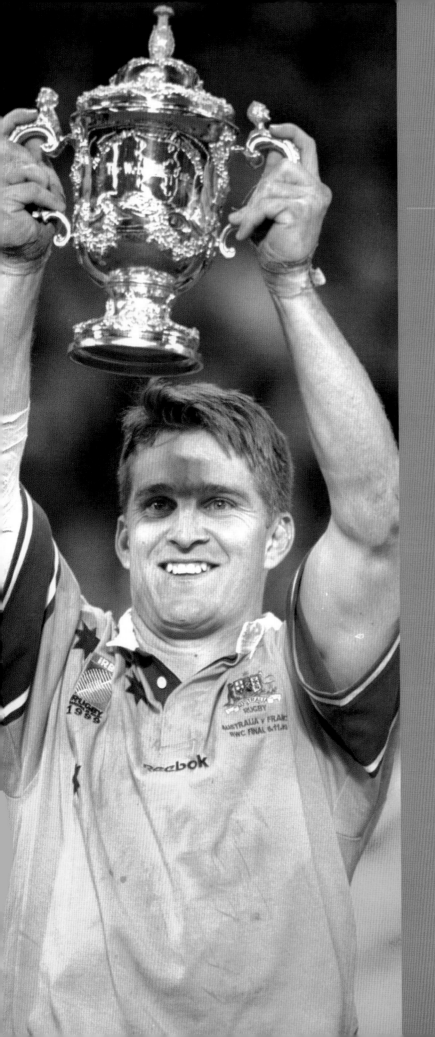

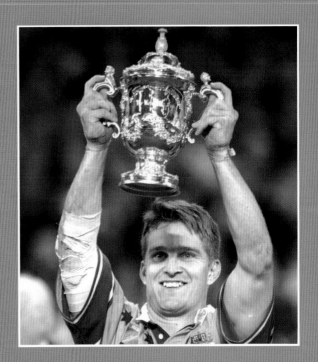

Australia

Australia were the first side to win the Rugby World Cup twice but if a certain member of the New South Wales parliament, Eldred Harmer, had got his way they wouldn't even have had a rugby team at the 1991 and 1999 tournaments. Harmer, in 1864, was disturbed by the sport and according to Jack Pollard's fascinating book *Australian Rugby*, tried to get it banned, telling the House that rugby matches were "vicious displays of brutish fist-fighting".

Luckily for the Wallabies and hundreds of thousands of Rugby Union fans across Australia, Mr Harmer failed to get his way and one of the most powerful rugby nations in the world was born.

Rugby Union was first established in Australia around 1864, with the first game played between Sydney University and the Sydney club. But, in spite of making a great start in the middle to late 19th century, Australia had one of the hardest tasks in establishing the game, it's position threatened by both Rugby League and Aussie Rules.

It took until 1899 for the first International to be played when an Australian side (nine from New South Wales and six from Queensland) took the field to face the touring British and Irish Lions in Sydney.

More than 28,000 people crowded into the

Sydney Cricket Ground to see those pioneering Australians beat the British Isles tourists 13-3, Ginger Colton having the honour of scoring Australia's first try. Some of the early clubs had their roots in associations with cricket clubs so it wasn't a surprise to see the national side taking the field at the SCG.

New Zealand and South Africa became regular early opponents but not until 1989 did the British and Irish Lions attempt another tour to Australia only. Instead, Australia became merely a stop-off on the way to New Zealand.

It was only a matter of time before the Australians would leave their own shores for a rugby tour and the first of these was in 1905 when they made the short journey to New Zealand. This Australian side lost 14-3 and it would be another 44 years before they returned from New Zealand victorious.

Before that, the Australians had their own version of England's big split, as professional Rugby League emerged in 1907. As an amateur sport, Rugby Union was becoming just too big a commitment for those not paid to play the game. In-so-saying Rugby Union had a foot-hold and Australia undertook a major tour of Britain in 1908-09. This is probably most famous as the tour that gave the Australians the nickname they still play under today. The name was

• Above
Australia take on Devon during their 1908-09 tour of Britain.

• Inset & opposite
Australia's first ever international match was against the 1899 touring Lions at Sydney.

inspired by the captain of that tour, Dr Herbert Moran, as much to stop the British calling them the Rabbits as anything else. There was considerable debate in the English press about what to call the Australians and letters poured in to newspaper offices. Wallabies, Kangaroos, Kookaburras and Wallaroos were all suggested, and Dr Moran said: "The decision demanded a conference. For a brief day we, who for six weeks had been Rabbits were Waratahs, but that was only emblematic of NSW. All were agreed that any name would be preferable to the Rabbits, and Wallabies won by a couple of votes."

Those first Wallabies played 31 games, winning 25, drawing one and losing five. The draw and most of the defeats came in Wales, but they beat England 9-3.

1908 also saw success for Australia in the London Olympics where they took the rugby gold, albeit against a team from Cornwall, the English county champions, who were representing the United Kingdom. Either way they were despatched quite comfortably 32-3, the Australians scoring eight tries.

The game continued on an even keel but, in a period before the First World War the Wallabies saw their side ripped apart by professionalism. The rift had begun in 1909 when a series was staged between the Wallabies and the Rugby League side, the Kangaroos. Both sides were paid to play by a New Zealand-born entrepreneur James Joynton Smith and once the series was over the Australian Rugby Union had little choice but to ban for life those chosen and, unfortunately, this group contained some of their best players.

With the best Wallabies ensconced in the Kangaroos camp, it wasn't long before league became the premier winter game and in fact union has spent most of the rest of its existence trying to

catch up with its league counterpart in Australia, such has been the interest in the Kangaroos.

Union began to struggle in the period up to the First World War not even prospering in its New South Wales hotbed and it must have come perilously close to going out of existence. A 3-0 seies whitewash by New Zealand as war was declared did little to help its cause. League played through the First World War while union didn't and afterwards only six clubs restarted in Sydney and none in Queensland, so it was inevitable that financial problems would surface.

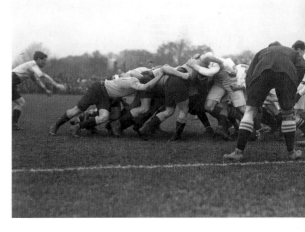

With the game almost dying out in Queensland it was NSW (or the Waratahs) who would take on other nations in Test matches in the 1920s. The team played in light blue and wore the Waratahs logo but did have the occasional Queenslander or Victoria player in their side.

NSW was lucky to have the support of the New Zealanders after the First World War as the income from matches against the Kiwis was crucial in keeping the Union buoyant. South Africa, who played NSW in 1921, also played their part in keeping the game going throughout the 20s. It is necessary to acknowledge how important those Waratahs were after the First World War and when the Wallabies lifted those World Cups in 1991 and 1999, it was with a debt to those pioneers. They also developed a style of rugby that still exists today, with every player expected to contribute both in attack and defence.

• Above
Australia in action, Sydney 1899.

• Below
Australia take on Cambridge in 1908 as part of their tour of Britain.

By the time the New Zealanders crossed the Tasman in 1929, it was to again play an official Australian side, as the Queensland Rugby Union was back in business. The schools were crucial to the re-establishment of rugby in Queensland and the Union there was reformed a year earlier. Although caps were later awarded for games played in the 1920s when NSW took over the national side, the first Test was billed as the rebirth of the Australian side.

The Sydney Morning Herald explained in its preview to the match: "When Lawton leads out his green-clad fifteen on to the field today many will recall the last occasion New Zealand faced an Australian team. War had been declared. New Zealand won, as it did each of three Tests in the 1914 series, and Rugby Unionists, almost to a man, discarded jerseys and

sprigged boots for sterner uniform.

"For some of the participants, those matches 15 years ago were destined to be the last of their rugby careers. They did not return."

In the 1929 series Australia never looked back from their 9-8 opening win in Sydney, taking the second Test in Brisbane 17-9 and the third 15-13 back in Sydney. They were one of the finest sides in Australia's history, and although the All Blacks were in something of a 'development stage', the achievements of this Australian side shouldn't be underestimated. Skippered by Queenslander Tommy Lawton – who did so much for the establishment of

the game in the northern state – and including such rugby legends as Cyril Towers, Syd Malcolm and prop Bill Cerutti, they carved out their own place in rugby history. And to confirm this wasn't a set of freak results, a year later they beat the British and Irish Lions, who were on their way to New Zealand, 6-5 in Sydney. Between the two wars the only other contact between the Australian national team and sides from the northern hemisphere was when NSW undertook a tour of the British Isles and France in 1927-28.

NSW and Queensland provided the players for the national side until 1931, when the emergence of Victoria as a third rugby state was significant in the development of the Wallabies. A Melbourne Rugby Union club started in 1888 and, after a number of different manifestations, was reformed as the Victoria Rugby Union in 1926. This area of Australia had the most trouble establishing itself as the state is solid Australian Rules and Rugby League country. However, It was crucial that a strong Victorian Rugby Union set-up emerged and in the 1930s, with Sturtridge the inspiration, the side hosted the British and Irish Lions and earned a reputation for playing fast, exciting rugby.

Australia were conspicuous by their absence at the top of world affairs after the Second World War, although they did enjoy some isolated successes, including an 11-0 win at Twickenham in 1948 and a 2-0 series victory in New Zealand a year later. However, during 1949 the All Blacks already had a squad in South Africa, and so Australia only faced the third-string side.

The Lions were still far too strong for the Wallabies, beating them six times on the trot, in 1950, 1959 and 1966, and between 1950 and 1963 Australia played 36 Tests against major nations, winning just four. Rugby League was still a great predator in those days, with many of the better players moving to the professional code before they were able to make a big impact on the union stage,

• Above left
The 1948 Australian team. Their tour of Britain included an 11-0 defeat of England at Twickenham.

• Above right
Trevor 'Tubby' Allan, captain of the 1949 Australia team who beat the All Blacks 2-0 in New Zealand in their two Test series.

and it was difficult to see the Wallabies ever becoming a real force.

Then, in 1961, one of Australia's greatest players, Ken Catchpole, made his debut, providing the backbone for the great Aussie comeback in the early 1960s. This comeback saw two Test wins in South Africa in 1963 (9-5 and 11-9) in a drawn series, and then in 1965 a 2-0 series win over the Springboks in Australia, with a side captained by John Thornett.

But it still wasn't enough for Catchpole, who said after the second Test win in 1965: "We didn't play anywhere near as well as we had before but we still won."

The drawn 1963 series was also a big breakthrough for the Wallabies as South Africa had won every other series between the sides since the first one in 1933. Apart from Catchpole, the loose forwards stood out – Greg Davies, Jules Guerassimoff and John O'Gorman.

This resurgence also prompted the Australian

Union to seek an official home for the Wallabies. In the early years of Australian rugby, not only did the sport struggle to raise its profile in competition with Rugby League and Aussies Rules, but it had also failed to establish a home. In England they had Twickenham and in Wales the National Stadium in Cardiff, but in Australia it was a case of squatting on Rugby League grounds. That all changed in 1966 when the AU bought Ballymore in Queensland. The first Queensland against NSW game took place there in 1967 and the New Zealanders were to visit a year later.

However, neither Catchpole's success nor the new ground seemed to inspire the Wallabies and in fact it was an ignominious defeat that really spurred them on. Big defeats are the making or breaking of most sides, and when the Australians suffered the embarrassment of being tagged the 'Woeful Wallabies' in 1972 it started their rise to the top of the world rankings. In that season they

• **Main**
Norman Hughes played 14 Tests for Australia at No 8 during the 50s.

• **Inset**
The flying Ken Catchpole from a 1966 match against the Southern Counties. Catchpole is one of Australia's greatest ever players and sparked their comeback in the 60s.

• Above
*Australian prop
Steve Finnane
(middle) watches on
as Captain John
Hipwell spins the
ball out to the backs
during the 1975 first
Test victory over
England in Sydney.*

were beaten three times by New Zealand and, under Bob Templeton, were beaten in eight of their 13 games. The coach said: "In terms of international rugby we weren't good. If people want to say woeful, so be it."

The side that lost to New Zealand was missing some great players, including John Hipwell, but no excuses could be made on 30 June 1973 when, in Brisbane, they suffered one of their worst ever defeats, losing 16-11 to Tonga. No 8 Mark Loane said: "The loss itself was a shock and I've always considered that to be the absolute rock-bottom of Australian rugby."

The fightback started with a drawn series against New Zealand in 1974, and then the arrival of England in 1975 for a series won 2-0, with one draw, by the Wallabies. Hipwell was chaired off the pitch after the first Test win, 16-9, in Sydney over England, and in the second, a week later in Brisbane, the Wallabies scored five tries for a 30-21 victory. The draw against New Zealand in that 1974 series ended a run of seven successive victories for the All Blacks over the Wallabies.

If Australia had been creeping back up the world rankings in the early 1970s, they arrived back in the elite with a bang in 1979, when a win over New Zealand returned the Bledisloe Cup to Australia. It was the first time the cup had been on offer in a one-off match. The season started badly with a defeat to Ireland but then New Zealand were sent back from Sydney on the wrong end of a 12-6 defeat.

Perhaps more remarkable than winning that Bledisloe Cup in 1979 was the way in which the side defended it in 1980, this time in a three-Test series, taking the deciding match 26-10 in Sydney. That 2-1 series victory for the Wallabies was their first series triumph over New Zealand since 1949. Wallaby skipper Tony Shaw said at the time: "In 1979 we had beaten the All Blacks in a war of attrition. We'd gone from that to this open, free-flowing style in 1980. We'd won it fair and square and played fantastic rugby. We had to nail them in that last Test and we knew from the Hika Reid try in the second Test that they were never dead.

"I remember being in the guys' faces, real finger-

in-the-chest stuff, urging them on and telling them: 'We've come this far, we've got to go on with it'. It's the most intense I've been in a game."

The free-flowing style that Tony Shaw alluded to in 1980 was to be the watchword of Australian rugby for the next two decades as they built a side feared throughout the world. The next warning came in the form of that famous 1984 side which will go down in history as one of the best from any nation to visit Britain and Ireland. Two years earlier, Shaw's side came to the UK and beat just Ireland, but the Wallabies weren't about to make the same mistake.

The 1984 side contained many players who would acquire legendary status by the time their careers ended, men like David Campese, Michael Lynagh, Andrew Slack, Simon Poidevin, Nick Farr-Jones and Mark Ella, who scored a try in every Test match on that tour.

This side completed the Grand Slam of wins over England, Ireland, Scotland and Wales and they did it in style, setting new standards for those that were to

follow them. They scored an incredible 51 tries, 12 of them in their four Tests, the biggest win coming in the last Test at Murrayfield, when they destroyed Scotland 37-12. They didn't finish the tour unbeaten, but in the games that really mattered, the Tests, they always rose to the occasion.

Alan Jones, the coach of the 1984 side, said of them: "I prefer the Gucci outlook. Long after you've forgotten the price, you remember the quality."

They started with a 19-3 demolition of England and the closest they came to defeat was in Dublin, where they won 16-9. Mark Ella scored the vital try in Dublin after great work by Campese and a young left wing named Matt Burke (not the current Wallaby).

Ella recalls: "Campo went inside with a big step. He took a couple of guys with him. Then he stepped out. Sometimes it's hard to get the ball off Campo, but he saw I was free and gave it."

After the scare in Dublin, Wales were hammered 28-9 in Cardiff before the Scotland victory confirmed just how good this 1984 side was.

• Above
David Campese races in to score against Wales at Cardiff Arms Park during their 1984 Grand Slam tour.

One disappointment for Australia was that Mark Ella retired after the tour, but his place was to be taken by a guy who'd made his debut the same year – Michael Lynagh. Nobody in Australia need have worried.

Two years later in 1986 the Wallabies won the Bledisloe Cup for the first time in six years and for the first time in New Zealand since 1949, securing a 22-9 victory at Eden Park to complete a 2-1 series win.

In this great form Australia were many people's favourite to win the inaugural World Cup in 1987. They looked like justifying this position after sailing through their group, but in the semi-final they had the misfortune of running into a French side at its sublime best. Legendary French full-back Serge Blanco was the hero of their 30-24 victory as he finished off a length-of-the-field move to send France into a Final with New Zealand. A dejected Australia went on to lose their third-place play-off with Wales, in Rotorua, 22-21.

But four years later, with many of that 1984 team maturing, they swept all before them in a World Cup tournament staged in England, Wales, Scotland, Ireland and France. Australia weren't overjoyed with their performance in the final, beating England 12-6 in a game that never flowed, and they probably reserved their best form for the wins over Ireland and New Zealand in the preceding matches. It was left to prop Tony Daly to grab the vital score in the Twickenham final.

New Zealand coach John Hart left nobody in any doubt about who he hoped would win that 1991 final. After England had mounted a forward-dominated campaign, Hart said: "God help the game if England wins the World Cup. Australia epitomize what is good about rugby. My criticism of England is that this game is played to run the ball, not just to kick and chase."

Australia came into the 1995 World Cup on the back of a famous 1994 Bledisloe Cup victory. Australia held a four-point lead, 20-16, as the game moved into its final minutes, with New Zealand attacking with all their might. All Black wing Jeff Wilson had already beaten two defenders and was about to dive over the line when a missile, in the shape of Australia scrum-half George Gregan, popped up to smash the ball out of his hands and so bring the Bledisloe Cup back to Australia.

"It's one of those experiences you know will only ever happen once in your career, and it's something I'll never shake off," Gregan admitted. "People still

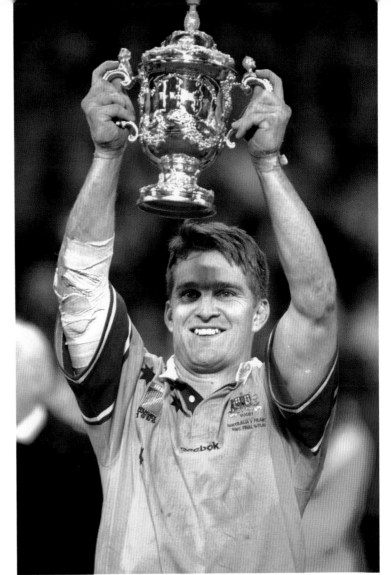

want to talk about it, but I think it made such an impact because of when it happened, in the dying stages of the game."

Australia only made the quarter-finals in 1995, losing 25-22 to England after a late Rob Andrew drop-goal in Cape Town, but they were back on top of the world four years later.

In between, things didn't go all their own way as the victory over the All Blacks in 1998 was their first over their greatest rivals for almost four years.

But by the time they lined up in the 1999 World Cup, back in the northern hemisphere, Australia stamped their mark on the tournament, conceding just one try in the competition and beating France 35-12 in the final. Captain John Eales said: "It was a special team effort throughout this tournament and I am convinced that we improved with every performance, and the final was our best display. We didn't want to be playing our best rugby against Romania in the opening match of the tournament,

and I am very pleased with how we progressed. Belief in yourself is everything, and we had a terrific will to win.

"People like Tim Horan were outstanding, but we had unsung heroes right across the board. Our prop Andrew Blades, who retired after this tournament, is a classic example of that."

Professionalism helped no nation more than Australia, because at last they could compete financially with League, and even sign some players from the 13-man code, like Wendell Sailor and Mat Rogers. As we move through the first decade of the 21st century, their place near the top of the world order seems guaranteed for a long time to come.

New Zealand

For rugby in New Zealand, think football in the UK and then double it. Everyone has played, everyone loves the game and everyone pays

• **Above left**
John Eales and Tony Daley celebrate as the final whistle is blown at the end of the 1991 World Cup final against England at Twickenham.

• **Above right**
Tim Horan lifts the Webb Ellis trophy after victory over France in the 1995 Rugby World Cup Final at the Millennium Stadium.

• **Above**
*Members of the
1926 Maori team in
London. Maoris
have been touring
Britain since the
1888-89 tour.*

attention when the All Blacks are in town so it is perhaps no wonder that the All Blacks have had so much success and that so many of their sides should be spoken of in reverential tones.

The first game in New Zealand, between Nelson College and Nelson Football Club, was staged on 14 May 1870, even before the formation of the (English) Rugby Football Union.

Rugby's introduction in New Zealand is credited to Charles John Monro. Monro, son of Sir David Monro, Speaker in the House of Representatives from 1860 to 1870, was born at Waimea East, but picked up his love of Rugby Union when he attended Christ's College, London. When he returned to New Zealand, he suggested that the local football club in Nelson try out the rugby rules.

After a visit to Wellington, Monro organised a game between them and Nelson and Rugby Union began to take hold. Today it is not only the pre-eminent winter sport but the pre-eminent sport at any time of the year in New Zealand.

New Zealanders have been spreading the gospel of rugby since the late 19th century, with the first national side being chosen for a trip to play New

South Wales in 1884. Like many touring parties of its time, it had its problems but was at least selected from each of the four major Unions at the time. They started as many New Zealand sides have followed, with eight wins in eight matches. The first main tour from New Zealand was in fact undertaken by a Maori team in 1888-89, and what a tour it was. It lasted 14 months as the Maoris played an astonishing 107 games, 74 of which took place in the British Isles.

The Maoris have played alongside and with the All Blacks ever since and no history of New Zealand rugby should omit the debt the All Blacks owe to them. To this day they are an incredibly strong team in their own right and many believe Maori matches warrant full Test status, as it is accepted that they would easily make it into the world's top eight sides. They still provide a stern test for any tourists.

That 1888-89 tour also unleashed the famous 'haka' on the British and Irish and one can only imagine what they made of it back then! It is still a key weapon in making the All Blacks the most feared side in international rugby. They aren't the only team to perform a war dance, as many of the sides from the South Sea Islands do so as well, but only with the

presence of the All Blacks does the haka strike real fear into the opposition. Before every Test match the whole All Blacks side, led by a Maori player, takes part in the haka in the centre of the pitch, an event to send chills down the spine of everyone who witnesses it.

The first New Zealand side to be considered as fully representative of their land was the 1893 team, that again made the trip to New South Wales, this time captained by Tom Ellison. New Zealand played at home for the first time in 1894, beating NSW 8-6. As NSW weren't themselves truly representative of Australia, the New Zealanders had to wait until the turn of the century, in 1903, for their first Test match, which again resulted in a victory, this time over Australia, 22-3. Billy Wallace had the honour of scoring the first points and the great Albert Asher

the first of his many tries for the New Zealand All Blacks.

In those early years of rugby, British teams would make regular journeys to the southern hemisphere, but two New Zealand sides coming the other way changed the face of the game. The first, 'The Originals', arrived in 1905 when Dave Gallaher captained a side that won all but one match of an incredible 33-match tour, scoring 868 points and conceding a paltry 47. Before they left, the New Zealand press was calling them world champions, following their 14-3 victory over Australia. The only defeat on the tour came against Wales, by 3-0, but even that was in controversial circumstances as the All Blacks believed they should have been awarded a try when Bob Deans appeared to go over the line, only to see his effort disallowed. Gallaher's team

• **Above**
The All Blacks perform the haka before their match against South Africa at Richmond in 1916.

were not only successful but also innovative, showing the British and Irish sides and their supporters an array of new moves, and promoting a new-look scrum with two players in the front row, and an extra scrum-half or 'rover' behind the pack. They rucked like no side before and introduced moves that had their opposition gasping. Modern international coaches talk about players being able to play anywhere on the pitch but Gallaher had pioneered this at the turn of the century, saying: "Our principle is that every forward should be a potential back."

Billy Wallace headed the scoring charts for the 1905 side, with 246 from 26 matches, while Jimmy Hunter crossed the line 42 times.

This 1905 tour is also credited with coining the nickname by which the New Zealand team is known throughout the world. One story has it that a British newspaper editor incorrectly transcribed a journalist's comment that the remarkable Kiwis played like they were 'all backs'. However, is it not more likely that they received the nickname because their kit was 'all black'? Whatever the true origin, the nickname and the team colours have never changed since.

The next great team after Gallaher's side was the 1924 All Blacks, 'The Invincibles', who swept all before them. Those who saw the All Blacks in the 1920s will never forget the way players like George Nepia, Bert Cooke and Maurice and Cyril Brownlie played the game, and they won every one of their matches on this tour including victories over Ireland 6-0, Wales 19-0 and England 17-11. Scotland refused to play the tourists after a row on the 1905 tour and that was the only thing that stopped New Zealand taking the Grand Slam.

Although tours to the British Isles are important, historically New Zealand's fiercest opponents are South Africa and the first All Blacks tour of the republic came in 1928. In 1921 when the Boks arrived in New Zealand the series was tied 1-1, with the last titanic Test being drawn 0-0. In 1928 there was again nothing to separate the two nations, this time ending 2-2. These two series launched one of the sport's greatest rivalries.

The 1930s saw mixed results for the All Blacks. They kicked off the decade with a 3-1 series victory over the Lions, under the captaincy of Cliff Porter, but also lost to both England (3-0 at Twickenham in 1936) and Wales (13-12 at Cardiff in 1935), and suffered a 2-1 home series defeat to South Africa in 1937.

They fared little better in the games immediately after the war, and their performance in 1949, when they lost every one of the six Tests they played, made what was about to happen even more amazing. For, in 1950, they embarked on an incredible run, as they chalked up series win after series win, losing just five of their next 24 Tests.

The 3-0 series victory over the Lions in 1950 started the renaissance as the All Black players proved that they could never be written off.

Bob Scott, the prolific full-back, was one of the first to stand up and be counted and he was followed by a teenage sensation, Don Clarke, who went on to become one of the most famous All Blacks of all time.

In 1956 this great run ensured that New Zealand won a Test series against South Africa for the first

time, with Clarke, or 'Superboots' as he was known, taking control on his debut in the third Test, which the All Blacks won 17-10. They completed the 3-1 series victory two weeks later at Eden Park with an 11-5 win, and South Africa were defeated in a Test series for the first time in 60 years. They followed this up in 1959 with a 3-1 series victory over the Lions.

In 1961 France became the first European country to tour New Zealand on their own, as all previous tours had been undertaken by the British and Irish Lions. France, who over the years have had some mighty clashes with the All Blacks, had won or shared the previous three Five Nations Championships before arriving in 1961 so were seen as a stern test to their dominance. But this good form counted for little, as they were whitewashed by the All Blacks 3-0, coming closest to causing an upset in the second Test in Wellington, before losing 5-3. In the first Test the All Blacks fielded two sets of brothers (Colin and Stan Meads, and Ian and Don Clarke) and triumphed 13-6 at Eden Park.

A year later came another first with a home-and-away series between Australia and New Zealand. This five match series was won 4-0 by New Zealand with the first Test, in Wellington, a 9-9 draw.

The team went from strength to strength

culminating in the greatest winning sequence in their history from 1965 to 1969 as they went 17 Tests without losing. The team were feared throughout the world and Brian Lochore's 1967 All Blacks are thought to be the finest New Zealand side ever. Their tour of the British Isles was sensational with just one draw, against East Wales, preventing them from establishing a perfect record. They were only stopped from completing a Grand Slam by the fact that they didn't play Ireland, due to an outbreak of foot-and-mouth disease in England.

The 21-15 victory over France, who were to win the Grand Slam in 1968, was described thus in the book *Men In Black*: "This had been a match in which the All Blacks had displayed one of the finest exhibitions of 15-man rugby in a hard, vigorous and exciting encounter."

Lochore had been appointed New Zealand captain for the 4-0 victory over the Lions in 1966 and achieved iconic status. Another New Zealand legend, Colin Meads, wrote of Lochore in his biography: "At the peak of his career, from 1966 through to 1969, he was everything I would want in a No 8. He spared himself not an ounce working away in the tight-loose covering, winning great lineout ball in the deep, backing and filling and playing his part in the rolling drive-and-feed.

• Above
Brian Lochore introduces his 1967 All Blacks to the Queen prior to their match with England at Twickenham. This team was considered by many to be the greatest ever.

• **Above**
Scrum-half Dave Loveridge passes the ball during the All Blacks 13-12 victory over Wales in their Grand Slam tour of 1978.

• **Inset**
Graham Mourie, captain of that 1978 team.

"As a captain he could be so self-effacing, for this was the very nature of the man, yet in his way he was as effective as Whineray had been."

In the 1970s the All Blacks had two colossal series with the Lions, but it was the 1978 team that broke a long-standing record. Graham Mourie, though not necessarily one of the best players in history, will go down as one of the best captains of an international side. It was his 1978 All Blacks that became the first to complete a Grand Slam in Britain and Ireland. They beat Wales 13-12, Ireland 10-6, England 16-6 and Scotland 18-9. The only side to lower their colours on their 18-match tour were Munster, who won 12-0 on an historic day in Limerick.

Two years before this 1978 Grand Slam, the New Zealand Rugby Football Union had formed the National Provincial Championship with a view to toughening competition amongst the domestic sides. The NPC allowed all 27 Unions to compete in three divisions with the First Division featuring 11 teams. In hindsight, and with the northern hemisphere following their path in later years, the establishment of the NPC was ground-breaking and this fiercely-fought competition helped New Zealand stay at the top of the world game throughout the 1980s.

Considering the way New Zealand had been such a powerful force throughout rugby history, it was fitting that they should lift the first Rugby World Cup in 1987 and fitting too that the team should be coached by All Black icon Brian Lochore. This side were so good they took the loss of their captain, Andy Dalton before the tournament, in their stride, finding another great leader in David Kirk to take them into battle. With backs like full-back John Gallagher and wing John Kirwan, this side oozed

class, from the first game when they beat Italy 70-6, to the last where they overcame the impressive France side 29-9. The 23-point margin in the final was the closest any side got in this World Cup to beating these All Blacks. Surprisingly, this remains the All Blacks sole World Cup success.

They have had a great deal more success in the Tri-Nations, which many in the southern hemisphere feel is as hard to win as the World Cup, winning four of the seven titles since its 1995 inception.

Before and during their first Tri-Nations win in 1996, the All Blacks fielded an unchanged pack for 10 consecutive Internationals. Little wonder with great players like Sean Fitzpatrick, Robin Brooke, Zinzan Brooke, Ian Jones and Michael Jones to select from? And even though they lost their title in 2000 and 2001, they bounced back in 2002, a 12-6 win over Australia helping them to clinch the tournament. Although New Zealand had to settle for third in the 2003 World Cup they came into the tournament in great form, after having won the Tri-Nations competition.

• **Above**
Doug Howlett hugs Dave Hewett as the All Blacks celebrate their win in the first 2002 Bledisloe Cup match between New Zealand and Australia played at Jade Stadium, Christchurch.

• **Below**
David Kirk, the captain of New Zealand, lifts the Webb Ellis trophy after their victory over France in the 1987 Rugby World Cup final at Eden Park in Auckland.

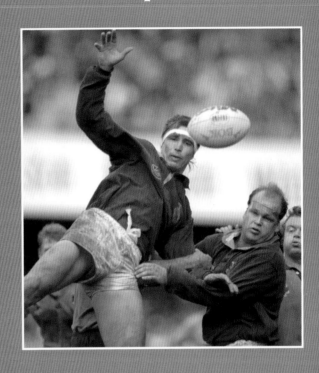

Chapter
EIGHT

South Africa

South Africa were quick to embrace the new game of rugby football and most historians place the first game in the republic at 1862, when a Civilians v Military match took place in Cape Town. Rugby thrived in the following years but it was the visit of the 1891 British and Irish Lions, two years after the formation of the South African Rugby Board, that gave the sport the kick-start it needed. These Lions were unbeaten and and only conceded one try in 20 matches. Charles (Hassie) Versfeld had the honour of scoring that first try and the ground the Springboks still play at in Pretoria bears his name.

But when the next tourists arrived five years later they found a much better South African set-up. Although the Lions won the first three Tests, the South Africans took the fourth, 5-0, to register their first ever Test victory against them. This 1896 Test is also reputed to be the first time the South Africans wore their famous green jerseys, although the choice of official colour was not made until 1906. Those 19th century defeats by the Lions clearly hurt the South Africans and it was to be another 78 years before they lost a series at home – to the 1974 Lions.

South Africa's improvement was clear when the Lions arrived again – in 1903 – to suffer their first series defeat on South African soil, drawing two Tests and losing the last one 8-0 in Cape Town. This win, according to Chris Greyvenstein's book

Illustrated History of Springboks Rugby, was "one of the real mileposts in the history of South African rugby". Barry Heatlie captained the side and Joe Barry and Alex Reid scored the vital tries.

With sides arriving in South Africa around the turn of the century, it was only a matter of time before the South Africans left their own shores, and in 1906 Paul Roos took the Springboks to the British Isles. The team included the legendary 'Thin Red Line' from Stellenbosch – the threequarters Johannes Loubser, Jacob Krige, Henry de Villiers and Antonie Stegmann. Anyone unaware of the pedigree of South African rugby was left in no doubt after they drew 3-3 with England, beat Ireland 15-12 and beat Wales 11-0. Although they lost 6-0 to Scotland they won 25 of their 28 matches with Loubser the star of the show, scoring 24 tries in 21 games. It was on this 1906 tour, their first overseas trip, that the South Africans picked up the nickname that was to stay with them, and become a national emblem. As with the All Blacks and Wallabies, the nickname arrived at the insistence of the British media who asked captain Paul Roos what the team was to be called. 'De Springbokken' (plural of 'Springbok') was how Roos requested that the reporters should refer to his side.

The springbok, as a rugby emblem, dates from 1903. In March of that year Gerald Orpen (Transvaal) suggested that the national rugby team play against the visiting British touring team in green and gold jerseys with a springbok on the left chest.

• **Above**
A dusty scene from the 1891 British and Irish Lions victory over South Africa.

When Roos led his team onto the field at Northampton, on September 27 1906, they were fully clad in green and gold, and the importance of that Springbok crest to the team remains to this day.

In 1910 South Africa were to confirm their place in the high echelons of the world game with a 2-1 series victory over the Lions – how things had progressed in 20 years!

After the First World War, South Africa produced some fantastic players, including the Morkel brothers, Jack and Gerhard, and between 1924 and 1933 Springbok supporters worshipped the great Bennie Osler.

This devotion began with Osler's role in the first Test on South African soil against New Zealand in 1928. It was known simply as 'Osler's match' as the Springboks ran out 17-0 winners, making Bennie a national hero after he collected 14 points. Osler is still regarded as one of the greatest players the country has ever produced. He was a master tactician and linked up for seven Tests with 'Mr Rugby', Danie Craven.

Irish international JD Clinch remembered Osler when he said: "He is the hardest to bring down and I do not believe that he can be knocked out."

Bennie Osler's place as one of the Springbok greats was confirmed on the 1931-32 tour of Britain and Ireland, when they completed that rarest of feats, the Grand Slam, with victories over Wales 8-3, Ireland 8-3, England 7-0 and Scotland 6-3. Under the captaincy of Osler, this side lost just one match, to Midland Counties at Leicester. "We played to our strengths on that tour," Osler explained. "We had a magnificent set of forwards, outstanding scrum-halves in Craven and De Villiers and a match-winning full-back in Gerry Brand."

Even better than that Grand Slam team was the South African side of 1937, regarded by many as the best side to leave South African shores. They won both Tests in Australia, and then went on to win in New Zealand by two Tests to one. Captained by great lock Philip Nel, this team included Fanie and Boy Louw, Danie Craven at scrum-half and, as the last line of defence, Gerry Brand. Their pack was immense with Louw and so many of this men at the peak of their careers. The South Africans won 9-5 and 26-17 in the two Tests against Australia in Sydney, before the fantastic comeback victory in New Zealand, when, having lost the first Test 13-7 in Wellington they roared back with wins in Christchurch, 13-6 and Auckland, 17-6.

• **Above**
The 1906 South Africans on their way to an 11-0 victory over Wales at Swansea.

• **Below**
A fascinating memorial to England's 3-3 draw with South Africa in 1906.

That final Test at Eden Park was billed by the media as a match that would decide the 'world rugby crown' so it was South Africa who became the unofficial world champions.

On the boat returning home, Nel announced his retirement by throwing his boots into the sea, handing the baton on to Danie Craven. Craven was an innovator of the highest degree and left footprints on the world game, as a player, coach and administrator, that are still visible today. His incredible ability, firstly as a scrum-half, allowed him to play international rugby in a number of other positions, including outside-half, centre and eighth man (not No 8 but an extra loose forward). He was also passionately committed to breaking down the barriers that existed between black and white.

Craven led his side to a 2-1 series victory over a touring Great Britain side just before the Second World War, but South Africa weren't to play another Test match for over a decade until, in 1949, they took on the mighty All Blacks on home soil. Whitewashes against the All Blacks are as rare as hen's teeth but the South Africans managed it in this unforgettable series. Under the captaincy of Felix du Plessis, the Springboks inflicted a 4-0 thrashing, starting with a 15-11 win in Cape Town and finishing the series off in Port Elizabeth, 11-8.

Sadly, one of the most memorable series in South African rugby history was tainted as New Zealand's first-choice half-back, Vince Bevan, was a Maori and the New Zealanders, under South African orders, made him ineligible for selection.

At this time the South Africans had no peers in the world game and they signalled their intention to dominate the decade when they sent a truly incredible side to Great Britain and Ireland in 1950-51. England, Ireland and Wales were beaten but South Africa saved the best for the Scots, who succumbed 44-0, leaving one Scottish newspaper to pronounce: "We were lucky to get nothing!" This Springbok side was a try-scoring machine but the effort was based on the forwards and particularly the fearsome front row, which included William Delport and Chris Koch who were joined later in the 1950s by Jaap Bekker.

Yet this form couldn't continue and as the 1950s came to a close, the Springboks suffered defeat at the hands of the All Blacks, losing a series 3-1, and in 1958 they lost 9-5 at home to a great French side, causing consternation in South Africa. Many felt they had turned their backs on the forward-orientated game, but back they came with a fearsome pack for the 1960 series, at home to New Zealand. Captained by the sensational Avril Malan at lock, and with giants like Johann Claasen, Pier du Toit, Chris Koch and Doug Hopwood alongside him, South Africa steamrollered the All Blacks, winning the series 2-1, with one draw.

This great side were more than just a forward pack as a year later they hammered Australia, romping to two huge wins 28-3 and 23-11. They also travelled to Europe in 1961, again taking a Grand Slam and only failing to win one Test match, a 0-0 draw with France at the Stades Colombes. They had great backs in Ian Kirkpatrick, Hennie Muller and, at their axis, the fly-half Keith Oxlee. Oxlee was also at the helm in 1962 as South Africa cruised to a 3-0 series victory over the Lions after drawing the first match 3-3 in Johannesburg. However, their form

began to dip as the '60s progressed, with many blaming the widening anger at the South African government's apartheid regime.

In discussions about South African rugby it is with regret that one immediately thinks of apartheid, such was its effect on sport in the Republic through the decades. Things seemed to come to a head in the late 1960s and early 1970s with demonstrations, opposing apartheid, almost wherever the Springboks played.

New Zealand refused to tour without their Maoris in 1967, and when the Springboks arrived in Australia, in 1971, 139 people were arrested during the first tour match in Adelaide, and more than 5,000 protestors marched to the match to vent their anger at the South African rugby side and police were forced to confront them. The Sydney Morning Herald called it "an embarrassing tour" and added: "Sport which has to be conducted behind barbed wire is, in this country, an ugly absurdity and we can do without it."

In 1980, the Springboks awarded a cap to Errol Tobias, the first black player to play a Test for South Africa, but it took until after unification for another black player to wear the green and gold – Chester Williams, who later became the first black player to score a Test hat trick.

In Mark Keohane's book, *Chester*, he revealed that from the first day South Africans started playing Test rugby, and until the 2002 Tri Nations, the Springboks selected 729 individuals, and only 15 were black.

In South African captain Francois Pienaar's book, *Rainbow Warrior*, Nelson Mandela explains how sport was a big factor in the fall of apartheid: "Today we can claim that we are truly one people, united within the treasured richness of our diversity.

"None of this could have been achieved by the political leadership on its own... The sportsmen and women of our country played a very crucial role in this regard, for sport reaches where politicians can never hope to.

• Above
South African scrum-half Piet Uys prepares to kick against England in 1961. South Africa won 5-0 at Twickenham on their way to taking a Grand Slam.

• Below
Will Carling and Rory Underwood in conversation with Errol Tobias, the first black player to gain full Springbok colours.

and one of the sports the South African people had missed the most was Rugby Union.

When Australia had won the Rugby World Cup a year earlier, there were many in South Africa who refused to recognise them as true world champions and it was fitting therefore that it wasn't long before the Wallabies toured South Africa.

The first meeting between the official world champions and the nation that thought they would have won it came on 22 August 1992. The political situation was still tense and no anthems were played at the match but South Africa's isolation had told on the players and, not surprisingly, the Wallabies won 26-3. It was a difficult occasion for all concerned and Australians were quick to praise the Springbok performance. "The last 40 minutes were as good as the first 40 in last year's World Cup semi-final against New Zealand," proclaimed captain Nick Farr-Jones.

Before that clash with Australia, the Springboks were formally welcomed back into the international arena with a 27-24 defeat by New Zealand. New Zealand hooker Sean Fitzpatrick was soon toe to toe with Naas Botha as the All Blacks were keen to 'welcome' them back.

"Amongst those sports leaders, Francois Pienaar stands out. It was under his inspiring leadership that rugby, a sport previously associated with one sector of our population and with a particular brand of politics, became the pride of the entire country."

South Africa's political system at last began to crumble in the early 1990s and in 1992, after apartheid was banished, a new governing body, South African Rugby Football Union (SARFU), was formed on a non-racist basis to take the country into a new, enlightened era.

With the apartheid regime crushed, it was time to allow South Africa back from their sporting isolation,

The problems that apartheid brought to sport ensured that when that political system fell, it was with great joy that the Springboks were welcomed back into the rugby fold. To endorse this, they were invited to host the 1995 Rugby World Cup. The Rainbow Nation, as they were known by the time the World Cup arrived in South Africa, made a dream start to their first World Cup, lifting the trophy in front of their own supporters with a nervy 15-12 victory over New Zealand. As President Mandela handed the trophy over to the Springbok captain Francois Pienaar, he said: "Thank you for what you have done for South Africa." Pienaar replied: "We

could never do what you have done for South Africa."

It was difficult for the Springboks to follow that World Cup victory and they went through a number of coaches in the subsequent years with perhaps the most successful of them being Nick Mallett, the Oxford University-educated coach.

Mallett's side equalled the world record held by New Zealand for consecutive Test victories, winning 17 from 1997 through to 1998. His side, captained by Gary Teichmann and containing Springbok greats such as Mark Andrews, Joost Van Der Westhuizen, James Small, Percy Montgomery and Andre Joubert, kicked off their great run with a huge 61-22 victory over Australia in Pretoria.

Mallett's men unfortunately seemed to peak in the years between the two World Cups but it did bring them the Tri-Nations title in 1998, which included victories in Wellington and Perth. Their run eventually came to an end at Twickenham, when they lost 13-7 to England.

After that loss to England and failure to beat the record, Teichmann said: "The results over the past year speak volumes. We have played all the top sides in the world and won. We have lost today, but it is consistency that really counts.

"We'd equalled the record and it was somewhere in the back of the mind to beat it. But the idea was just to beat England. They might have used the record to motivate themselves."

Mallett said: "I'm not too disappointed because we have equalled the record and that has been a fantastic achievement. It's been a hell of a year and there have been times when we have flirted with danger and got away with it – this time our luck ran out."

Their good form continued into the 1999 World Cup with their luck again running out after an epic semi-final tussle with Australia. The game went into extra time after fly-half Jannie de Beer levelled the scores 18-18 with a penalty six minutes into added time, but Australia went on to win the try-less semi-final 27-21.

Their form in the new Millennium has been patchy to say the least. After a 2002 European tour that saw them lose by a record 53-3 to England they failed to reach the semi-finals of the World Cup in 2003. They lost to England in the pool stages and New Zealand in the quarter finals.

• **Above**
Andre Venter of South Africa celebrates a 19-15 victory over Australia in the 1998 Tri-Nations match at Ellis Park in Johannesburg. South Africa went on to win the Tri-Nations title.

• **Above**
Lisandro Arbizu of
Argentina kicks
during the 2002
Ireland v Argentina
test match held at
Lansdowne Road.
Although Ireland
won the game 16-7
the Pumas have
beaten every nation
in the world.

Argentina

Although not in the same league as the three
giants of southern hemisphere rugby, the Argentine
Pumas are still a force to be reckoned with,
particularly on home soil. Argentine rugby shares a
similar birth to most countries – the first rugby balls
travelled on boat with British settlers, mostly arriving
in Argentina to work for the railway companies in the
mid 1800s. With cricket already established in the
country (now only a minor sport), the first official
rugby game was played by two teams made up of
expats in 1873, making them one of the first nations
to take up the game. The first official club game was
played between the Buenos Aires Football Club and
Rosario Athletic Club in 1886.

By 1899, five clubs decided to organise a
championship, and that association evolved into the
Unión Argentina de Rugby. Four of those clubs still
play in First Division today, the fifth having long-since
disappeared.

The first team to tour Argentina was a British side
in 1910 but it would take a further 17 years for the
second tour, again a British team that included 14
present and future internationals. Only after the
Second World War did teams start to tour Argentina
on a more regular basis.

The breakthrough for Argentine rugby and where
the nickname Puma was coined was on their first
overseas tour, in 1965 to South Africa. A team that
had been written off made history by defeating the
Junior Springboks. There has been no looking back

of 'South America Jaguars' in 1982) were followed by three sour World Cups in which they failed to advance to the quarters, winning only one of nine games, a feat they finally achieved by beating Ireland 28-24 in 1999.

since. Tours by the three home unions followed and Buenos Aires became an almost impregnable outpost – Wales, Scotland and Ireland losing matches there from 1968-1970. England were invited in 1973, but political problems and an invitation to tour New Zealand forced the cancellation.

Wins against every nation in the world (except a 21-21 draw with the All Blacks and a South Africa side actually beaten by an Argentine XV in the guise

Whilst Los Pumas gained world notoriety, the game at home was also growing. There are currently 23 Provincial Unions, 330 clubs and approximately 60,000 players, the best of whom are signed up with clubs in England, Italy and France. This has been a blow to the domestic game but has been beneficial for the Test team which is now a competitive force in world rugby.

• Above
Argentinian players celebrate the final whistle of the Rugby World Cup quarter-final play-off between Ireland and Argentina from the Stade Felix Bollaert, Lens.

• Inset
Agustin Pichot in action during a 2002 Test against Australia. Pichot is one of the Argentine stars to ply his trade in Europe.

• Above left
Fijian fans, including 4 men in a coconut tree, watch the incredible 1977 victory against the Lions from Buchurst Park, Suva.

• Above right
Pio Bosco Tikoisuva makes a break for Fiji in the same game.

• Opposite
Pat Lam of Samoa races towards the tryline against Wales during the 1999 Rugby World Cup Pool D match at the Millennium Stadium.

South Seas Islanders

No history of rugby could be complete without acknowledging the huge part the South Sea Islands, predominantly those of Samoa, Tonga and Fiji, have played in our great game.

They have been playing rugby in Fiji almost as long as anywhere else in the world, the first recorded match taking place in 1884. They embraced the game with great passion and have always brought their own innovative style to the rugby world, becoming the dominant force in Sevens.

Fiji's first international was in 1924, when they beat Western Samoa 6-0. Australia were the first nation to give an international against Fiji full Test status when the Fijians arrived in their country in 1952. In the first Test, Sailosi Valewai scored a try after just 15 seconds but the popular Fijians were unable to hold on, losing 15-9. It wasn't long before Fiji turned that defeat into a victory, in a second, hastily arranged, Test. Phil Tressider in The Sunday Telegraph described Fiji's 17-15 victory as the biggest upset in Australian rugby history.

To prove that this win wasn't a fluke, Fiji won again in 1954, 18-16, but that was when the winning run over Australia ended, as by the end of 2002 they still hadn't added to those two victories.

Fiji came to Europe for the first time in 1964, losing both matches, against a Wales XV and France, but they left their mark on British and Irish rugby in 1977. The Lions, who had lost in New Zealand, stopped in Fiji on the way home and lost there as well, 25-21.

Fiji's record established them as the leading South Pacific nation and their performances in the World Cup have illustrated this.

In 1999 they should have beaten France to make the quarter-finals, eventually losing 28-19, but they had made the last eight in 1987, again losing to France.

If Fiji's victory in Australia in 1952 was described as a huge upset, that is nothing compared to the fall-out that occurred when Tonga came to Brisbane in 1973 and won 16-11, inspiring a top-to-bottom restructuring of the Australian game.

Australian teachers are credited with introducing rugby to Tonga at the start of the 20th century and, as with Fiji, Australia were the first to welcome Tonga into the rugby world, touring there in 1954. But it wasn't until 1973 that they had a Test match against the Wallabies. Tonga's other famous victory came against France in 1999, 20-16 in Nuku'alofa.

Mention Western Samoa in the rugby world and the word 'Wales' appears next to them, quickly followed by 'shock'.

Samoa left their mark on the World Cup by beating Wales 16-13 in 1991 and they repeated the trick in the 1999 tournament, with a 38-31 victory. The Samoans had developed considerably after the First World War and they gained independence in 1962, when the country was administered by New Zealand. It was therefore inevitable that rugby would become a major sport.

The future of the South Sea Island teams looks extremely bright. Just as the British and Irish Lions have done for many decades, the islands made their debut as a united team in 2004. A combined Pacific islands team played Australia, New Zealand and South Africa in Test matches. Australia coach Eddie Jones said the Wallabies were honoured to welcome the united Pacific team to the international fold.

"The Pacific Islanders will be a formidable challenge for the Wallabies. Like the British and Irish Lions, they are made up of the best players from top quality international teams," Jones said.

"The Islanders generally play with a lot of flair and natural talent. They like to throw the ball around and run it from anywhere, which usually makes for a fast, free-flowing match."

Fiji, Tonga and Samoa will then combine again for a tour of the northern hemisphere in 2005, as agreed by the International Rugby Board.

"It is exciting news for rugby in the Pacific," said Charlie Charters, chief executive of the Pacific Islanders Rugby Alliance (PIRA).

"It potentially represents a step into the big time for the countries of Fiji, Samoa and Tonga."

The Pacific Islanders team was set up to give players from the three individual nations more experience against high-profile rugby powerhouses. "We have campaigned hard that the Islanders represents a crucial lifeline in the playing and commercial development of rugby in the Pacific," Charters added.

There are certainly exciting times ahead.

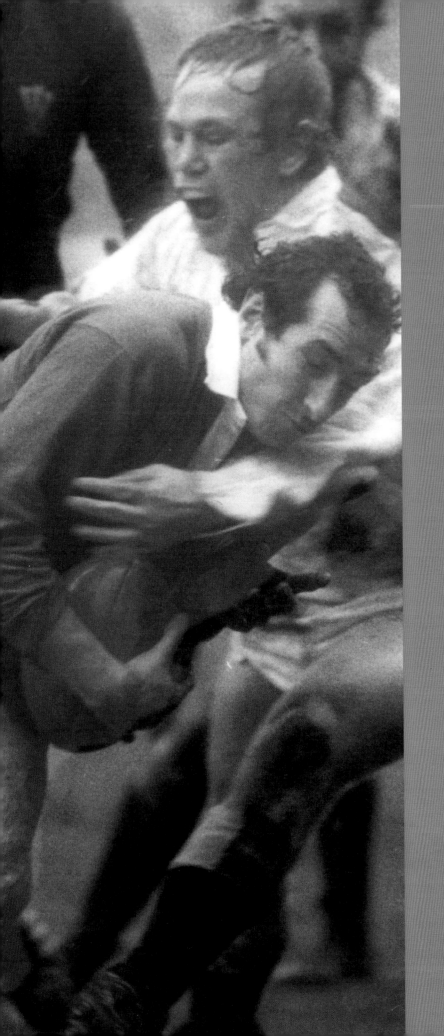

The Greatest
Ever XV

Chapter
NINE
9

Ever since the first sporting encounter, the arguments have raged about who are the best players. Well, in Rugby Union they rage even harder with world-class players on both sides of the globe, dozens of whom would justify a place in a team selected from the history of Rugby Union.

Britain's *Rugby World* magazine's search for the game's greatest ever team took over a year, speaking to players with 638 caps' worth of knowledge and experience.

The New Zealand All Blacks took centre stage in the side and made up the majority of the 120 players selected for the shortlist. Ten were selected for each shortlist but, for example, there was only one shortlist for centres and it wasn't broken down into inside and outside-centres.

The final composition of the 120 best players in the world was New Zealand 25%, France 13.3%, England and Wales both 12.5%, South Africa and Australia both 11.6%, Scotland 6.6%, Ireland 5.8% and Argentina 0.8%.

This is the ultimate Rugby Union side, as chosen by 25 experts.

Full-back – No 15

Serge Blanco

France (1980-91). Tests: 93. Points: 233.
The Venezuelan-born Blanco made his debut in 1980 against South Africa at Newlands and, despite a few appearances on the wing, was soon established as the world's greatest full-back. Laid-back both on and off the field – and with a 60-a-day smoking habit to boot – Blanco used the rugby pitch to unleash his creative genius. By the end of the 2002-03 season, only David Campese, Rory Underwood, Christian Cullen and Jeff Wilson had passed Blanco's 38 international tries. Blessed with pace, vision and the courage to launch counter-attacks from deep within his half, Blanco was responsible for some stunning tries. Scores against Australia in injury time of the 1987 Rugby World Cup semi-final and his hand in Philippe Saint-André's amazing try against England in 1991 will forever be etched in the memory. Blanco retired after the 1991 World Cup. He was a runner-up with France in the 1987 World Cup and also won Grand Slams in 1981 and 1987. He was appointed captain in 1990, eventually leading his country 17 times,

including during the 1991 World Cup. A member of the Biarritz Olympique club, he served as club president from 1991 to 1998 and also served as president of the French League.

VERDICT: Blanco was everything good about French rugby. He had the flair, imagination and know-how to open any defence. He was no slouch when it came to kicking either and by the end of the 2002-03 season only four Frenchmen had scored more than Blanco's 233 international points.

The shortlist – Full-back:

2: George Nepia (NZ), 3: A Irvine (Sco), 4: JPR Williams (Wales), 5: J Gallagher (NZ), 6: C Cullen (NZ), 7: M Burke (Aus), 8: G Hastings (Sco), 9: G Brand (SA), 10: B Scott (NZ).

Right-wing – No 14
Gerald Davies

Wales (1966-78). Tests: 46. Points: 72.

For the first three years of his Test career, Gerald Davies played at centre. Twelve Tests and a place on the 1968 Lions tour to South Africa came his way before he was moved to the wing during Wales' tour to New Zealand and Australia in 1969. Any notions, however, that he was being put out to grass – a

victim of the growing trend for crash-bang centres – were dispelled as he reinvented himself as possibly the greatest winger the game has seen. He had always had good hands and a shrewd rugby brain, but what made Davies such a potent winger was his ability to sidestep and dummy opponents without taking his foot off the accelerator. The result? Twenty tries in 46 Tests for Wales during a career that lasted 12 years and included a second Lions tour, to New Zealand in 1971. He studied at Loughborough University before appearing for Cambridge University, Cardiff, Barbarians and London Welsh. He will be remembered in Wales for many scintillating tries but none were more precious than one he scored against Scotland at Murrayfield in 1971. In the dying moments of a match that had seen the lead change hands many times, Scotland looked to have won. But that was before Davies fizzed past the home defence to score in the corner, setting up flanker John Taylor for a wide-angled conversion which gave Wales a 19-18 win and the first of three Grand Slams in the decade. Davies is now a journalist with *The Times*.

VERDICT: Ex-Lions team-mate John Taylor said of Davies: "His acceleration, swerve and sidestep, his acute sense of awareness and his unselfishness, make him the best wing I've ever seen."

• Opposite
Serge Blanco of France during his final appearance for his country in the 1991 World Cup quarter final match against England at Parc des Princes in Paris.

• Above
Gerald Davies of Wales runs with the ball during the 1978 Welsh tour to Australia.

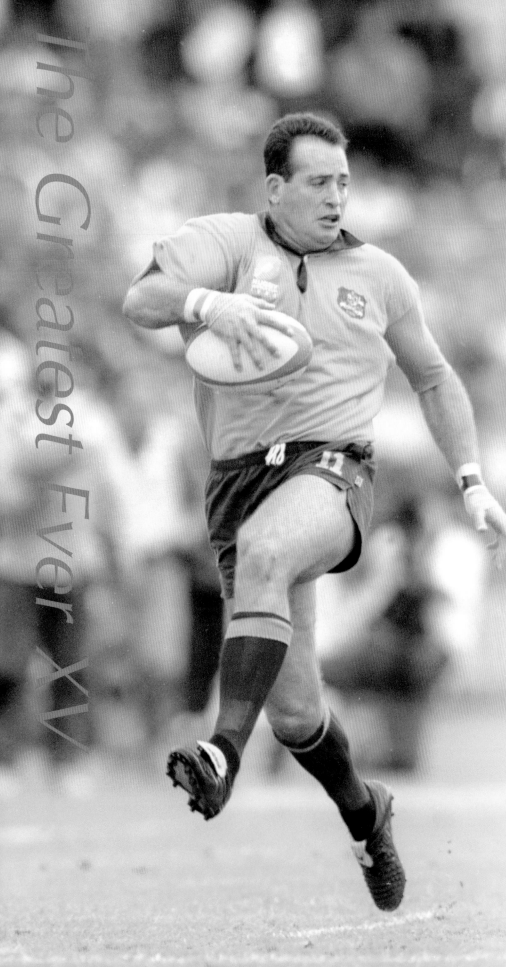

Left-wing – No 11
David Campese

Australia (1982-96). Tests: 101. Points: 315.
A maverick and a loner, Campo, who played for NSW and Randwick, was an entertainer who liked the sound of his own voice nearly as much as he liked ripping opposition defences to shreds. A record 63 tries in a record 101 Tests, for a wing, is proof he could walk the walk as well as he could talk the talk and he is one of the biggest stars of the modern era. He kicked off his career with a try against New Zealand in 1982 and two years later announced himself on the world stage as part of Australia's Grand Slam side. The Player of the Tournament at the 1991 World Cup, where he was a winner, his ex-Wallaby coach Bob Dwyer said: "His tries are like Don Bradman's centuries. Most were brilliant, but because there were so many of them they're not easy to single out." One of Dwyer's favourites came in Campo's first Test. Receiving the ball for the first time in international rugby, Campese found himself face to face with Stu Wilson, one of the greats himself. Campo stood Wilson up and "ran round him so easily he might have been playing Test rugby for years." Campese was the first player to reach 50 Test tries and once he had retired he managed the Australian sevens squad, taking them to a bronze medal at the Commonwealth Games in 1998. He was awarded an Order of Australia Medal for services to rugby in January 2002.

VERDICT: Some critics pointed to Campese's fragile defence but his strengths as a finisher easily outweighed any flaws.

The shortlist – Wings:

3: J Wilson (NZ), 4: B Williams (NZ), 5: J Roff (Aus), 6: J Engelbrecht (SA), 7: P Jackson (Eng), 8: I Evans (Wales), 9: J Kirwan (NZ), 10: I Smith (Scotland).

Outside-centre – No 13

Philippe Sella

France (1982-95). Tests: 111. Points: 125.

"I remember taking my son to see Sella play in Dublin a few years ago," recalls Irish international Dick Milliken. "Instead of ball-watching we just watched him for 20 minutes. He seemed to have everything: powerful, quick and elusive in attack and yet so strong in defence. In my opinion he was the complete player." One of his great rivals, England's Jeremy Guscott, said facing him was like tackling a swinging phonebox. One of the key players of the French sides of the 1980s and 1990s, he was another Frenchman who starred in the 1987 World Cup.

Sella was first capped for France against Romania in 1982 and in the next 13 years he amassed the most caps ever in international rugby – 111. Only two Frenchmen have scored more than his 30 Test tries and it's doubtful whether any have made more thunderous tackles. Even the ex-England hooker Brian Moore, not noted for his love of Frenchmen, conceded that Sella, who stayed loyal to Agen throughout his Test career, was a phenomenal defender. His final Test was in the 1995 World Cup,

where he helped France to third place, beating England 19-9 in the play-off. Once his international career had ended, he headed, along with Michael Lynagh, to English club Saracens, helping them to a Tetley's Bitter Cup victory over Wasps in 1998.

VERDICT: Sella's battle honours include two French titles, the Tetley's Bitter Cup, a Grand Slam and a World Cup runners-up medal. Yet even this record does scant justice to his talents.

Inside-centre – No 12

Mike Gibson

Ireland (1964-79). Tests: 69. Points: 112.

Mike Gibson MBE once said: "The best guys are those who can do the simple things – kicking, passing, running – better than everybody else. Work on the basics and everything else will fall into place."

Everything fell into place for Gibson during a career that spanned 15 years and 69 Irish caps, which was still a record at the end of the 2002-03 season. He also won 12 Lions caps and went on five tours, a record for the side he holds jointly with another Irish legend, Willie John McBride. On the trip to New Zealand in 1971, he slotted in perfectly with the

• **Opposite**
David Campese demonstrates his famous 'goose step' that helped him to 63 tries in a record 101 Tests for Australia.

• **Above left**
Philippe Sella of France goes over to score during their 1991 World Cup match against Fiji.

• **Above right**
Mike Gibson passes the ball in the Five Nations match against Scotland in 1979, his final season for Ireland.

mesmerising Welsh backs and helped the Lions to an historic series victory. Although he played some Tests at fly-half, Gibson was rated a far better centre with his range of passing, strong tackling, shrewd tactical brain and lethal acceleration causing headaches in opposition midfields. A fierce and committed trainer, he appeared 40 times at centre, 25 at outside-half and four on the wing. As well as his physical prowess, Gibson was also mentally indomitable and he epitomised the 'focused' athlete long before the word became trite in a sporting context. He went out on a massive high when, aged 36, he helped Ireland to a famous win over Australia in his last Test in 1979.

VERDICT: Dick Milliken, who played alongside Gibson in the 1970s, remembers him as being at his absolute peak during the 1971 Lions tour. "Mike was unbelievable on that tour," he said.

The shortlist – Centres:

3: J Guscott (England), 4: T Horan (Aus), 5: D Gerber (SA), 6: B Robertson (NZ), 7: J Maso (France), 8: J Butterfield (England), 9: R Poulton-Palmer (England), 10: G Stephenson (Ireland).

Outside-half – No 10

Hugo Porta

Argentina (1971-90). Tests: 56. Points: 582.
With the number of great Welsh fly-halves in our game, some will be surprised to see an Argentinian lining up in the No 10 shirt. But Hugo Porta's brilliance put Argentina on the rugby map and he is accepted as the greatest player the country has ever produced.

For a long time establishing a definitive total of international points for Porta was something of a problem, for records of Argentine rugby Tests weren't readily available and British-based historians tended not to recognise matches against 'minor' international opponents. But thanks to the work of historians like Frankie Deges of the *Buenos Aires Herald*, it is now recorded that Porta played 56 times for Argentina in a career that spanned 19 years. In the process he helped himself to 582 points for the

Pumas, including all 21 in a draw with the All Blacks in 1985. He also helped the Pumas to a draw with France in 1977 and an incredible 24-13 win over Australia in 1979.

In addition, Porta played in all six Tests when the South American Jaguars side visited South Africa (1980, '82 and '84) and in one of those games in 1982 he grabbed a 'full house' of try, conversion, penalty and a drop goal as they shocked South Africa 21-12.

Although a natural runner, Porta was equally proficient at the kicking game. After former Lions coach Carwyn James saw him play in 1980, he said: "It was a question of having one's faith restored in the aesthetic and artistic possibilities of back play."

Porta played in the 1987 World Cup before retiring, returning to the Test arena at the age of 39 when Argentina came to England in 1990. He moved into politics after his rugby career finally ended, becoming Argentina's ambassador in South Africa, a post he occupied until 1996, and later their Minister of Sport, until 1999, when President Carlos Menem stepped down. In 2003 he returned to his family's bathroom business.

VERDICT: Porta played for Argentina against a World XV in 1999 – and still looked a class act at 47.

• *Above*
Hugo Porta of Argentina in action during a 1990 match against Ireland at Lansdowne Road in Dublin.

The shortlist – Outside-half:

2: C Morgan (Wales), 3: R Andrew (England), 4: M Lynagh (Australia), 5: P Bennett (Wales), 6: B John (Wales), 7: J Davies (Wales), 8: M Ella (Aus), 9: J Kyle (Ireland), 10: J Rutherford (Scotland).

Scrum-half – No 9

Gareth Edwards

Wales (1967-78). Tests: 53. Points: 88.
Capped by Wales at the age of 19 and by the Lions a year later, Gareth Edwards MBE was Wales' youngest ever captain (20), played a record 53 consecutive times for his country, scored the then record number of tries for Wales (20) and played 10 Tests for the Lions in a prestigious stint in the red jersey that brought series wins in New Zealand (1971) and South Africa (1974). He had the lot, phenomenal upper-body strength, electrifying pace, a vast array of kicks and superb passing. His bonhomie hid a fiercely competitive streak that helped him become the most complete player of all time and his impact is demonstrated by the fact that, once he was selected for his debut, against France in 1967, he was never dropped. He was Wales skipper 13 times and as a player he helped his country to three Grand Slams and five Triple Crowns.

VERDICT: Edwards' try for the Barbarians against the All Blacks in 1973 was class, but for sheer individual brilliance the one he got against Scotland the previous year takes some beating.

The shortlist – Scrum-half:

2: D Loveridge (NZ), 3: N Farr-Jones (Aus), 4: R Howley (Wales), 5: S Going (NZ), 6: C Laidlaw (NZ), 7: K Catchpole (Aus), 8: H Tanner (Wales), 9: J van der Westhuizen (SA), 10: D Jeeps (England).

Prop – No 1

Ray McLoughlin

Ireland (1962-75). Tests: 40. Points: 4.
Willie John McBride called McLoughlin a man of "profound depth of thought", while Colin Meads paid tribute to him after the 1971 Lions tour to New Zealand when he said: "His intelligent appraisal of the game meant more to the Lions than most are aware."

McLoughlin, from Ballinasloe and capped 40 times by Ireland, was a rugby revolutionary who spent hours studying the complexities of the front row and how best to disrupt opponents. He also

• Above
Gareth Edwards under attack from Peter Wheeler during his 50th International in 1978.

• Below
Ray McLoughlin kicks the ball away from Wales' Mervyn Davies in the 1975 Five Nations match. It was his last for Ireland.

insisted code names be given to back-line moves so the pack would know what to expect. McLoughlin made his Ireland debut against England in 1962. Capped by the Lions in 1966, work commitments and injury meant he had to wait five years before resuming international rugby. Had McLoughlin not been injured against Canterbury during the 1971 Lions tour, he would have undoubtedly played in the Test series.

VERDICT: Tough as old boots and a deep thinker who opponents underestimated at their peril.

The shortlist – Loosehead prop:

2: O du Randt (SA), 3: I McLauchlan (Scotland), 4: C Koch (SA), 5: E Rodriguez (Australia), 6: S McDowell (NZ), 7: K Skinner (NZ), 8: J Iracabal (France), 9: J Leonard (England), 10: C Faulkner (Wales).

Hooker – No 2

Sean Fitzpatrick

New Zealand (1986-97). Tests: 92. Points: 55.

In your face, on your back, up your nose – there was no escaping Sean Fitzpatrick for a generation of hookers during the 1980s and 1990s. If he wasn't busy offering his opinions on their hooking skills, the Auckland and All Blacks hooker was dominating the set-piece, popping up on the wing to take a pass or chin-wagging with the ref.

Former All Blacks coach John Hart reckoned him as strong a scrummager as any international prop and his lineout throwing was as reliable as his repartee. The son of 1950s All Black centre Brian Fitzpatrick, Sean came to international notice as a member of the 'Baby Blacks' and started his first Test in 1986, aged 23, against France. He went on to gain 92 caps (63 of them consecutively over an eight-year period), a World Cup winners' medal and series wins against all the major nations and he led his country more than 50 times. His career prompted Hart's predecessor, Laurie Mains, to call Fitzpatrick "the best example of the meaning of an All Black". In the years after his departure from the international scene, his shadow remained long over the All Blacks, as they tried and failed to replace him.

VERDICT: It took the All Blacks a year to recover from the loss of Sean Fitzpatrick.

The shortlist – Hooker:

2. P Wheeler (England), 3: K Wood (Ireland), 4: T Lawton (Aus), 5: J Pullin (England), 6: P Kearns (Aus), 7: B Meredith (Wal), 8: C Deans (Sco), 9: P Dintrans (Fra), 10: B McLeod (NZ).

Prop – No 3

Robert Paparemborde

France (1975-83). Tests: 55. Points: 32.

With his sloping shoulders and unorthodox scrummaging technique, Robert Paparemborde was the king of the castle for nine seasons between 1975 and 1983. First capped against South Africa in 1975, 'Papa', as he was universally known, showed his talent for try-scoring with five in his first nine Tests. That try-scoring record continued and he ended his 55-cap career with eight, which was still, in 2003, more than any other prop in rugby history. Unusually for a French prop, Paparemborde played his rugby clean, likening the front-row contest to a "loyal man-to-man struggle". The man from Pau was twice a member of Grand Slam sides, in 1977 and 1981, and he captained his country five times. It was more than a struggle for a succession of opposition looseheads who failed to cope with the Frenchman's strength and technique.

Welshman Graham Price always knew when Paparemborde was about. "You could feel the effect on my side of the scrum of his influence on the other side," he said. Paparemborde went on to manage the French side at the start of the 1990s, sadly succumbing to cancer, after a long battle, in April 2001.

VERDICT: A side would always go forward with the great Paparemborde amongst its number.

The shortlist – Tighthead prop:

2. Ken Gray (NZ), 3: Graham Price (Wal), 4: Jeff Probyn (Eng), 5: Fran Cotton (Eng), 6: Piet du Toit (SA), 7: Jean-Pierre Garuet (Fra), 8: Iain Milne (Sco), 9: Courtenay Meredith (Wal), 10: Hannes Marais (SA).

Lock – No 4 Colin Meads

New Zealand (1957-71). Tests: 55. Points: 21.

"The thing I despise most about that chap Meads," an England lock was once heard to say, "is the way the terminal traces of your jockstrap hang out of the corners of his mouth at the end of a game." Capped 55 times by New Zealand, Colin Meads MBE evoked strong emotions in rugby fans by playing the game with a ferocity that caused sensitive types to blanch. Even Fergi McCormick, a long-time team-mate of Meads, called him "a terrible man with the silver fern on". A farmer by trade, when he played his last match for New Zealand, against the Lions in 1971, he'd amassed a then world record number of caps, seven of them in the position where he made his debut – flanker. Yet despite this reputation, 'Pinetree', as he was better known, was a world-class second-row. With a strength derived from years of

• **Opposite**
Sean Fitzpatrick of New Zealand runs with the ball during the 1991 Rugby Union World Cup match against England played at Twickenham.

• **Above left**
Robert 'Papa' Paparemborde runs out onto the Cardiff Arms pitch to play Wales in the '78 Five Nations.

• **Above right**
New Zealand's Colin Meads in action against England during the 1964 Test at Twickenham which the All Blacks won 14-0.

hard labour on his King Country farm, Meads' rucking and mauling wore down the resistance of opposition packs for over a decade. He led the controversial and unofficial New Zealand Cavaliers to South Africa in 1986 but he still managed the All Blacks from 1984 to 1995, taking them to the World Cup Final in 1995. His services to rugby were rewarded in 1971 with an MBE and again 30 years later when he was named a Distinguished Companion of the New Zealand Order of Merit.

VERDICT: Meads was once asked if he worried about his reputation. "You don't play to make yourself popular, do you?" came the reply.

Lock – No 5

Frik Du Preez

South Africa (1961-71). Tests: 38. Points: 11.

Frik Du Preez was the most complete second-row in the history of the game. He could jump as high as an elephant's eye in the lineout, he was a mighty scrummager and slick ball-handler. And his pace was such that when he scored a 40-metre try for the Springboks against the 1968 Lions, Gareth Edwards was left trailing in his slipstream. Edwards's fly-half in that Test was Barry John and he later said of Du Preez: "One of the marks of a great player is a willingness and the confidence to do the unorthodox. Frik had this ability to do the 'wrong' things that turned out to be right."

Du Preez also played flanker, which helped develop his pace off the mark and unlike many forwards of his day was a superb ball-handler and great kicker. He may have played in the 1960s and 70s, but the Springbok rugby public never forgot the great man from Western Transvaal as they voted him the greatest Springbok of the 20th century. First

• **Above**
Ian Kirkpatrick playing for New Zealand against the 1977 Lions.

• **Below**
A portrait of Frik Du Preez, voted the greatest Springbok of the 20th century.

capped in 1961, Du Preez, who was born in Rustenberg, won 38 caps for South Africa in a career that encompassed 11 seasons, six overseas tours and prompted the father of Springbok rugby, Danie Craven, to call him a "once-in-a-lifetime phenomenon".

VERDICT: Du Preez had so much talent he could have played anywhere. He chose lock and the fact he keeps John Eales out of our side shows the talent he possessed.

The shortlist – Locks:

3: J Eales (Aus), 4: B Dauga (France), 5: G Brown (Scotland), 6: I Jones (NZ), 7: WJ McBride (Ire), 8: M Andrews (SA), 9: L Mias (France), 10: R White (NZ).

Blindside Flanker – No 6

Ian Kirkpatrick

New Zealand (1967-77). Tests: 39. Points: 57.

Once complimented by a New Zealand selector for being a 'bash-wallop' player, there was much more to Kirkpatrick's game than just putting in big hits. Against the Lions in 1971, this Canterbury, Poverty Bay and New Zealand flanker scored one of the greatest ever tries by a forward when he broke from a maul on halfway and, through a combination of

pace and hand-offs, made it to the try-line. He won the first of his 39 caps against France in 1967 and became an All Black in an era of New Zealand dominance that saw them go five years and 52 matches undefeated. Former Wales and Lions flanker John Taylor, who played against Kirkpatrick six times, remembers the Gisborne farmer as his "greatest adversary" and a "big man, with great pace and wonderfully athletic".

Kirkpatrick was captain of the New Zealand side that played the Barbarians in 1973 and was on the receiving end of rugby's greatest try, scored by Edwards. At 6ft 2in and 16st and with a resting pulse rate of 48, Kirkpatrick had the size and stamina to make Rugby League coaches drool. Wigan dangled a £20,000 contract in front of his nose in 1971, but found their offer rejected. His last 37 appearances for New Zealand were in consecutive Internationals, an ever-present in the side until he retired in 1977, following the Lions tour, but not before he had helped the All Blacks gain revenge for their series defeat in 1971. When he retired he'd scored more tries than any other New Zealand forward (16), a

record later overtaken by Zinzan Brooke.

VERDICT: Grant Batty said of Kirkpatrick's display in 1974 against Australia: "It was the most dominant, powerful performance I've seen from an All Black."

The shortlist – Blindside flanker:

2: K Tremain (NZ), 3: P Greyling (SA), 4: A Whetton (NZ), 5: W Ofahengaue (Aus), 6: J-C Skrela (Fra), 7: M Shaw (NZ), 8: M Teague (England), 9: M Crauste (Fra), 10: J Prat (Fra).

Openside Flanker – No 7

Michael Jones

New Zealand (1987-98). Tests: 55. Points: 56.

Time was called on Michael Jones's incredible Test career in 1998 when injuries and age finally persuaded John Hart to drop the Samoan-born Auckland flanker from the All Black squad. It was the end of a 55-Test career that had started back in 1987 with selection for the inaugural World Cup. From the moment Jones, nicknamed the 'Iceman', scored the tournament's opening try against Italy, it was

• Above
Michael Jones in action during the 1991 World Cup match against the USA.

149

• **Above**
*Mervyn Davies of
the Lions in action
during the 1974 tour
of South Africa.*

The shortlist – Openside flanker:

2. F Slattery (Ire), 3: J Kronfeld (NZ), 4: P Winterbottom (Eng), 5: T Neary (Eng), 6: J Ellis (SA), 7: L Cabannes (Fra), 8: G Mourie (NZ), 9: S Poidevin (Aus), 10: J-P Rives (Fra).

No 8 – Mervyn Davies

Wales (1969-76). Tests: 38. Points: 7.

At the end of the Lions' Test series win against the All Blacks in 1971, one New Zealand paper wrote that "this elongated, gangling individual didn't look much like an international No 8 but it was a classic case of appearances deceiving."

It wasn't the first time that people had underestimated Merv 'the Swerve' Davies. The London Welsh legend, who was born in Swansea, had a stormer against the Scots on his Welsh debut in 1969 when Wales went on to win the championship. He starred for the incredible Welsh side of the 1970s and was not only a key figure for the 1971 Lions but again three years later, when the Lions won in South Africa. Dexterous and athletic, Davies was nigh on untouchable in the lineout while his vision in the loose put him head and shoulders above every No 8 of his era. Sadly a brain haemorrhage, sustained while playing for Swansea, ended his career in 1976. Many commentators believe he would have led the 1977 Lions to New Zealand instead of Phil Bennett.

VERDICT: Davies's battle honours are awesome: 38 Welsh caps, two series wins with the Lions (1971 and 1974) and two Grand Slams.

The shortlist – No 8:

2: Z Brooke (NZ), 3: D Richards (Eng), 4: J-P Bastiat (Fra), 5: W Shelford, 6: M Du Plessis (SA), 7: H Muller (SA), 8: M Mexted (NZ), 9: B Lochore (NZ), 10: L Rodriguez (Fra).

apparent that here was a flanker blessed with a unique ability. He was a key component of the All Black side that won the first World Cup and four years later he again scored the World Cup's opening try, this time against hosts England at Twickenham. Jones didn't take his God-given talent for granted, refusing to play on Sundays as he considered it a sacred day, even though it cost him a place in the 1995 New Zealand World Cup squad. In 1988 the man who is revered throughout New Zealand gave a string of performances that at times defied belief such was his athleticism. But in 1989 he tore three knee ligaments and many doubted he'd play top-flight rugby again. Nearly ten years later he continued to strut his stuff for Auckland and he completed a 12-year All Black career before moving into a coaching role with Samoa.

VERDICT: John Hart called Jones "the best player in my time". Many would say of all time.

Coach – Carwyn James

The late Carwyn James was one of the best man-managers the rugby world has seen, pulling the strings behind the 1971 Lions and guiding these great players to even greater heights.

As coach of those 1971 Lions in New Zealand, James, who won two caps for Wales in 1958, led the side to a first Test series win by a British touring team abroad in the 20th century.

He also coached Llanelli with stunning success, but his genius was in the way he handled world greats like Gareth Edwards and Barry John while being modest, some say shy, and constantly playing down his own abilities.

Described by his biographer Alun Richards as the "prince of coaches", Richards went on to say with overwhelming fondness: "What also needs to be said is that he was a Welshman who made you feel glad you were a member of the human race."

The Subs Bench

With an array of talent on the shortlists, coming up with seven substitutes was not easy. But we looked for a balance – one prop, one lock, one hooker, a back-rower, a scrum-half, a centre who could cover the outside-half position and a specialist full-back who could fit in anywhere along the back-line.

To anchor the scrum, should the worst happen or we needed an impact player for the last 20 minutes, we travelled to South Africa for a player who made a real impact on Springbok rugby – **Os Du Randt**

Du Randt was the rock on which the South African World Cup-winning scrum was built. He made his debut in 1994 against the hard scrummagers of Argentina, playing a further 38 times and scoring four tries in a career that ended in the third-place play-off at the 1999 World Cup.

• Above
Os du Randt hands off George Gregan of Australia during the semi-final of the 1999 Rugby World Cup played at Twickenham.

Covering the lock positions is a man who could easily slip into the back row such was his athleticism and who only just missed out on our team behind two legends of the game, **John Eales**.

The Queenslander was nicknamed 'Nobody' because, as they say, Nobody is Perfect! Eales was just 21 when he won his first World Cup in 1991 and eight years later he returned to the World Cup stage to lift the trophy as captain.

In our team of the century and beyond, Eales would bring more than just the displays of one of the best locks the world has ever seen as he was a world-class goal-kicker. He scored 173 Test points before he retired from the game in September 2001, having won 86 caps and captained the Wallabies a record 52 times.

Backing up Du Randt in the front row is an Englishman who many feel should have captained the Lions – **Peter Wheeler**.

Wheeler won 41 caps in a nine-year England career and when he retired in 1984 it was as the third most-capped Englishman ever. He was an all-round threat, working tirelessly in the loose and relishing the challenge of the set play. Wheeler was a key element in England's Grand Slam of 1980 – their first for 23 years – and played on two Lions tours, in 1977 and 1980. Now chief executive of his beloved Leicester, Wheeler was a great club man, leading the Tigers to English (John Player) Cup wins in 1979, 1980 and 1981.

In the back row, fans around the rugby world will never forget the influence and outstanding ability of our next member of the bench, **Fergus Slattery**.

The pinnacle of Slattery's career came in 1974 when he won the No 7 jersey for Willie John McBride's legendary Lions side, which toured South Africa undefeated. Slattery appeared in all four Tests on that trip and was crucial to the success of those famous Lions.

A nightmare for outside-halves all over the world, Slattery had an incredible international career with Ireland. His Test career – which included 17 games as captain – spanned 14 years and when he played his final International, in 1984 against France, he'd won 61 caps and was the world's most-capped flanker.

• Opposite
Australia captain John Eales emerges with the ball against France during the 1999 Rugby World Cup final at the Millennium Stadium.

• Above
Lions flanker Fergus Slattery takes the ball during the 1974 Lions tour match against South Africa.

• Below
Peter Wheeler captained England and won 41 caps for his country.

153

Our bench has four forwards of incredible ability but in the backs we are just as blessed. Covering the centre and outside-half positions is England's **Jeremy Guscott**.

A three-time Lion in 1989, 1993 and 1997, Guscott made his Test debut for England against Romania in May 1989 and in typical Guscott style celebrated with a hat-trick of tries. That performance led to an instant Lions call and he was touring with the world's most famous team, on their winning tour to Australia, with just one international cap to his name.

Crucial to that 2-1 series win in Australia, Guscott scored a try in the second Test, becoming the first Englishman since Jeff Butterfield to score tries on his England and Lions debut. He didn't miss a Test on either the 1993 or 1997 Lions tour.

He also played in one of the most famous England teams in the history of the game, helping them to the 1991 World Cup final and to Grand Slams in 1991, 1992 and 1995. He finally retired, pulling out of the 1999 World Cup with a groin injury, with 65 England caps and 30 international tries to his name, while he also helped his club Bath to a stream of domestic honours.

Guscott will be remembered on the world stage for many things, but not least the drop goal that won the 1997 Lions series in South Africa.

You always need a scrum-half on the bench and in our team if anything ever did happen to the great Gareth Edwards, in would step All Blacks legend **Dave Loveridge**.

One of the best half-backs ever to wear the famous black jersey, Loveridge made his debut against Wales in 1978, before enjoying an eight-year international career that brought him 24 caps and three tries. He was known for his swift, long pass and was captain of the All Blacks on their 1980 tour of Australia and Fiji.

Completing our bench is **George Nepia** and it sounds incredible in itself that such a player is not in the starting line-up. Nepia was the teenage sensation of the New Zealand 'Invincibles' that toured the world in 1924-25. A wing by trade, Nepia was switched to full-back before appearing in four matches in Australia, two in New Zealand, all 30 games in Britain and France and two in Canada, on the way home.

Nepia was the man the All Blacks felt they couldn't drop, being both sure in defence and a prolific goal-kicker.

The young Maori boy from Nuhaka on the east coast returned from the triumphant Invincibles tour to star throughout Hawkes Bay's golden Ranfurly Shield reign in the 1920s.

Nepia was denied a place on the All Blacks trip to South Africa in 1928 because of his colour, but he was back in 1930 and his final Test appearance helped New Zealand clinch a 3-1 series win for his country over the Lions.

He moved to Rugby League in the mid-1930s but was always regarded as one of the greatest All Blacks of all time.

- **Opposite**
Jeremy Guscott runs with the ball. His career includes three Grand Slams and a World Cup final for England as well as three Lions' tours.

- **Above left**
Dave Loveridge spins the ball out under the watchful eye of France's Pierre Berbizier during their 1981 first Test in Toulouse.

- **Above right**
New Zealand sensation George Nepia starred in the legendary All Black 'Invincibles' of 1924-25.

The knowledge of the following international players was chosen to compile the side:

Bryn Meredith (caps: 34 Wales & 8 Lions)	John Beattie (25 Scotland & 1 Lions)
Paul Rendall (28 England)	Roger Uttley (23 England & 4 Lions)
Norman Gale (25 Wales)	Tony Ward (19 Ireland & 1 Lions)
Jeff Probyn (37 England)	Joel Stransky (23 South Africa)
Pat Whelan (19 Ireland)	Alan Old (16 England)
Fran Cotton (31 England & 7 Lions)	Dick Milliken (14 Ireland & 4 Lions)
Bobby Windsor (28 Wales & 5 Lions)	Jamie Salmon (12 England & 3 New Zealand)
Iain Morrison (15 Scotland)	David Duckham (36 England & 3 Lions)
Andy Ripley (24 England)	Billy Steele (22 Scotland & 2 Lions)
Bernard Gadney (14 England)	Bill Cuthbertson (21 Scotland)
Steve Smith (28 England)	Brian Price (32 Wales & 4 Lions)
John Taylor (26 Wales & 4 Lions)	Bill Beaumont (34 England & 7 Lions)
Mickey Skinner (21 England)	

Record Breaking Players

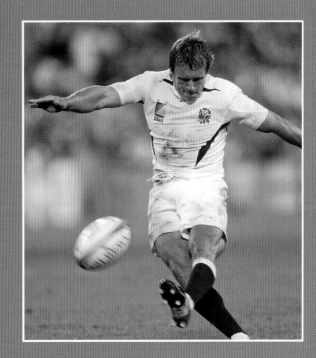

Chapter
TEN
10

In this chapter we pay homage to rugby's record-breakers.

1. MOST CAPPED PLAYER

Jason Leonard, England (1990-2004), Tests: 114
The Barking-born carpenter became the first England player – and first forward anywhere in the world – to win 100 caps and only the third member of the Test centurions club, along with France's Philippe Sella and Australia's David Campese.

With a career spanning two decades, he seamlessly made the transformation from amateur to professional in the most demanding role, of prop forward.

By the time he had made his 112th appearance for England (more than any player in the history of the game) in the 2003 World Cup he'd played in four World Cups, three Lions tours and had won an astonishing four Grand Slams.

Leonard began his rugby career at London club Barking, then moved to Saracens before beginning his long association with Harlequins in 1990.

He made his England debut that same year and was lucky, in some ways, to come up against the formidable scrummagers of Argentina on that first trip. With a hostile crowd it was a case of make or break for the young Londoner and as the rugby world knows it definitely made him, impressing England coach Geoff Cooke.

His England and Harlequins coach, Dick Best, said of Leonard after his debut: "England have found a prop for ten years."

Not known for his try-scoring exploits, his one international touchdown came on the day he became England captain, as they beat Argentina at Twickenham in 1995.

After returning from the 2003 World Cup Leonard was awarded the OBE (following his MBE in 2000), but not before he had suffered a serious neck injury that threatened to end his career in 1992. A piece of hip bone was removed and placed at the top of his neck, enabling him to continue his rugby career.

• **Above**
The England front row of Jason Leonard, Steve Thompson and Graham Rowntree prepare to scrummage during the 2003 Six Nations match against Scotland at Twickenham.

2. MOST CONSECUTIVE TEST WINS

New Zealand (1965-69): 17

After the 1956 All Blacks – the first to win a series against South Africa – restored post-war pride to a famous rugby nation, it was left to another side to pick up the gauntlet in the 1960s. Once that side of 1956 was broken up, new players were needed to maintain the great All Blacks tradition. This side – which really came to the fore in 1965, with Wilson Whineray as its captain – completed 17 consecutive Test wins, beating South Africa, Australia, England, Wales, Scotland, France and the British and Irish Lions along the way.

The rock on which this side was built was Colin Meads. A farmer, he was reputed to do his training either with a sheep on his back or with one tucked under each arm!

Around Meads and Whineray were men of steel like Kel Tremain, Ken Gray, Waka Nathan and the great Brian Lochore, and had there been a World Cup in the 1960s it wouldn't have been a question of whether these guys would have won it, just by how much. Theirs was a forward-dominated effort, although they also had genuinely world-class backs such as Don Clarke, Fergie McCormack, Chris Laidlaw, Earl Kirton and Sid Going.

Captain Lochore remembers the 1967 vintage saying: "Our pack was stuffed with provincial captains. We had utter confidence in each other. We were an arrogant team but only arrogant where a good team should be, on the field. We backed ourselves and we backed our mates.

"Fred Allen (the coach) was not nicknamed Fred the Needle because he loved to sew. He could strip a player of any pretensions with a withering look and a word. Imperfections in training were food and drink to him. The fear of not doing things well developed into pride in doing them well.

"There were elements of fear of Fred's vengeance in how good we became as a team. He was ruthless but his heart beat for rugby and for his players."

The record was equalled by Nick Mallett's South African team of 1997 and 1998, the All Blacks taking precedence as their run lasted five seasons.

• **Above**

Colin Meads (left of shot) and Brian Lochore (right) in amongst the England pack during their 1967 Test from Twickenham. New Zealand won the match 23-11.

3. MOST TESTS AS CAPTAIN

Will Carling, England

Tests as England captain: 59 (1988-96)

Love him or hate him – and most people did one or the other – there's no ignoring William David Charles Carling, the man who led England to three Grand Slams in five years and to the 1991 Rugby World Cup final.

Born in Bradford-on-Avon, Wiltshire, Carling made his England debut in 1988 against France, and in the same year he was handed the England captaincy by manager Geoff Cooke at the age of just 22.

The Harlequins centre was fortunate to have so many great players around him in the 1990s, but his durability was remarkable, as he captained his country an incredible 59 times – more than anyone else in the world.

A powerful, direct-running centre, who complemented his midfield partner Jeremy Guscott perfectly, he won 72 caps, playing his last Test against Wales in 1997, and scoring 12 tries in international rugby.

Carling's record-breaking run almost came to an end when he called the RFU committee "57 old farts" in an off-the-cuff remark at the end of a TV interview, a comment for which he was sacked as England captain in May 1995.

But after an uproar and the refusal of any other England player to take on the captaincy, Carling was reinstated within 48 hours in an embarrassing U-turn for the RFU.

Carling may have been the most successful England captain, but he often played down his role: "Captain on the field! People have an exaggerated idea of what that means, and of how much influence I can exert," he explained in his authorised biography *Will Carling*. "Tighten up, spread it, vary the lineout – I can say it but it's up to the team to implement it.

"Also, you not only have to react to the opposition but to the referee. That's why preparation is so important. There's no time once the match starts. The majority of my captaincy work is done by the time we run out. The hustle and bustle of a Dublin International is no place to be trying to work out a new strategy."

It is an exceptional record and the success he had as England captain is unlikely ever to be matched, let alone beaten.

• Above
Will Carling passes the ball during the 1995 England v France Five Nations Championship match.

• Inset
Portrait of England Rugby Union captain Will Carling during a photoshoot held in London, 1989.

4. MOST PROLIFIC

HALF-BACKS

Nick Farr-Jones and Michael Lynagh: 47 times for Australia between 1985-92

Partnerships come and go but some hang around a little longer than others, and that was certainly the case with Nick Farr-Jones and Michael Lynagh, the prolific Australian half-backs. The pair lined up together in the green and gold of the Wallabies 47 times between 1985 and 1992, more than any other half-backs in rugby history.

Scrum-half Farr-Jones, who made his debut on the Grand Slam tour of 1984 alongside Mark Ella, was one of the greats of Australian rugby, most famous for leading Australia to their first World Cup win in 1991.

He went on to lead his country a then record 36 times, finishing with 23 wins in those games, before John Eales surpassed him in the captaincy stakes.

Farr-Jones, who won 63 caps and scored 37 points, announced his retirement in 1992, but was persuaded to come back a year later, eventually finishing his career against South Africa.

Alongside Farr-Jones in those 47 Tests was Queenslander Michael Lynagh, who was a terrific running fly-half and one of the greatest goal-kickers the rugby world has seen.

He came into the side under huge pressure, being handed the job of replacing the great Mark Ella (Lynagh had played centre on the 1984 tour). But he filled the No 10 shirt superbly, winning 72 caps and scoring 911 points, which was a record on his retirement in 1995.

Farr-Jones's Wallaby coach Bob Dwyer was clearly a fan. He said: "He set high personal standards for himself, and because of his maturity and strength of character he was able to set high standards for the team quite naturally and easily.

"He understood from the outset when and how the team needed to concentrate, and when and how it needed to relax. His influence on the team in all its activities on and off the field has been vital to its success. Without it, I am sure we would not have won the World Cup [in 1991].

"Australia has always had good half-backs but until Farr-Jones came to the fore we had not had a great half-back for some time. For this reason I believe Farr-Jones gave the side another dimension."

Dwyer was similarly impressed with Lynagh, saying: "Michael was an outstanding organiser of the side. He is very controlled as a person and possesses tremendous composure. I cannot remember an occasion when I saw him panic. As a player he also had tremendous running skills and width of vision, not to mention his obvious kicking ability."

• **Above**
Nick Farr-Jones passes back to Michael Lynagh during the 1992 Australia v South Africa Test played at Newlands, Cape Town.

5. MOST POINTS IN A CHAMPIONSHIP SEASON

Jonny Wilkinson, England (1998-)
89 in 2001

So much, so young, Jonny Wilkinson has made one of the most dramatic impacts on international rugby in the history of the game.

After making his debut as an 18-year-old in the 1998 Five Nations Championship, he became indispensable for the England team. And by the end of the 2003 Six Nations he held 12 different England records, including most points in a championship season (89) and most points in a championship match (35). He had scored more points than any Englishman in the history of the game.

Yet Wilkinson's first start in an England shirt, in June 1998, was a nightmare, as a weakened England side was hammered 76-0 in Brisbane, on the so-called Tour to Hell, when England lost to Australia, New Zealand and South Africa in quick succession.

One of the most dedicated players of his generation, Wilkinson, a British Lion in 2001, is renowned for his relentless pursuit of excellence, and he spends hour after hour practising his kicking.

He scored 77 points in the 2003 Six Nations, more than any player, and attributes his success to winning the mental battle. "The mechanics need to be correct," he says, "but at the same time I have to be comfortable within myself. State of mind is as important as technique; success or failure is governed by feel as much as anything."

His incredible success with his goal-kicking belies how good he is with ball in hand and as his career develops, so does he as a running fly-half.

Wilkinson captained England for the first time in 2003, against Italy, in the same year when he dropped the winning goal in the World Cup final, against Australia.

In the 2001 Six Nations, 35 points against Italy and 13 more against Scotland put Rob Andrew's England scoring record in sight, and he only needed eight points against France to claim a place in rugby history by surpassing Andrew's 396-point mark, aged only 21.

One of the most humble players in international rugby, he said after breaking the England record: "Just to be mentioned in the same breath as Rob was an honour – he was my hero when I was growing up. To overtake his England total is an achievement to be proud of."

Named as the International Players' Player of 2002, Wilkinson also scooped the fans' vote when he was named Planet Rugby's Player of the Year for the second successive year. He was also awarded the MBE in the end-of-year Queen's Honours List – the youngest rugby player ever to receive such an award. Astonishing!

6. MOST POINTS IN TEST MATCHES

Neil Jenkins, Wales (1991-2003), 1,049

To say Neil Jenkins has had a roller-coaster ride in international rugby would be something of an understatement. Having to follow some of the greatest players in world rugby into the Wales No 10 shirt meant he was a villain one minute and hero the next.

He talks about how difficult it was to be a Wales outside-half in his autobiography *Life at Number Ten*.

Jenkins said: "An occupational hazard of being the Wales outside-half is that there is no settling-in period, and when you consider the players of international ability that Wales has had in the position in the past ten years, it is a travesty that so little has been seen of them.

"It is as well for the likes of Grant Fox, Michael Lynagh, Mark Ella, Joel Stransky and Andrew Mehrtens that they were not Welsh, because they would have struggled to have made a name for themselves."

But there's no question that Jenkins had the last laugh, loved by Wales supporters as his career moved into its final stages.

On Saturday 3 February 2001, against Ireland at Lansdowne Road, the fly-half from Church Village became the first player in rugby history to score a thousand Test points.

Jenkins's achievements are even more significant considering the fact that the majority of his caps came in a Wales side that was struggling.

"Reaching 1,000 points was the ultimate achievement," Jenkins admitted. "Becoming the first player to reach the four-figure landmark would mean more to me than breaking Michael Lynagh's record and Ieuan's (Evans) 72 Wales caps because records are there to be broken.

"Whatever figures I end with will be overtaken at some time in the future, but the first player to reach 1,000 points holds that honour for eternity."

Jenkins was just 19 when he made his Wales debut in 1991 against England. But he enjoyed his finest hour in a Lions shirt, when he selflessly answered the call by switching to full-back and helped kick the 1997 Lions to a 2-1 series victory over South Africa.

"The hardest thing about that tour was its end," said Jenkins. "The squad and management had been together for eight weeks on what was, for me, the journey of a lifetime. Part of me wanted it never to end.

"For the first few days when I returned home it was as if something was missing. Rugby Union may be a professional sport, but to play for the Lions was a privilege."

• **Opposite**
Jonny Wilkinson kicks a penalty during the 2003 Six Nations against France. England went on to win the match 25-17.

• **Above**
Neil Jenkins of Wales slides over to score the match winning try during the 2001 Six Nations match against France played at the Stade De France, in Paris. Wales won the match 43-35.

7. MOST CAPPED
WOMEN'S PLAYER

Liza Burgess, Wales (1986-2002) Caps: 72

The word legend is overused, especially in sport, but sometimes it is needed to describe the impact of a select number of rugby players. In the women's game if you hear the name Liza Burgess, and you know the women's game, it is difficult to stop the word legend popping into your head.

Burgess played in one of the first women's Internationals in 1986, when Great Britain took on France, and when she retired from international rugby 16 years later she had gained 72 caps, more than any other woman.

When she lined up for Wales in the 2002

Women's World Cup, she was playing in her third World Cup and was still at the top of her sport, aged 36.

Burgess first played in the late 1980s at Loughborough University under the guidance of Jim Greenwood, and she went on to represent the newly formed Great Britain side whilst still a student. A move to London followed and, after helping to found Saracens Ladies in 1988, Burgess spent the Nineties as one of the leading lights in the women's game.

Born and educated in Newport, she represented Wales as they hosted the inaugural Women's World Cup in 1991 and later captained her country many times. She also led Saracens to numerous league and cup triumphs before moving to Clifton in 2000, whom she led to their Premiership title in 2001 and their Rugby World National Cup triumph in 2002.

"The commitment involved and the standards of play have altered a lot," she says. "When I first started playing we didn't have that many international fixtures, whereas now the season is more or less ten months of the year. I've been training quite hard since I was at university, though, and we're given so much more information and support now that it's not hard to motivate myself."

It takes a lot to stay at the top of the international game for more than 15 years, but Burgess has defeated the critics by moving with the times. She has been rewarded by fellow players, coaches and journalists alike and is not only a former Welsh Rugby Union Player of the Year but also one of the original members of the Rugby World Hall of Fame.

Burgess played on for Clifton after retiring from international rugby but has one eye on the future.

She added: "Ultimately I want to coach Wales. Not in the next few years as I have so much to learn, but that's where I'd love to be in ten years."

• **Above**
Liza Burgess of Wales in action during the 2002 Women's International between England and Wales at Old Deer Park, Surrey.

8. MOST CAPPED SCRUM-HALF

George Gregan (1994-), Tests: 96

George Gregan is one of those sportsmen who has an on-field persona and an off-field personality that couldn't be further apart. Meet him off the field and it's hard to get a word out of the softly-spoken, Zambian-born scrum-half, but on it he is aggressive and triumphant, and basks in his victories.

"I try to keep my private life private," he says, "and as a result I'm sometimes portrayed as a cold fish. I'm not. I love my job, I love competing and when I'm on the field there is nothing more important to me in life than winning. The public only see that side of me."

Already he has won World Cup, Super 12 and Tri-Nations titles, and he was an integral part of the downfall of the 2001 Lions. He surpassed Nick Farr-Jones as Australia's most capped scrum-half and in 2002 he overtook Joost van der Westhuizen as the most capped No 9 in the history of the game, with 78 appearances.

Like Gareth Edwards in the 1970s, Gregan is a devastating attacking threat, as well as being a great passer of the ball, while in defence he has the ability to stop anyone.

Gregan made his Test debut against Italy in 1994 after some great displays for ACT and the Australian sevens side. His career took off in the same year, when he made one of the most famous tackles in the history of the game on Jeff Wilson, to win a Test against New Zealand.

Andrew Slack, captain of the 1984 Grand Slam Wallabies and later coach of Queensland Reds, believes Gregan's influence over the Super 12 has been immense, as his side the ACT Brumbies won back-to-back titles in 2000 and 2001.

Slack said: "You can list all these things and analyse any number of factors for the Brumbies' success. But when it all boils down, George Gregan is the most important thing. To have a great player in such a crucial position is a major, major factor. Take George out of the equation and the Brumbies' chances over the years would have been limited."

• Above
George Gregan of the Wallabies scores a try under pressure from Chris Paterson of Scotland during the 2003 Rugby World Cup Quarter Final match between Australia and Scotland.

• Inset
Gregan lifts the Webb Ellis trophy after victory over France in the 1999 Rugby World Cup final at the Millennium Stadium.

9. MOST CAPPED FLY-HALF

Rob Andrew (1985-97), Tests: 71

In the 1980s and 1990s, every England rugby fan had a view on the debate: who should be the country's fly-half, Rob Andrew or Stuart Barnes? Andrew was seen as the steadying influence, the man with the golden boot, while Barnes was portrayed as the guy with flair, the one to open up the tightest defence. Well, Andrew, who was made an MBE, certainly won the argument and his 71 caps for England make him the world's most capped fly-half.

Andrew made his debut against Romania in 1985, enjoying a 13-season career in an England shirt before being replaced by Paul Grayson at the end of the 1997 Five Nations Championship.

He scored 15 points on that debut and, although Simon Hodgkinson and Jon Webb were England's goal-kickers for large parts of his career, when Andrew played his final Test match it was as his country's most successful points-scorer, with 396, a mark later overtaken by Jonny Wilkinson.

Andrew only took up England's goal-kicking full-time in 1994 when Webb retired from the international game, and he didn't take long before setting a new record for points in a match, 30 against Canada later that year.

Andrew, who was a Lion in 1989 and 1993, helped England to Grand Slams in 1991, 1992 and 1995 and to the World Cup final in 1991, while his ice-cool temperament ensured England made the semi-finals in 1995, when he kicked a late drop-goal to knock out Australia.

His retirement in 1995 left a massive hole in the England team and he was even recalled in 1997.

Jack Rowell, his England coach in 1995, said when he heard the news: "I am stunned at Rob's retirement. It leaves a huge gap in the England firmament. His performances have got better as he has got older. He has underpinned the England team's performance and his retirement gives me a selection headache. There is Mike Catt and David Pears, but what a player, what a gentleman to lose.'"

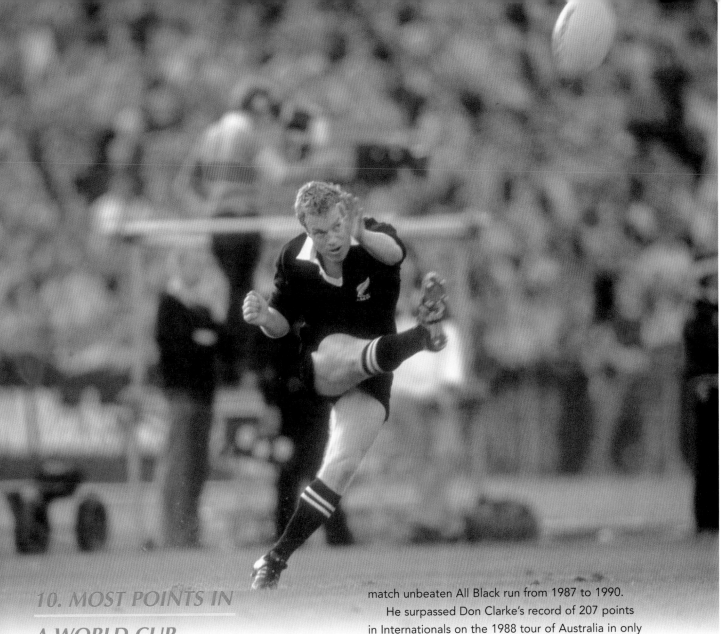

10. MOST POINTS IN A WORLD CUP

Grant Fox, New Zealand (1985-93), 126 in 1987

Grant Fox is one of the most prolific goal-kickers in the history of our game and in 1987 he managed to establish his points record without even scoring a try.

The New Plymouth-born outside-half made his debut for New Zealand in 1985, playing 46 Tests and scoring 645 points, before his last game, against Samoa in 1993.

Educated at Auckland Grammar School, Fox went on to star for Auckland but didn't play a Test match in New Zealand until the first game of that 1987 World Cup, where his country crushed Italy. The selectors were clearly as impressed as the spectators that day as he played in every Test from then until the next World Cup in 1991, participating in the 23-match unbeaten All Black run from 1987 to 1990.

He surpassed Don Clarke's record of 207 points in Internationals on the 1988 tour of Australia in only his second season as a regular-choice fly-half. His 433 points in first-class rugby during the 1989 domestic season was also a record.

New Zealand's reliance on his goal-kicking in that period often belied his abilities with the ball in hand, as he controlled the All Blacks back-line and read the game exceptionally well.

When Fox played his last Test match in 1993, the All Blacks knew they had a huge task to replace him.

Coach Laurie Mains said: "Grant Fox is a once-in-a-lifetime player. We could not attempt to produce another because there is nobody near his level.

"He is very meticulous in everything he does and because you cannot duplicate him our new fly-halves will have a different set of strengths. Ultimately it will mean our attack relies a bit more on passing the ball than the kicking style Grant specialises in."

• Opposite
Rob Andrew kicks the ball high in the England v Scotland match during the 1995 Five Nations Championships at Twickenham.

• Above
Grant Fox of New Zealand in action during the 1987 Rugby World Cup.

The World Cup

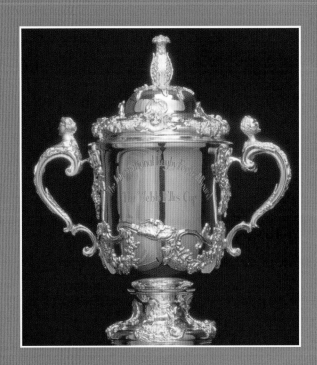

Chapter
ELEVEN

• Above
John Kirwan of New Zealand evades the tackle and goes on to score a try during the 1987 Rugby World Cup match against Fiji played at Lancaster Park, Christchurch, New Zealand.

The Rugby World Cup is now a multi-million pound global extravaganza that is only topped, in the sporting world, by the Olympics and Football World Cup. But when it was first mooted at the International Rugby Board in 1958, it received no more than a lukewarm response from many corners of the rugby world. Subsequent proposals faired no better until the mid 1980s. This proposal, which was backed by Australia, France and New Zealand, was only accepted after South Africa gave a new tournament its support.

The British and Irish Unions were opposed to the idea of a World Cup, but it still received enough support for the first tournament to be staged, in New Zealand and Australia, in 1987.

Such was the haste in which this first World Cup was organised that there wasn't enough time for a qualifying competition, so 16 unions, by invitation only, were asked to take part. It was, to date, the easiest one to predict, with only New Zealand, Australia and France in with a realistic chance of winning. South Africa were banned from the competition due to the sporting boycott instigated in response to the continued apartheid regime in the republic.

England and France may have fought over who would host the 2007 Rugby World Cup but back in 1987, due mostly to apathy, there was only one choice of venue, New Zealand and Australia.

Many people believed this tournament would be a one-off and the 16 teams struggled for any kind of profile on the global stage. The participating teams were the two hosts, the sides from the Five Nations Championship plus Argentina, Canada, Fiji, Italy, Japan, Romania, Tonga, USA and Zimbabwe.

The Home Nations certainly didn't take it as seriously as the big two from the southern hemisphere and hooker Brian Moore remembers the 1987 World Cup as "quaint", such was the haphazard way in which it was organised.

The way Moore and his England colleagues approached the tournament didn't stop some great rugby being played and the small television audience that saw it were treated to some of the greatest performances the World Cup has seen.

But there were, as there have been at all subsequent World Cups, some fearsome mismatches and New Zealand v Italy, which kicked off the tournament at Eden Park, Auckland, was a classic example. New Zealand thrashed the Italians 70-6,

the first of several big scores in the World Cup, many of which involved the Kiwis.

This opening match contained an incredible try by New Zealand wing John Kirwan, who went on to coach the Italians 15 years later. Kirwan collected the ball in his 22 and used his immense pace and power to take him through or past a host of Italian defenders and over the try-line.

The Home Unions may not have taken it that seriously but as so many nations were underdeveloped, England, Scotland, Ireland and Wales all made the quarter-finals, something that hasn't happened since. In fact, one of the main legacies of the Rugby World Cup is the way that it has contributed to the development – and not just financially – of some of the smaller rugby-playing nations. It has given many of them a focus and a path to allow the game to grow in those countries.

In those 1987 quarter-finals Scotland succumbed 30-3 to the All Blacks. The Scots, who lost their key man, fly-half John Rutherford, in their opening 20-20 draw with France, conceded two tries in the game. No other side in the tournament was to restrict the All Blacks to so few.

Australia were the pre-tournament favourites and they justified this tag by racing through their group stage without losing a match, beating England 19-6

along the way. Another UK team was to perish at the hands of the Wallabies in the quarter-finals, Ireland. Taking on the Australians in Sydney, and having already lost to Wales in the group stages, Ireland were rank outsiders and duly went down 33-15.

England and Wales also clashed in the quarter-finals but they produced a poor match, Wales winning 16-3. Their dubious reward was a semi-final meeting against the rampant New Zealanders.

Wales' three tries in the clash with England, by Gareth Roberts, Robert Jones and John Devereux, all stemmed from mistakes by their opponents. And as John Mason, in The Daily Telegraph, put it: "New Zealand will not be quaking."

In the fourth quarter-final the Fijians produced some breathtaking rugby against France and early in the second half looked as though they might be causing the first World Cup upset. But their hopes disappeared in one blundering moment when fly-half Severo Koroduadua dropped the ball as he glided unchallenged over the French try-line. France launched a fightback and booked a place against Australia in the first semi-final, with a 31-16 win.

France and Australia produced a classic in the last four and it still ranks as one of the best matches of all-time. It was another reason why the game deserved a Rugby World Cup.

• **Above**
Iain Paxton of Scotland battles for the ball with David Kirk of New Zealand during the 1987 Rugby World Cup quarter-final.

• **Inset**
Wade Dooley of England is challenged for the high ball by Richard Moriarty of Wales during their quarter-final match at Ballymore, in Brisbane.

• **Above**
Jonathan Davies runs with the ball during the 1987 Rugby World Cup semi-final match between New Zealand and Wales in Brisbane.

• **Below**
Serge Blanco of France scores a dramatic try to win their semi-final against Australia played at the Football Stadium in Sydney.

John Reason, writing in The Sunday Telegraph, said of the France v Australia match: "I never thought I would see a game to rival the one played between the Barbarians and the All Blacks at Cardiff, in 1973, but this one did.

"It had a few more mistakes and not so many great players. And Australia in 1987 are not of the same class as New Zealand in 1973. But so much was happening in so many places and for so much of the time that this game will be remembered as long as the World Cup is played."

The 30-24 victory for the French was achieved by a last-gasp try from the sensational Serge Blanco, who finished off a length-of-the-field move, that mesmerized the crowd and took his side into the first World Cup final.

The other semi-final was something of a foregone conclusion as Wales, who were by now missing five first-choice forwards, had to travel to Rotorua to play hosts New Zealand, and were blown away 49-6. It was in the forwards that New Zealand demolished the Welsh, who also had the ignominy of seeing lock Huw Richards sent off. Richards was dismissed for punching Gary Whetton but not before he was pole-axed himself by a retaliatory punch from Wayne Shelford.

Wales, despite their defeat, did have the pleasure of travelling further in this first World Cup than any of the other UK nations and they rounded off their tournament by beating Australia for third place.

They were punished for a sending-off in the semi-finals, but benefited from one in the third-place play-off as Wallaby David Codey was dismissed and his side had to play for 75 minutes with 14 men.

But even with that advantage Wales only just snatched victory, Adrian Hadley scoring a late try that Paul Thorburn converted from the touchline.

After so many great games and great individual performances, the final was something of an anticlimax.

The tournament showed in stark focus the widening gulf between the northern and southern hemispheres that would soon herald the end of the amateur game. And this was emphasized by the final, staged at Eden Park, when New Zealand triumphed 29-9.

The prolific Grant Fox formed the platform with six penalties, and even without skipper Andy Dalton, who had to withdraw through injury just before the tournament, the All Blacks never looked like losing.

Michael Jones was outstanding in the final, scoring a try and dominating the breakdowns.

Fox finished the tournament with 126 points and new captain David Kirk with the Webb Ellis Trophy in his hands. Those who were there or watched it on television enjoyed it but no one knew if there would be another.

The success of the 1987 World Cup convinced the powers-that-be that there should be another tournament, and the decision was taken to stage it in Europe, with matches in England, Wales, Scotland, Ireland and France.

For this tournament the IRB invited all member Unions to enter qualifying rounds. The eight 1987 quarter-finalists were guaranteed berths while 32 other nations competed for eight other spots. South Africa were still unable to compete due to the boycott.

The 1991 World Cup, complete with an official anthem, opened at Twickenham. Grand Slam winners England took on the reigning world champions New Zealand in a game that failed to live up to expectations. The All Blacks denied England possession for long periods, and Michael Jones's try gave them the foundation for an 18-12 victory.

But this World Cup will be remembered for one of the biggest shocks in rugby history as tiny Western Samoa beat mighty Wales at Cardiff's National Stadium. "What if they had been playing the whole of Samoa?" the newspapers asked cruelly.

With strong ties to New Zealand rugby, the Samoans surprised the Welshmen with bone-crunching tackles to book their place in the quarter-finals. The warning signs had been there for the Welsh ever since they finished bottom of the Five Nations Championship earlier that season and then endured a 63-6 hammering in Brisbane against Australia.

• Above
Robert Jones passes the ball during Wales' 1987 third place match against Australia in Rotorua, New Zealand.

• Below left
John Kirwan of New Zealand scores a try during the 1987 Rugby World Cup final against France at Eden Park in Auckland.

• Below right
Sila Vaifale beats Robert Jones on his way to scoring the 2nd try for Western Samoa during their 1991 Pool 3 victory over Wales.

a fearsome clash back at Lansdowne Road. Crucially the All Blacks were without back-rower Michael Jones, who refused to play on Sundays because of religious beliefs. And Australia, with David Campese at his dazzling best, triumphed 16-6.

All the quarter-finalists had to battle for their successes, with both Italy and Canada putting up competitive displays against the All Blacks.

Western Samoa's run came to an end at Murrayfield, when they went down 28-6 to a disciplined Scotland side, while New Zealand saw off brave Canada 29-13 on a rain-sodden pitch in Lille.

No one could deny that England deserved their place in the 1991 final, to face the Wallabies, after a mountainous route that took them past both Scotland at Murrayfield and France in Paris.

France and England met in a highly charged Parc des Princes quarter-final. England had moved through the tournament with a reliance on their forwards and they soon turned this match into a confrontation, Mickey Skinner's massive tackle on Marc Cecillon personifying England's no-holds-barred commitment.

Even the great Serge Blanco was guilty of throwing punches, at England wing Nigel Heslop, as

But nothing could have prepared this proud rugby nation for a 16-13 defeat by Western Samoa, and the embarrassment of not making the quarter-finals of the World Cup.

Both Wales and Western Samoa had been drawn in their group with Australia, so the Welsh agony was prolonged only until they succumbed to the Wallabies, 38-3 in Cardiff, and bowed out.

Australia, in contrast to the Welsh, continued to make giant leaps and came into the 1991 event as favourites following a 21-12 win over New Zealand in August. They had a mighty scare in the quarter-finals, only overcoming Ireland 19-18, with a Michael Lynagh try in the closing minutes. And in the semis they were drawn with the holders, New Zealand, for

• Above
Donal Lenihan of Ireland rotates the ball out of a maul during their 1991 Rugby World Cup quarter-final match against Australia at Lansdowne Road in Dublin.

• Inset
Nick Farr-Jones gets to grips with Gary Whetton in the 1991 Australia v New Zealand semi-final at Lansdowne Road.

French organisation and discipline deteriorated. Heslop was hit after charging Blanco following a high ball but while England's aggression was disciplined, the French lost their composure. Pascal Ondartes infringed and Jonathan Webb finally put England ahead 13-10, before captain Will Carling booked England's place in the last four; after he caught Blanco fielding a garryowen, Carling dispossessed him and dived over the line for the try that sealed a 19-10 victory.

For Blanco it was a sad end to one of the greatest careers the game has seen, as he retired after the match.

England then moved to foreign soil again in the knowledge that if they won on their travels again, the reward would be a World Cup final at Twickenham.

While there was no doubt in Paris, England were let off the hook in Edinburgh as Gavin Hastings missed a penalty in front of the posts, with the scores tied at 6-6 midway through the second half.

Rob Andrew eventually delivered the win for England, kicking a drop-goal from the final scrum to secure a 9-6 victory.

The climax of the 1991 Rugby World Cup took place at a packed Twickenham and England committed the unforgivable sin of changing their game plan.

They had steamrollered the opposition to make the final with a forward-dominated pattern. But, stung by criticism that they were boring to watch, England adopted a wider, more free-flowing strategy in the final, and this played into Aussie hands as England found themselves frustrated at every turn.

The only try came midway through the first half when the impressive Willie Ofahengaue won the ball

at the tail of the lineout and drove for the England line. The Australian forwards took up the charge, finally collapsing over the line with prop Tony Daly claiming the try.

England had to wait for the second half before a Webb penalty got them onto the scoreboard, but Lynagh responded to make it 12-3. Soon afterwards England had their best scoring chance when Peter Winterbottom tried to exploit a clear overlap on the left wing. His pass to Rory Underwood was knocked on by David Campese, who was penalised for a deliberate knock-on. Webb converted the penalty, but Derek Bevan's failure to award a penalty try is still debated to this day. Late in the match, England had their final chance to score, only for a knock-on to deny them. At the final whistle the Wallabies were victorious, 12-6.

Ireland, though only making the quarter-finals, had the leading points-scorer in the tournament in Ralph Keyes (68), while Campese and France's Jean-Baptiste Lafond were joint top try-scorers, with six each.

The 1991 Rugby World Cup signalled the era when rugby union arrived on the world scene and rugby's rulers knew they had a global product on their hands. For the first time, players became household names and the tournament took the sport to new heights.

• **Above**
Nick Farr-Jones holds up the Webb Ellis trophy after Australia beat England to win the 1991 Rugby World Cup.

• **Below**
Gavin Hastings disappointed after missing a crucial penalty kick during the 1991 Rugby World Cup semifinal match between Scotland and England at Murrayfield.

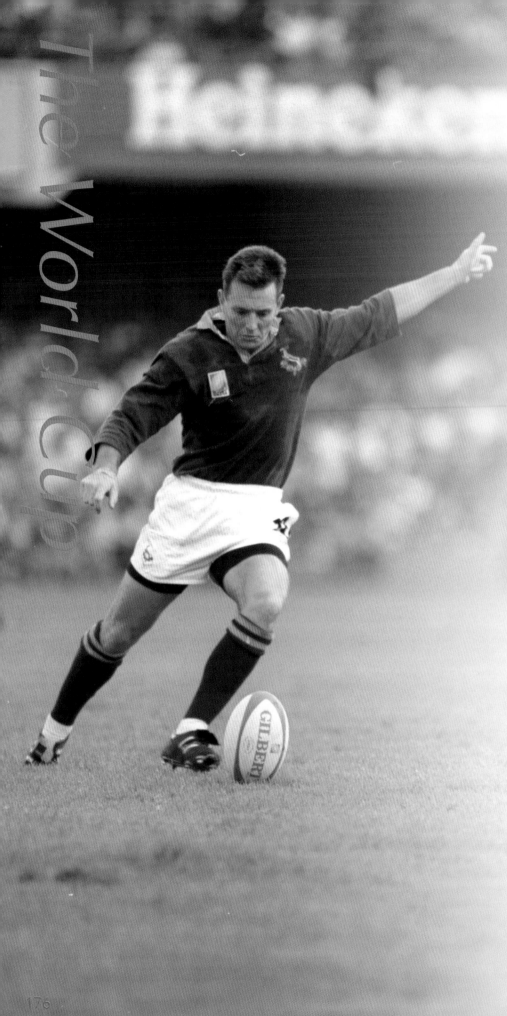

TV audiences were huge but with the demands on players' time getting heavier and heavier, the tournament also confirmed that it was a question of when and not if rugby union turned professional.

Meanwhile, the political revolution in South Africa led to the lifting of the sporting boycott on the republic.

In 1992 they made their first trip to England for 22 years, and it was therefore fitting that the South Africans were awarded the 1995 Rugby World Cup, to complete their return to the rugby world.

The country was still struggling to come to terms with economic problems, so it was a massively important gesture by the IRB to award the tournament to South Africa. It not only poured much-needed finance into the country but confirmed that rugby was a sport that was prepared to welcome one of its favourite sons back into the fold.

This third World Cup was, for many, more emotional than the first two. The bandwagon rolled into town amidst fears that the country's infrastructure would be unable to cope with the third biggest sporting event in the world. But President Nelson Mandela pledged his support for the tournament and at the opening ceremony at Newlands in Cape Town, he welcomed the 16 countries to the 'Rainbow Nation'.

South Africa put on a memorable tournament and it was the first World Cup to be staged in just one country. It proved a massive success and in the opening ceremony, Mandela summed up what the Rugby World Cup meant to his reborn nation and what a tournament like this can bring to a country. He said:

"Your presence affirms the unity in diversity, the humanity in healthy contest, that our young democracy has come to symbolize. South Africa keenly appreciates your love and support. South Africa opens its arms and heart to embrace you all."

The opening game of pool A was as exciting as the pre-match ceremonies, with the hosts surprising the reigning world champions Australia 27-18. Joel Stransky did the damage in Cape Town, scoring 22 points in front of president Mandela.

Canada and Romania were the other teams in the group and were able to test the top two, but the so-called Battle of Boet Erasmus saw the game between Canada and South Africa deteriorate into a brawl which did nothing to enhance the image of rugby. The game started 45 minutes late due to floodlight failure, and ended with James Dalton, the Springbok hooker, Rod Snow, the Canadian prop, and Canadian captain and fly-half Gareth Rees being sent off. Springbok Pieter Hendriks and Canadian Scott Stewart were also suspended after the match.

In pool B, England were Grand Slam champions and favourites, but though they won all three games they were far from fluent. They struggled against Argentina 24-18 and Italy 27-20, but got into their stride against Western Samoa (who claimed the second qualifying spot), beating them 44-22.

The 1991 tournament had David Campese but the real star of the 1995 event didn't come from the winners, South Africa, but from runners-up New Zealand. He was a young man called Jonah Lomu, who'd earlier sent out a warning to the rugby world with a destructive performance at the Hong Kong Sevens and in pool C he left an indelible mark on the tournament.

New Zealand were expected to win the pool with ease, with Wales and Ireland slugging it out for second place. Against Ireland, the All Blacks unleashed Lomu. With his strength and power he swept aside Irish 43-19 and Welsh 34-9.

New Zealand fielded their second string side but were still able to record a record win of 145-17 over Japan. Ireland just managed to hold off Wales 24-23 to take second spot.

In pool D, Scotland and France were the two big guns, with Tonga and Ivory Coast hoping to gain valuable experience from the competition. Emile Ntamack scored in injury-time to give France a 22-19 win over Scotland in what was one of the games of the tournament.

Tragically, Ivory Coast winger Max Brito suffered a serious injury against Tonga that has left him paralysed.

Three of the quarter-finals went to form. France dominated Ireland up front and the reliable boot of Thierry Lacroix gave them a 36-12 win. Chester Williams wasted no time in getting into the record books as he became the first South African player to

• **Opposite**
Joel Stransky of South Africa during the 1995 Rugby World Cup final against Australia.

• **Above**
Jonah Lomu breaks free of the Welsh during the 1995 Pool C match at Ellis Park, in Johannesburg.

score four tries in a Test match, as they beat Western Samoa 42-14.

The Lomu legend continued to grow as New Zealand rolled over Scotland 48-30 in the third quarter-final. But the brave Scots made sure that one of their greatest players, Gavin Hastings, departed the international scene with his head held high. They became only the second side, after Australia, to score 30 points against the All Blacks, their tries coming from lock Doddie Weir (two) and Gavin's brother, Scott.

England v Australia in Cape Town was a re-run of the 1991 final and the toughest of the quarter-finals to predict. It was incredibly tight and it was decided in dramatic fashion. With the scores tied at 22-22, and the game heading into injury-time, Rob Andrew landed a spectacular 45-metre drop-goal, after a lineout catch by Martin Bayfield, to give coach Jack Rowell's side victory and a meeting with New Zealand.

The first semi-final featuring France and South Africa was almost abandoned as torrential rain made the pitch at King's Park in Durban unplayable, and pictures of women sweeping the rain off the pitch flew around the world.

It was a nail-biting time for South Africa, as they knew that if the game was abandoned they would go out of the competition because of the red card they had incurred against Canada.

When the game got underway Andre Joubert turned in a superlative performance and was the rock on which the Springboks prospered. Joel Stransky kicked a penalty and Ruben Kruger powered over for a try, while Thierry Lacroix kept France in the game with his boot. With three minutes to go, France trailed 19-15. Abdelatif Benazzi drove for the line but was stopped an inch short and South Africa weathered a series of crucial scrums as France went for the pushover try. South Africa won a scrum and Stransky cleared his lines. All eyes were on referee Derek Bevan as he signalled the lineout before blowing the final whistle. South Africa were through to the final.

Jonah Lomu destroyed England in their semi-final. England captain Will Carling called Lomu a "freak" and it took the All Black one minute to stamp his mark. The 18st 8lb, 6ft 5in wing picked up a kick and raced to the try-line, steamrollering past Carling, Tony Underwood and Mike Catt. England never got to grips with Lomu that day in Cape Town and he went on to score an incredible four tries, as the Kiwis won 45-29.

John Mason, in The Daily Telegraph, described the scene: "In defying the tenets of a team game, here was one player who spent the semi-final of the 1995 World Cup reducing a previously competent, well-drilled England team, seeking an 11th consecutive victory, to bedraggled also-rans. It was embarrassing; it was also inspiring, a sporting occasion to remember."

England's tournament went from bad to worse as they then suffered defeat in the third-place play-off, 19-9 to France.

These play-offs are often irrelevant but this one had great significance as only three sides plus the hosts were to qualify automatically for the 1999 event. So the defeat to France left England having to qualify for the next World Cup.

Two sides who were never in danger of having to qualify were New Zealand and South Africa as their next date was 24 June, at Ellis Park, Johannesburg, where they would contest the World Cup final.

All the portents pointed to a South Africa win. Their stadium, their supporters and their readmission to the sporting world following the boycott. Oh, and they also had the small matter of one Mr Nelson Mandela, one of the world's leading statesmen, in the crowd to cheer them on, appearing in the Springboks' No 6 shirt, like the one worn by captain Francois Pienaar.

But New Zealand, though undermined by sickness in the squad in the days before the final, were the favourites after their demolition of England. However, the script writers were to have their way, but only just as the Springboks emerged triumphant in the first Test match in the history of the game to go into extra time.

It wasn't a thriller, but then finals rarely are, all the points coming from kicks, four for South Africa's Joel Stransky and three from All Black Andrew Mehrtens.

At the end of a compelling 80 minutes the scores were locked at 9-9. Mehrtens kicked the All Blacks ahead with 18 minutes to go only for Stransky to kick a penalty and the winning drop-goal, after Zinzan Brooke had knocked on and given the Springboks the scrum and the field position they needed, for a 15-12 win.

But the plaudits must go to the inspired Springbok defence that stopped Lomu and everything else the All Blacks could throw at them, in a way every other side in this tournament had failed to do. The Springboks, led by Joost van der Westhuizen and Japie Mulder, proved that Lomu could be tamed as they hit him often and hard. No tries were scored but Ruben Kruger was unlucky when referee Ed Morrison declared that the ball had been held up.

The final whistle triggered an emotional outpouring as Mandela in his Springbok jersey was there to present the trophy to Pienaar.

Pienaar summed up what it meant when he said: "We did not have 63,000 fans behind us today, we had 43 million South Africans."

One sour note was the allegation made by the All Blacks that they had been poisoned before the final.

Frenchman Thierry Lacroix finished the tournament as the leading points-scorer, bagging 112, eight ahead of Gavin Hastings. The leading try-scorers were Lomu and his colleague Mark Ellis. They both scored seven, Ellis profiting from the huge win over Japan.

The 1995 World Cup was a huge success, continuing the march to professionalism, and the feeling around the rugby world was that the game was about to change beyond all recognition. We did not have to wait too long... Rugby Union turned professional in August 1995 so the game had to wait a further four years for its first fully professional Rugby World Cup, hosted in Wales, but again with matches in England, Scotland, Ireland and France.

The one-nation, one-cup concept that had been so successful in 1995 was ignored for the 1999 event and with it came problems, not least in empty stadiums and a lack of an overall central organisation.

• **Above**
Nelson Mandela presents the 1995 World Cup to Francois Pienaar, the South African captain.

179

• **Above**
General view of the Millennium Stadium during the opening ceremony of the 1999 Rugby World Cup.

• **Inset**
Juan Menchaca of Uruguay in action during the 1999 Rugby World Cup match against Spain played in Galashiels, Scotland.

On the field the tournament entailed the most comprehensive qualification campaign the game had seen. The IRB ruled that only four teams (the top three from 1995, South Africa, New Zealand and France, plus the hosts, Wales) would qualify automatically, sending every other nation, including England and Australia, on a circular route to the Finals. They also expanded the tournament from the 16 it had been in 1987, 1991 and 1995 to 20, based in five pools of four and they also introduced a complicated play-off system between the group stages and the quarter-finals for those who emerged from those groups as 'lucky losers'.

That group system was to come in for a great deal of criticism at the end of the tournament as the minnows were hammered, in empty stadiums, while some sides were penalised by having to play that extra match in those play-offs.

The new format also increased the number of matches from 32 to 41 and the tournament stretched six days longer, to 37.

For 2003 the much more sensible system of four groups of four, with the top two in each qualifying for the quarter-finals, was restored.

Sixty-five teams started out on the road to fill those 16 extra places for 1999. There were some new faces although of the teams that had made past Finals only Ivory Coast and Zimbabwe weren't there in 1999. Spain, Namibia and Uruguay made their debuts.

South Africa put on a show no one will forget in 1995, but the Welsh at least matched them for pageantry and occasion.

The opening game was in the magnificent new Millennium Stadium in Cardiff, built to house 75,000 fans to take the place of the National Stadium, next to Cardiff Arms Park.

The professional era delivered the numbers that everyone sought. In 1987 the event had a cumulative audience of 300 million viewers, but this now ballooned to three billion viewers in 140 countries in 1999. Rugby had arrived on the global stage!

Pool A was a cakewalk for the defending champions, South Africa, and they were even able to give some of their squad players a run-out in the matches against Spain and Uruguay.

Their only test came at Murrayfield against Scotland, but they even cruised home in that one, 46-29, to ease into the quarter-finals.

But it was crucial that minnows like Spain were invited to rugby's greatest party and not sidelined into a small tournament of their own. Spain manager Alfonso Mandalo explained: "The important thing is to be here in the Finals, the results are secondary."

Spain's 'final' came in the pool game with Uruguay, the South Americans emerging 27-15 winners.

England's World Cup campaign was 'Lomu-ed'

again, four years after he destroyed them in the 1995 semi-finals. The record books will tell you that England lost in the quarter-final to the South Africans in Paris, but their exit was engineered at Twickenham by that man Lomu.

Placed together in the same group, with Tonga and Italy, it was always going to come down to the clash between the big two, New Zealand and England.

It looked to have been going so well for England but, as captain Martin Johnson had predicted in the run-up to the game, it all hinged on "the fine line".

In the second half, after New Zealand turned over England ball, Lomu crossed Johnson's fine line, smashing through English tacklers in a stampeding 50-metre run to the try-line. It was déjà vu for England and although they weren't eliminated immediately, once they had lost to New Zealand they were only postponing the inevitable. England scored

101 points against Tonga and New Zealand the same score against Italy, both teams qualifying for the next stage.

But England never recovered from that defeat to New Zealand and although they hammered Fiji 45-24 in the play-off, their energy was spent and they performed poorly in the quarter-finals, losing to South Africa (and five drop-goals from Jannie De Beer), 44-21.

The closest thing we got to a shock in the pool stages came in pool C where everyone knows that Fiji should have beaten France, on what was still a great day for south seas rugby, in Toulouse.

France had endured a poor Five Nations Championship in 1999 and only just got past Canada before Fiji rolled into town.

The game was full of passion and when Fiji led 19-13 in the second half it seemed a shock was on the cards. But referee Paddy O'Brien made a series

• **Above**
Jonah Lomu of New Zealand brushes aside Tim Rodber of England during the 1999 Rugby World Cup Pool B game at Twickenham.

of mistakes, and sent two Fijian props, Dan Rouse and Joeli Veitayaki, to the sin-bin. France edged ahead, with the benefit of a try that looked to include a forward pass, to a 28-19 victory.

For France the group was a nightmare but as with all good sides they saved their best until they really needed it.

After the match referee O'Brien acknowledged his poor performance, but that did little to help the Fijians as defeat sent them to Twickenham for a daunting play-off.

Pool C saw Namibia welcomed into the Rugby World Cup family, Heino Senekal having the honour of scoring their first try, as they lost to Fiji.

Most sides would have killed to swap groups with Wales, as the hosts were paired with Argentina, Samoa and Japan. But the Welsh only just made it out of pool D, finishing on the same points as Argentina and Samoa.

History repeated itself for the unfortunate Welsh

as they blundered once again, as they had done in 1991, against a Samoan side.

This time the Samoans scored five tries, one an embarrassment for the Welsh as they overthrew a lineout on their own line for a gift of a score. There was something for Welsh fans to cheer in their second Samoan debacle as Neil Jenkins moved to 913 points, overtaking Michael Lynagh as the leading scorer of all time.

The defeat ended a ten-match winning run for the Welsh and as Argentina, Samoa and Wales had all lost once they finished tied on top of the group, with seven points.

All three qualified for the knockout stages. Argentina, as a lucky loser, had to play Ireland, Samoa went to Scotland and Wales hosted Australia in the quarter-finals.

Ireland were never going to qualify from their pool as winners, not with Australia as company, but their campaign ended in disaster as they went out in

the play-offs to an inspired Argentina, 28-24 in Lens.

In the three previous World Cups Ireland had always made the last eight. Ireland's cause wasn't helped by the fact they were drawn in the same group as the unstoppable Australians, who beat them 23-3 in Dublin, not only making sure they couldn't win their group but inflicting a big blow on their morale.

Another significant sighting in this pool was USA Eagle Juan Grobler getting over the line against Australia. Remarkably, it was the only try Australia conceded in the tournament, such was their domination.

Yet the Wallabies came close to defeat in a glorious semi-final at Twickenham, when a massive extra-time drop-goal from Steve Larkham took them past South Africa in a 27-21 triumph.

De Beer beat England with the drop-goal in the quarter-finals and revealed that he continually practised the skill, but for Larkham it was something he rarely worked on.

Larkham said: "I might have had five or six [drop] kicks in training. I think I got one of them.

"Actually I don't think I've ever landed a drop-goal in senior rugby at any level. Tim Lane [assistant coach] mentioned the possibility just before we went out for extra time. When I got the ball I looked up and saw just a wall of South Africans in front of me. The ball was in an awkward position and I thought there was no chance here."

South African coach Nick Mallett added: "That was a fantastic game of rugby, hard and fast, so it was easy to go into the changing rooms and congratulate them."

The two semi-finals were staged on consecutive days at Twickenham and the second one produced arguably the biggest shock in World Cup history.

New Zealand came into this semi-final as hot favourites, having beaten Scotland far more convincingly than a 30-18 scoreline suggests. The All Blacks faced a French team that had done no more than limp into the last four, although they did show some signs of recovery when beating Argentina 47-26 in the quarter-finals. But anyone who believed France could actually win was reminded that four months before the World Cup they had lost 54-7 in Wellington, and conceded seven tries.

• Above
Argentinian players celebrate victory following the 1999 Rugby World Cup quarter-final play-off against Ireland from the Stade Felix Bollaert, Lens,

• Below
Juan Grobler of the USA is tackled by Nathan Grey and Jason Little of Australia on his way to the line.

183

Crucially, however, the French side knew they had to match the Kiwis try for try, and they scored four to win the game 43-31.

At France's core was outside-half Christophe Lamaison, who scored 28 points, which included a full house of a try, penalty, conversion and drop-goal.

In Ian Robertson's *Complete Story of the Rugby World Cup 1999*, legendary commentator Bill McLaren described this great game thus:

"In four World Cup tournaments and some 42 years of rugby coverage, I cannot recollect a match of such substantial enthrallment, extraordinary physical output and complete disregard of the betting odds as France's incredible performance in showing the door to the mighty All Blacks before an enraptured 72,000 capacity audience at Twickenham, who reacted to the magical events placed before them with all the unfettered enthusiasm they usually reserve for the pride of England."

New Zealand were clearly broken by their defeat and they failed to recover in time for the third-place play-off, losing 22-18 to South Africa without scoring a try.

The final was never likely to live up to the France v New Zealand semi-final. Indeed, it was something of an anticlimax as France never got close to reaching those heights again.

It was a cautious match, which played into the hands of the efficient Wallabies, and they ran out 35-12 winners, scoring two tries through Ben Tune and Owen Finegan.

The keys to Australia's victory were their incredible defence and the way they controlled the tackle area, ensuring the inventive French backs didn't get the quality ball they needed to weave their magic.

"Fantastic is the only way I can describe it," said Australian centre Tim Horan, who played in both the 1991 and 1999 campaigns.

"It did take some time to sink in. My thoughts on winning the first World Cup were that there would be plenty of time for me, but a second World Cup is unbelievable.

"It's not a dream come true because I never dreamt that I would win two World Cups. It's a fantastic achievement that has been building for two years."

Away from the final there were some other magnificent achievements, most notably by the Argentinians, who made the quarter-finals. And therefore it was fitting the Pumas did win one prize as their prolific goal-kicker, Gonzalo Quesada, crept past the 100-point mark (102) to score more than any other player at the tournament. Canadian Gareth Rees slotted all of his 19 attempts at goal.

Jonah Lomu, for the second World Cup running

and this time on his own, was the leading try-scorer, with eight.

It was written all over the faces of those England players on 22 November 2003. They wanted their lap of honour to last forever. Clive Woodward's England team had just won the World Cup. With Oasis' anthem Wonderwall blaring out over the loudspeakers at Sydney's Olympic Stadium, it was clear that every England player was doing all they could to take it in, all they could to make that lap of honour last for the rest of their lives.

For around 110 minutes of rugby they had captivated an 85,000-strong crowd in the Olympic Stadium and the millions watching on television back home. Although they didn't do it without putting those fans through the mill more than once.

When they went into the break 14-5 ahead – courtesy of a Jason Robinson try and the boot of Jonny Wilkinson – those fans were looking forward to one last score and 30 minutes of relaxed enjoyment.

But Australia – to their eternal credit – roared back to send the game into extra time, the scores tied at 14-14.

Only referee Andre Watson knows exactly why he gave that last penalty against Phil Vickery to allow Elton Flatley to send his kick over and the game into 20 minutes of extra time.

For the whole match Vickery and his front row partners, Trevor Woodman and Steve Thompson, had held more than the upper hand in the scrums.

However, despite this advantage they still fell foul of Watson six times and the bemused look on Vickery's face when the last one was awarded summed up the majority of the crowd.

But give that last penalty Watson did and England, under the incredible leadership of Martin Johnson, responded with one last effort in extra time.

• Above
Gonzalo Quesada of Argentina was the highest points-scorer in the 1999 Rugby World Cup with 102.

During this period Wilkinson and Flatley exchanged penalties to tie it up again and then it was left to the last act, to send the Webb Ellis Cup to Twickenham.

A line out on the Australia 22. Two phases and then Matt Dawson drove into the Australia 22 to set up the opportunity. Johnson took it on a few more hard yards and then back to Wilkinson.

It slipped on to his weaker right foot and two nations held their breath. The ball travelled true and through the posts and England were champions.

"It is a great team," said England coach Clive Woodward after the final. "It was an immense effort by a great team and about the crowd, I was just so proud to see so many there, and so many millions of supporters back home and I am so proud of the team they really stepped up to the mark.

"It was incredibly close, I think that we should have won the game with something to spare before the end, we made a lot of errors and I am sure that it was an exciting game to watch.

"We had a saying that it was going from good to great and they have always been a very good team and I think that they proved it against all adversity.

"Every decision seemed to go against them and yet they still won and that is the sign of a champion team and they are a great bunch of players with a great captain. I am just very, very proud and privileged to be in charge of them. "

The Australian team and their management were incredibly dignified in their praise of England after the World Cup final, some even coming into the winning dressing room after the match to congratulate the new owners of the Webb Ellis Cup.

"Even as disappointed as they were you had players like Brendan Cannon, Bill Young and Ali Baxter coming in to see us at the end," revealed England prop Jason Leonard.

"You know they are very low but despite that they came into the changing rooms for a beer and a chat.

"You can only respect people who do that when you know personally they are at a very low point in the day, after the game.

"You don't mention the game or what's going on. You know many of those players so you ask about family. That part of the game is still there."

• **Above**
English players flanker Richard Hill, fly-half Jonny Wilkinson and fly-half Mike Catt salute fans after England's victory in the 2003 Rugby World Cup final at the Olympic Park Stadium.

The Australian World Cup will always be remembered as the best of the first five. A mini-Olympics staged in a country that had hosted sport's greatest show on earth in 2000.

Much of the infrastructure from the Sydney Olympics was used at the Rugby World Cup, including the Olympic Stadium, which hosted the final.

Almost 100 nations started on the road to qualification, a far cry from the first tournament in 1987 when 16 teams were invited to play. The first game of the 2003 qualification process was staged between Norway and Luxembourg in 2000.

Another huge factor in the success of the World Cup was the 16th man – the Australian public.

The Australian Rugby Union decided on the risky strategy of holding the tournament across Australia, taking it into cities where rugby league or Australian rules was king.

The strategy proved an overwhelming success and the World Cup was welcomed from Perth on the west coast to Sydney on the east.

The sensational support was never better shown than in Tasmania, where they were awarded one game, between Romania and Namibia. The Tassies treated the game as their World Cup final, with the mayor of Launceston coming up with an idea for every citizen to support one team or the other. Those born on odd days were asked to back Namibia and those on even days, Romania.

The support of the Australian people ensured that all the ticketing records for a Rugby World Cup were broken in 2003.

Lessons learned in previous tournaments enabled the IRB and Rugby World Cup Ltd to implement structural changes, which avoided problems of the past, and the Australian Rugby Union proved a fine and able partner. This was reflected in the commercial success of the Tournament, which realised a net profit in excess of £64 million, an increase of 36.81% on RWC 1999. This was accompanied by record gates and strengthening commercial relationships. In 1987 600,000 people went through the turnstiles to watch World Cup matches, but in 2003 this had increased to 1.9m, 300,000 more than in 1999.

The reach of the World Cup has also increased

• Above
Jason Robinson scores a brilliant try for England.

187

beyond all recognition since 1987. Just 17 countries televised the 1987 tournament but by the time of the 2003 competition 194 countries tuned in.

Notable was the very substantial growth in 2003 of ticket sale receipts, leaving a tournament surplus of £30.4 million.

Equally notable was the increase in total commercial revenues of almost £12 million, which has contributed to a £17 million increase in the surplus that RWC Ltd will remit to the IRB Trust.

The Trust will use these monies to run the game and, in particular, to fund rugby's development over the course of the next four years. The success of RWC 2003 means that there is a very significant sum of money available to the IRB to apply to the challenges which the sport now faces, but upon these reserves there are many and growing demands.

Some £4 million was made available in the form of participation contributions to the 20 Unions who reached Australia. All teams received £150,000 and, reflecting the additional time spent in Australia, the last eight received an additional £100,000 and the last four a further £50,000. In other words, each team received at least £150,000, the quarter-finalists received £250,000 and the semi-finalists £300,000.

Another key aspect of RWC 2003 was its anti-doping programme, the most extensive in the history of the game. In all, a total of 511 doping controls were conducted, 307 of which were no-notice out of competition tests and 204 in competition. These controls included tests for the new drug THG. Every single test proved negative.

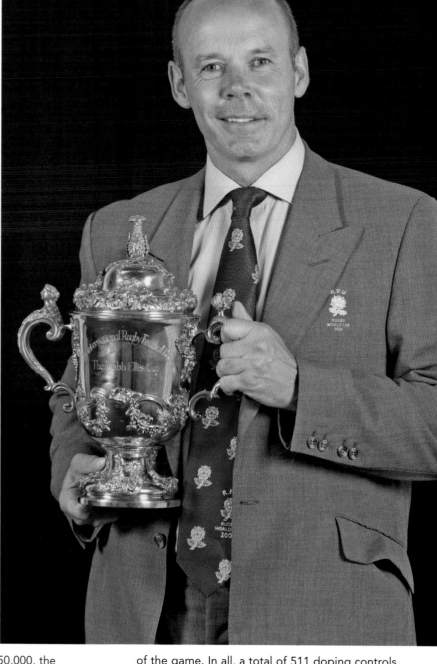

• **Above**
A proud Clive Woodward with the Webb Ellis Cup.

RUGBY WORLD CUP	1987	1991	1995	1999	2003
Hosts	New Zealand	England	South Africa	Wales	Australia
Number of unions	16	31	52	69	83
Spectators	600,000	1,000,000	1,100,000	1,600,000	1,900,000
Broadcast to (countries)	17	103	124	214	194
TV audience	300 million	1.75 billion	2.67 billion	3 billion	3.4 billion
Total Receipts	£3.3 million	£23.6 million	£30.3 million	£70.0 million	£81.8 million
Surplus/net contribution	£ 1.0 m	£ 4.1 m	£17.6 m	£47.3 m	£64.3 m

THE POOL STAGES - 2003

Pool A

The pool of the horrendous mismatches, this one came down to one game, Australia v Ireland in Melbourne, to decide which side was to head the group. Like the World Cup Final the game between the Wallabies and Ireland came down to one drop goal. Unfortunately for Ireland, however, their drop, from David Humphreys, sailed agonisingly wide and Australia won the game, 17-16.

That victory sent Australia through as the top side in the pool and to a quarter-final against the weakest nation in the last eight, Scotland.

Ireland's World Cup hung on that Humphreys drop goal but at least they made the quarter-finals this time as group runners-up.

In 1999 Argentina knocked them out and they had to qualify for 2003. But in 2007 they go straight to the

Finals after beating the Pumas, 16-15 in Adelaide.

When Ireland beat the Pumas it was skipper Keith Wood who earned the plaudits, coach Eddie O'Sullivan saying: "It was the performance of a great captain. Cometh the hour, cometh the man!"

Namibia – shorn of some of their best players in a row over finances – proved to be the weakest team in the tournament. Their 22-try, 142-0 hammering by Australia was hard for the rugby world to watch! It was the biggest winning margin in a World Cup Finals game and a mismatch that did rugby union no good.

"It was men against boys," said Namibia coach Dave Waterston. "Australia were ruthless."

The Namibian World Cup final arrived in their pool game with the Romanians, on a memorable day in Tasmania. Romania won the battle of the minnows in Pool D, Argentina's victories over both of them left them third behind Australia and Ireland.

Argentina kicked off the 2003 World Cup, playing in the first game, as they had done in 1999, this time

• **Above**
Brian O'Driscoll scores a try as he is tackled by Elton Flatley during the Rugby World Cup Pool A match between Australia and Ireland. Australia were the narrow victors.

losing to hosts Australia, 24-8. After finishing third in the group the Pumas will suffer the ignominy of having to qualify for the 2007 tournament.

Namibia finished the World Cup with the worst record. They conceded an astounding 310 points in four games, and scored just 28.

POOL A RESULTS:

Australia 24 **Argentina** 8	**Ireland** 45 **Romania** 17
Argentina 67 **Namibia** 14	**Australia** 90 **Romania** 8
Ireland 64 **Namibia** 7	**Argentina** 50 **Romania** 3
Australia 142 **Namibia** 0	**Argentina** 15 **Ireland** 16
Romania 37 **Namibia** 7	**Australia** 17 **Ireland** 16

POOL A TABLE

	P	W	PD	PTS
Australia	4	4	241	18
Ireland	4	3	85	15
Argentina	4	2	83	11
Romania	4	1	-127	5
Namibia	4	0	-282	0

Pool B

Before the start of the World Cup, Pool B looked to be the most open. France, Scotland and Fiji vying for top spot, with the dangerous USA and Japan lying just behind.

But once the matches got underway it was clear that a young French team – that went on to win the 2004 RBS Six Nations Grand Slam – was going to dominate Pool B.

France were rarely troubled in any of their four games and matched New Zealand, in Pool D, as the two countries to emerge from the pool stages with a perfect record, picking up a maximum of five points in every game.

Scotland followed France into the quarter-finals but only just, beating Fiji in the final game, in Sydney, 22-20.

Scotland had to wait until four minutes from time to score their only try and coach Ian McGeechan said: "I told the players sometimes you don't win until the

The Pool B minnows, USA and Japan, were never embarrassed, unlike some of the sides in the other pools, the USA winning their showdown 39-26 to avoid finishing bottom of the pool. This was the USA's first finals win since beating Japan in Brisbane 12 years earlier.

POOL B RESULTS

France 61 **Fiji** 18	**Scotland** 32 **Japan** 11
Fiji 19 **USA** 18	**France** 51 **Japan** 29
Scotland 39 **USA** 15	**Fiji** 41 **Japan** 13
France 51 **Scotland** 9	**Japan** 26 **USA** 39
France 41 **USA** 14	**Scotland** 22 **Fiji** 20

POOL B TABLE

	P	W	PD	PTS
France	4	4	134	20
Scotland	4	3	5	14
Fiji	4	2	16	-16
USA	4	1	-39	6
Japan	4	0	-84	0

last ten minutes. They took me too literally!"

Fiji produced one of the World Cup's most explosive players in Rupeni Caucaunibuca and he had a tournament he and no-one else will forget.

Wing Caucaunibuca scored a sensational length-of-the-field try against France before getting sin-binned, and subsequently banned, for a clash with Olivier Magne.

• Above
Gordon Bullock and Bruce Douglas of Scotland celebrate victory over Fiji.

• Inset
Fijian winger Rupeni Caucaunibuca smashes his left forearm into French flanker Olivier Magne's face during their World Cup match against France.

• Above
Will Greenwood of England scores a try during the Rugby World Cup Pool C match between South Africa and England.

Pool C

Jonny Wilkinson applied the killer blow but England's journey to that World Cup final in Sydney had begun six weeks earlier when they were based on the other side of Australia, in Perth.

Four games played, four games won and only 47 points conceded are the bare statistics of England's progress through the pool stages of the World Cup. However, they don't tell half the story of the way Clive Woodward's side set the foundations for their victory in the Webb Ellis Cup.

England could have played Georgia and Uruguay a hundred times and the result would have stayed the same but the clashes with both South Africa and Samoa were impressive victories for a team building

an unstoppable momentum.

The 25-6 win over South Africa – in Perth – set the tone for England's World Cup and contributed as much as any other match to their eventual victory in the final.

The game turned in the 63rd when Lewis Moody charged down a Louis Koen kick, the ball breaking free to Will Greenwood who pounced to score.

Samoa posed some very different problems in Melbourne, playing their own brand of total rugby, against an England side which showed seven changes from the side that beat South Africa.

England were trailing 16-13 after 52 minutes before a treble substitution, including try-scorer Phil Vickery, turned the game in their favour.

The Uruguay game brought a record-fest, with England running in a magnificent 17 tries to go past the 100 point mark, their 111 points being the second biggest total in their history.

Samoa stunned England and could easily have won that game in Melbourne but it was the two big sides that made it into the last eight.

Most of the rugby world, outside England and South Africa, would have loved to have seen Samoa make the quarter-finals but they had to be content with third in the pool, after wins over Georgia and Uruguay.

The Uruguayans celebrated as if they had won the World Cup when they won their biggest game against Georgia, 24-12, diving into the crowd on a lap of honour.

"Both teams need more games and experience but it's the World Cup and there were 28,000 spectators. It's a great day," acknowledged the Georgian vice president, Zaza Kassachvili.

It was indeed an historic day for those Uruguayans, who had never before won a game at the World Cup finals.

POOL C RESULTS:

South Africa 72 **Uruguay** 6	**England** 84 **Georgia** 6
Samoa 60 **Uruguay** 13	**England** 25 **South Africa** 6
Georgia 9 **Samoa** 46	**South Africa** 46 **Georgia** 19
England 35 **Samoa** 22	**Georgia** 12 **Uruguay** 24
South Africa 60 **Samoa** 10	**England** 111 **Uruguay** 13

POOL C TABLE

	P	W	PD	PTS
England	4	4	208	19
South Africa	4	3	124	15
Samoa	4	2	21	10
Uruguay	4	1	-199	4
Georgia	4	0	-154	0

• Above
Uruguay's players cheer on their fans after victory against Georgia.

• **Above**
Doug Howlett scores with 10 minutes to go to finally shake off a spirited Welsh side in their Rugby World Cup Pool D match.

Pool D

There was a dominant side in every one of the 2003 World Cup pools and never before had it been so easy for pundits to select the sides that would contest the quarter-finals.

New Zealand were the top seeds in Pool D and looked to be the side to beat in Australia as they whipped through the early stages, scoring at will.

They almost matched their opening match against Italy in 1987 (then they won 70-6) and it was only a matter of time before they qualified for the last eight.

They only conceded 20 points in their first three games but the soft underbelly of the Kiwis that was eventually to see them spinning out of the tournament, at the semi-final stage, was exposed for the first time by the Welsh in the penultimate round of pool matches.

The Kiwis finally ran out 53-37 victors against the Welsh but they only went 43-37 ahead with a Doug Howlett try ten minutes from time, in one of the most exciting games in the World Cup pool stage.

"We learnt a lot about the way we have to defend against sides who recycle the ball quickly," admitted scrum-half Justin Marshall, after seeing his side concede four tries. "We hadn't been tested like that to date."

Later in the tournament many blamed their easy pool matches for their eventual semi-final exit to Australia.

Wales coach Steve Hansen knew his World Cup rested on the final game, against the Italians, so he threw a young team at the All Blacks with dramatic results.

New Zealand looked beatable after the Wales game, their invincibility gone, and few expected them to win the tournament after the four tries they conceded in the Telstra Stadium.

But win Pool D they did, actually with ease, scoring a remarkable 42 tries in their four-game pool stage.

Italy's ability to challenge Wales for second spot was undermined by a ludicrous schedule that saw their matches crammed into a short period and they arrived at the last and decisive game with Wales battered and bruised by the Tongan and Canadian onslaught. They eventually lost 27-15, allowing Wales to take their place in the last eight.

That crucial defeat to Wales will mean the Italians have to qualify for the 2007 tournament but they will be favourites to grab the Europe One spot that sends them on a collision course with New Zealand, again, and Scotland.

Canada's World Cup heights of 1991 and 1995, when they made the last eight themselves, looked a long way away for a nation that has lost ground on the big guns since the game turned professional.

The Canadians emerged victorious from their bottom of the pool clash with Tonga 24-7 but not before losing inspirational captain Al Charron to injury. "We tried to push his injury to the back of our minds," said Canada wing Winston Stanley. "We just said 'ten more minutes for Al'."

POOL D RESULTS

New Zealand 70 **Italy** 7	**Wales** 41 **Canada** 10
Italy 36 **Tonga** 12	**New Zealand** 68 **Canada** 6
Wales 27 **Tonga** 20	**Italy** 19 **Canada** 14
New Zealand 91 **Tonga** 7	**Italy** 15 **Wales** 27
Canada 24 **Tonga** 7	**New Zealand** 53 **Wales** 37

POOL D TABLE

	P	W	PD	PTS
New Zealand	4	4	225	20
Wales	4	3	34	14
Italy	4	2	-46	8
Canada	4	1	-81	5
Tonga	4	0	-132	1

• *Above*
Welsh Scrumhalf Dwayne Peel celebrates with his team after winning over Italy in their crucial group D game.

195

• Above

Nathan Sharpe crashes through the brave Scottish defence as Australia's victory takes them through to the semi-final.

• Inset

Will Greenwood scores for England against Wales.

The Quarter Finals

Once again England's ability not to panic came to their aid as they battled back from going behind, against Wales, to move into the last four.

Clive Woodward picked the most experienced team in the history of international rugby (689 caps) and it showed in the way they reacted to being 10-3 down to the Welsh at half time.

Will Greenwood kick-started the recovery with a try, Jonny Wilkinson's boot followed up, although helped by the overwhelming influence of Mike Catt, as England powered home 28-17.

"England are getting stronger game by game and we have played a lot of rugby over the years and won," said England coach Woodward.

"We are playing some pretty average rugby at the moment and still winning. I think that it is sheer bloodymindedness and the will of the team that has seen us through.

"It is pretty frustrating for the team for the amount of work that they do. They are an outstanding group of players but they are just not playing well. It happens, it is not a perfect world. You cannot be a Rolls Royce every week."

In the first quarter-final South Africa departed at this stage for the first time, losing 29-9 to a Carlos Spencer-inspired New Zealand.

"As a team, of course we are disappointed," admitted Springbok coach Rudi Straeuli, who was replaced after the World Cup by Jake White. "We came here to win the World Cup and didn't!"

Hosts Australia struggled to put away the weakest side in the last eight, Scotland, only getting the upper hand five minutes into the second half by virtue of a try from Stirling Mortlock.

"We can go home with our heads held high," said Scotland's Director of Rugby, Jim Telfer.

Ireland failed to make the quarter-finals in 1999 and never looked like going into the last four this

time around, blown away by the enigmatic French.

The Irish did score three tries to France's four but they only came when the game was lost after coach Eddie O'Sullivan saw his side go 37-0 down.

"It took a lot of character in the second half to come out and play good rugby," said O'Sullivan. "There's something about this French side that's menacing. They have phenomenal speed and class."

QUARTER FINAL RESULTS
England 28 **Wales** 17
France 43 **Ireland** 21
New Zealand 29 **South Africa** 9
Australia 33 **Scotland** 16

The Semi Finals

ENGLAND seemed determined to win the Webb Ellis Cup the hard way and continued their trend of winning from behind after seeing France score the first try in their semi-final in the Olympic Stadium.

France went into the game as slight favourites but the sight of the rain in Sydney dampened French hopes and they were defeated.

England coach Clive Woodward dismissed the rain as the reason for his side's win saying: "It rains in France as well, I know because I go there on holidays."

Jonny Wilkinson was named Zurich man of the match, after kicking all of England's 24 points, and

• *Above*
Stirling Mortlock of Australia scores the first try of the Australia New Zealand semi-final which sets up their surprise 22-10 victory.

197

Woodward added: "I have to say first of all we are extremely lucky having him (Wilkinson) in our team, he is the world's best number ten. He is just a brilliant guy to be with and to coach, but it is a team game, the ultimate team game.

"We like to score tries but if a team gives away penalties you have to kick goals and without a goal kicker in your team you can come unstuck. We put a lot of pressure on the French. They had two yellow cards, it was such a good night."

That early try – from Serge Betsen – was France's only points in the game and they saw Jason Leonard emerge as an early substitute, his 112th cap, a new world record.

Australia sprung a surprise in the other semi-final, 24 hours earlier, knocking out New Zealand, who had looked, along with France, the in-form side at the World Cup.

The New Zealand–Australia semi-final turned in an incredible 60 seconds early in the game when All Blacks full-back Mils Muliaina saw a try disallowed and soon after Stirling Mortlock took an interception and sprinted almost the length of the field to score.

All Blacks coach John Mitchell refused to resign after the defeat but was soon replaced by Graham Henry.

Mitchell said: "Our execution was poor and we did not deserve to win but I will not resign. This is a fantastic group to be part of."

SEMI FINAL RESULTS
Australia 22 New Zealand 10
England 24 France 7

• **Above**
Jonny Wilkinson kicks his final penalty goal against France.

• **Opposite**
Jason Leonard comes on against France in the Rugby World Cup semi-final to win his 112th cap.

THE WORLD CUP FINAL 2003
STAT ATTACK

1. ENGLAND FIELDED THE MOST EXPERIENCED STARTING XV in the history of the game, boasting 638 caps before the game, 208 more than Australia which meant the teams had an average number of caps of 42.53 and 28.66 respectively. When you add the Australia bench caps to the starting team the combined total was 693 compared to England's 952, a figure swelled by the world record 112 caps Jason Leonard had amassed.

2. THE PLAYER WITH THE LEAST CAPS IN THE TWO starting line ups was Al Baxter with six, the prop coming into the Wallaby front row as a result of the neck injury suffered by Ben Darwin in the semi-final against New Zealand.

3. IN TERMS OF CAPS AUSTRALIA HAD THE EDGE ON England in only one category, the half back pairing, with Gregan and Stephen Larkham having 158 caps to Matt Dawson and Jonny Wilkinson's 107.

4. ENGLAND HAD A SIGNIFICANT CAP ADVANTAGE IN the forwards with 375 compared to the 167 of Australia. Amazingly there was nothing between the backlines with each team's back division totalling 263 caps.

5. MUCH WAS MADE OF THE AGEING ENGLAND PACK with the 'Dad's Army' tag being used regularly over the last couple of years, so how did the statistics compare when you take a closer look at the combined ages? Well, England did have the older of the two packs with 234 years to the 208 of Australia, although there was less than four years difference in the average ages of the forwards with England at 29.25 years and Australia at 26 years.

6. THE AVERAGE AGES OF THE STARTING LINE UPS WERE equally close with England the older at 28.33 years compared to the 26.6 of Australia with the total figures being 425 and 399 respectively.

7. THERE WAS LITTLE DIFFERENCE WHEN YOU CONSIDER the weights and heights of the packs with England having an 18 kg advantage in the weight division (890-872), which equates to an average of 111.25 to 109 kg per man.

8. IN THE HEIGHT DEPARTMENT THE TALLEST PLAYER ON the pitch was Aussie lock Justin Harrison at 203cm, three centimetres taller than his Wallaby team-mate Nathan Sharpe and England captain Johnson. The other lock on the park, Ben Kay, stands at 198cm.

9. BY COMPARISON THE SHORTEST PLAYERS WERE England full back Robinson and Wallaby scrum half Gregan, who both stand at 173cm in their socks. Four others in the starting XV's – Back, Dawson, Wilkinson and Flatley – are only a little taller at 178cm.

10. AUSTRALIA SCORED THE MOST POINTS OF THE TWO finalists (328-307), before the final, although still 33 points behind Tournament points scoring leaders New Zealand.

11. THE WALLABIES SCORED SEVEN MORE TRIES THAN England in their six matches en route to the final (42-35), while conceding only five tries in the process, one fewer than England, who had conceded four of their six tries in the knockout phase.

Statistics from The Rugby World Cup 2003 media centre

WORLD CUP 2003 STAT ATTACK

TRY SCORERS:
Doug Howlett (NZ): 7
Mils Muliaina (NZ): 7
Joe Rokocoko (NZ): 6
Will Greenwood (Eng): 5
Chris Latham (Aus): 5
Josh Lewsey (Eng): 5
Mat Rogers (Aus): 5
Lote Tuqiri (Aus): 5

POINTS:
Jonny Wilkinson (Eng): 113
Frederick Michalak (Fr): 103
Elton Flatley (Aus): 100
Leon MacDonald (NZ): 75
Chris Paterson (Scot): 71

RUGBY WORLD CUP 2007

World Champions England will meet a familiar foe during the 2007 World Cup finals as they have been drawn with South Africa in Pool A of the next tournament, which will be hosted by France, but held in France, Wales, Scotland and Ireland.

If South Africa and England are well acquainted in Rugby World Cups, Ireland and Argentina have even more entwined histories in this competition. If Argentina qualify in top place from the Americas qualifying group (Americas 1), the two sides will find themselves together for the third RWC in a row.

Ireland and Americas 1 are drawn in Pool D alongside France, in what will undoubtedly be seen as the Group of Death.

RWC 2003 runners up Australia are joined by Wales in Pool B whilst New Zealand are joined by Scotland in Pool C.

RWC Chairman Dr Syd Millar and President of the Fédération Francaise de Rugby, Bernard Lapasset, made the draw, which was overseen by Michael O'Neill of Price Waterhouse Coopers.

"Here we go again," said England coach Andy Robinson. "South Africa, and it could very well be Samoa as well (England also have Oceania 1 in their pool). It smells of Perth 2003.

"There's no way around it – we will treat the big teams and the smaller teams the same, and prepare for the games in exactly the same way as ever."

Clive Woodward's counterpart Jake White, the newly appointed head coach of South Africa, was extremely positive about the repeat match-up.

"It's a blessing for South Africa being drawn in the same pool as the champions. England weren't favourites for 2003 when the pools were set, but ended up winning it," said White.

"In order to win the Rugby World Cup you have to win the big matches. South African rugby is turning a corner and the national team is going in the right direction.

"I've now got a lot of the players I coached at under 21 level coming through and making names for themselves. We're positive about this."

France head coach Bernard Laporte added: "It's a good draw for us – we are happy. Playing in France of course has its advantages, but also there will be the added pressure of the exposure and spotlight on the players. We are looking forward to it though."

Wales coach Mike Ruddock was looking forward

• **Above**
Mils Muliaina of New Zealand scores one of his 7 Rugby World Cup tries as Matt King of Canada attempts to tackle him during their Pool D match.

England Rugby World Champions 2...

to the potential prospect of playing at the Millennium Stadium. "I'm delighted with the draw, especially if we get to play in front a home crowd. It will be an utter privilege to play against Australia in a Rugby World Cup.

"We've got a good young team that performed well in 2003. I am lucky to have inherited such a talented core of players who can go on from here to the next step."

"We're delighted with the draw," said Scotland captain Chris Paterson. "Playing at Murrayfield is going to add an extra dimension for us, and although we've never beaten New Zealand before there's a first time for everything, and why not at Murrayfield?

"We were also pleased to avoid Argentina from the third tier of sides – they are a real danger."

The full draw for the 2007 Rugby World Cup

Pool A: England, South Africa, Oceania One, Americans Three and Repechage Two.
Pool B: Australia, Wales, Oceania Two, Americas Two and Asia One.
Pool C: New Zealand, Scotland, Europe One, Europe Two and Repechage One.
Pool D: France, Ireland, Americas One, Europe Three and Africa One.

Following Australia's staging of the 2003 World Cup, there was a fight to see who would host the 2007 tournament. The Council of the International Rugby Board decided, by a massive majority of 18 votes to three, to award the competition to France,

rejecting the only other bid, from England. Dr Syd Millar, IRB Acting Chairman, said: "In making this decision, the Council of the IRB was faced with a difficult choice.

"We had received fine bids from two of the most powerful and influential rugby nations in the world, and there is no doubt that both could – and without doubt would – have staged a wonderful Rugby World Cup."

A statement from the FFR said: "An immense festival of rugby awaits for the sixth edition of this formidable competition. This result is a dream."

Back in 1987 the joint New Zealand-Australia bid was the only one on offer, but this intense rivalry just to host the tournament shows how much the Rugby World Cup has grown. It was always going to be staged in the northern hemisphere after the 2003 World Cup was awarded to the south and then it was left to the two most powerful nations in Europe to fight it out.

In the run-up to the vote France changed their initial bid so as to give some of the pool matches to Wales, Ireland and Scotland. This, coupled with the fact that the English wanted to host the event around June time, as opposed to the September/October preferred date of the French proposal, meant that the French victory was expected. But the ease by which they achieved it shocked everyone in the rugby world. With England, as a foundation Union, getting two votes themselves, the 18-3 defeat means that only one other nation, likely to be Canada, voted for them.

• Above
England hope to repeat the jubilant scenes which greeted their 2003 Rugby World Cup triumph by winning the 2007 Rugby World Cup in France.

• Inset
Francis Baron the RFU Chief Executive pictured during the 2002 RFU launch of England's ill-fated bid to host the 2007 Rugby World Cup.

Index

Ackford, Paul 88
Aitken, Jim 86
Albaladejo, Pierre 77
All Blacks 32, 39, 41.43, 47, 51, 55, 56, 58, 60, 62, 64,
. . . . .69, 114, 116, 118-125, 130-132, 135, 140, 144-150,
. . . . .155, 159, 167, 171-179, 182, 184
Andrew, Mark 133
Andrew, Rob 63, 64, 89, 99, 119, 160, 162, 175, 178
Army Rugby Union 30
Asian Games 26
Australian RFU 23, 113
Back, Neil 12, 21, 34, 52, 105
Bancroft, Jack 73
Barry, Joe 128
Bastiat, Jean-Pierre 84, 150
Bateman, Allan .20, 67
Batty, Grant 60, 149
Baxter, James 21, 22
Baxter, Jim 53
Bayfield, Martin 178
Beaumont, Bill .60, 69, 84
Bedell-Sivright, Dr 51
Beer, Jannie de 133, 181, 183
Bekker, Jaap 130
Benazzi, Abdelatif 178
Bennett, Phil 33, 34, 60, 83, 145, 150
Bentley, John 67
Best, Dick 64, 158
Betsen, Serge 21, 95, 198
Bevan, Derek 175, 178
Bevan, Vince 130
Billups, Tom 44
Blackheath 12, 30
Blanco, Serge 17, 85, 118, 140, 141, 172, 175
Boniface, Andre 77
Boniface, Guy 80
Botha, Naas 132
Brand, Gerry .129, 141
Brezoianu, Gabriel 33
Brito, Max 177
Brooke, Robin 125
Brooke, Zinzan 31, 52, 125, 149, 150, 179
Brown, G 148
Brownlie, Cyril 122
Brownlie, Maurice 122
Burke, Matt .117, 141
Bush, Percy 33
Butler, Eddie 41
Butterfield, Jeff 54, 55, 78, 144, 154
Cabannes, L 150
Calder, Finlay 62
Calder, Jim 86
Cambridge University 14, 23, 30, 36, 44, 45, 141
Campbell, Alastair 86
Campbell, Ollie 61, 86
Campbell-Lamerton, Mike 56
Campese, David 63, 117, 140, 142, 158, 174, 175, 177
Capendeguy, Michael 80
Cardiff 21, 31, 35, 37, 41, 46, 62, 80, 83, 84, 88, 91,
. . . . .115, 118, 122, 141, 172-174, 180, 185
Carleton, John 85
Carling, Will 64, 65, 88, 89, 90, 93, 160, 175, 178
Carpmael, William Percy 30, 31
Carrere, Christian 80
Catchpole, Ken .115, 145
Catt, Mike 166, 178, 196
Caucaunibuca, Rupeni 191
Cecillon, Marc 175
Celaya, Michel 77, 78
Cerutti, Bill 114
Chalmers, Craig 90
Chapman, Frederick 74
Chilcott, Gareth 88
Claasen, Johann 130
Clark, Jack 44
Clarke, Ben 64, 99
Clarke, Don 39, 55, 123, 159, 167
Codey, David 172
Cohen, Ben 95
Commonwealth Games 26, 42, 142
Connell, Gordon 81
Cooke, Geoff 64, 101, 158, 160
Cootes, Vanessa 45
Cotton, Fran 67, 147
Courage Leagues 22, 61
Cove-Smith, Dr Ronald 52
Crabos, Rene 78
Crauste, Michel .79, 149
Craven, Danie 53, 59, 129, 130, 132, 148
Crawford, Jen 44
Cullen, Christian 140, 141
Currie Cup .23, 39, 40
Currie, John 78
Cuthbertson, Bill 86
Cutler, Steve 63
Dallaglio, Lawrence 34, 48, 72, 91, 93, 104
Dalton, Andy 62, 124, 173
Dalton, James 177
Daly, Tony 13, 118, 175
D'Arcy, Gordon 95
Darwin, Ben 199
Davies, Dave 74
Davies, Gareth 61
Davies, Gerald 57, 58, 60, 82, 141
Davies, Greg 115
Davies, Jonathan 33, 34, 46, 145, 172
Davies, Mervyn 34, 150
Davies, Phill 88
Dawe, Graham 88
Dawes, John 31, 57, 81
Dawson, Matt 199
Dawson, Ronnie 55
Deans, Colin 62, 86, 147
Delport, William 130
Devereux, John 171
Dods, Peter 86
Dominguez, Diago 32
Dooley, Wade 88, 171

Dourthe, Claude 46
Drysdale, Dan 75
Du Preez, Frik 39, 148
Duckham, David 57
Dwyer, Bob 63, 142, 161
Eales, John 40, 67, 119, 148, 152, 161, 184
Edwards, Gareth . . .31, 34, 57, 58, 59, 60, 80, 82, 83, 145, 148,
. . . . .149, 151, 155, 165
Ella, Mark 117, 118, 145, 161, 163
Ellis, Jan 39, 150
Ellis, Mark 179
Ellis, William Webb 40, 173
Ellison, Tom 121
European Nations Cup 25, 33
Evans, Eric 78
Evans, Ieuan 63, 64, 90, 142, 163
Farr-Jones, Nick 63, 117, 132, 145, 161, 165, 174, 175
Finlay, N J 46
Fitzgerald, Ciaran 62
Fitzpatrick, Sean 21, 125, 132, 146, 147
Five Nations 34, 38, 39, 41, 42, 56, 72-96, 101, 103,
. . . . .104, 123, 162, 166, 170, 173, 181
Flatley, Elton 185
Fouroux, Jacques 84
Fox, Grant 163, 167, 173
Frost, Clare 46
Frost, Simon 23
Gabe, Rhys 73
Gadney, Bernard 53
Gale, Norman 80
Gallagher, John 125, 141
Gallaher, Dave 21, 51, 121, 122
Gibbs, Scott 20, 64, 67, 91
Gibson, Mike 38, 57, 83, 143, 144
Going, Sid 145, 159
Gould, Roger 41
Gray, Ken 56, 147, 159
Greenwood, Will 94, 193, 196
Gregan, George 118, 119, 165, 199
Guerassimoff, Jules 41
Guransescu, Andrei 42
Guscott, Jeremy 63, 66, 67, 88, 89, 143, 144, 154, 160
Hancock, Frank 21
Hands, David 82, 103
Hare, Dusty 84
Harmer, Eldred 112
Harris, Iestyn 21, 46
Harrison, Justin 199
Hart, John 118, 146, 149, 150
Hartley, Jack 46
Hastings, Gavin 64, 90, 141, 175, 178, 179
Heatlie, Barry 128
Heineken Cup 35, 37
Hendriks, Pieter 177
Henry, Graham 67, 68, 69, 198
Heslop, Nigel 175
Hignell, Alastair 23
Hill, Richard 34, 68, 88
Hipwell, John 116
Hodges, David 43, 44
Hodgkinson, Simon 88, 166
Hopwood, Doug 130

Horan, Tim 119, 144, 184
Howlet, Doug 194
Howley, Rob 35, 68, 103, 145
Hudson, 'Doc' 44
Humphreys, David 23, 189
International Olympic Committee 26
International Rugby Board 13, 14, 17, 22, 24, 25, 27, 32,
. . . . .36, 39, 42, 45, 46, 100, 102, 103, 105, 106, 137,
. . . . .170, 173, 176, 180, 186
Irvine, A 35, 141
Isherwood, Carol 45
Jackson, Peter .34, 78, 142
James, Carwyn 57, 58, 78, 144, 151
Japan 24, 25, 32, 36, 170, 177, 179, 182, 186
Jarrett, Keith 80
Jeeps, Dickie 55, 78, 145
Jenkins, Neil 32, 91, 163, 182
Jervey, Patty 44
Jimsheladze, Paliko 33
John Player Cup 22, 41
John, Barry 33, 34, 57, 58, 82, 145, 148, 151
Johnson, Martin 12, 37, 48, 66, 67, 89, 93-94, 100, 104,
. . . . .181, 185, 199
Joinel, Jean-Luc 85
Jones, Alan 117
Jones, Cliff 33
Jones, Ian 125, 148
Jones, Ken 53, 54, 78
Jones, Lewis 54
Jones, Michael 125, 149, 150, 173, 174
Jones, Robert .63, 171, 173
Joubert, Andre 133, 178
Kay, Ben 199
Keyes, Ralph 175
Kiernan, Michael 87
Kiernan, Tom 56, 80, 81
Kirk, David 124, 171, 173
Kirkpatrick, Ian 130, 148, 149
Kirwan, John 93, 125, 142, 170, 171, 173
Koch, Chris 130, 146
Koen, Louis 193
Koroduadua, Severo 171
Krige, Jacob 128
Kronfeld, J 150
Kruger, Ruben 178, 179
Kyle, Jackie 33, 36, 37, 54, 76, 77, 81, 145
Lacans, Pierre 85
Lacroix, Thierry .177, 178, 179
Lafond, Jean-Baptiste 175
Laidlaw, Chris 56, 145, 159
Laidlaw, Roy 86
Lamaison, Christophe .92, 184
Lane, Tim 183
Laporte, Bernard 94
Larder, Phil 11, 46
Larkham, Steve 183, 199
Lawton, Tommy 114, 147
Leicester 35, 37, 41, 98, 129, 152
Lenihan, Donal 62, 63, 67, 68, 174
Leonard, Jason 15, 21, 22, 146, 158, 198, 199
Leslie, David 86
Lewsey, Josh 11

Lions, British & Irish 21, 22, 30, 33-39, 41, 46, 47, 50-69,
. . . . .78, 104, 112, 114, 122, 123, 124, 128-130, 136,
. . . . .137, 141-155, 159, 163, 165
Llewellyn, Willie 73
Loane, Mark 41
Lochore, Brian .56, 123, 150, 159
Lomu, Jonah 12, 15, 31, 47, 177, 178, 179, 181, 185
Loubser, Johannes 128
Louw, Boy 53, 129
Louw, Fanie 129
Loveridge, Dave 145, 155
Lowe, Cyril 74, 75
Lyle, Dan 44
Lynagh, Michael . . .117, 118, 143, 145, 161, 163, 174, 175, 182
Magne, Olivier 191
Malan, Avril 55, 130
Malcolm, Syd 114
Mallett, Nick 133, 159, 183
Mandalo, Alfonso 180
Mandela, Nelson 40, 132, 176, 179
Marais, Hannes 147
Marshall, Justin 194
Martin, Allan 83
Martin, Greg 63
Mason, John 144, 171, 178
Maton, Leonard 12
McBride, William-John 33, 38, 55, 57, 58, 59, 61, 83,
. . . . .143, 145, 148, 153
McCarthy, Jim 76
McCrae, Ian 81
McDowell, S 146
McFarren, Krista 44
McGeehan, Ian 64, 65, 67, 109
McKay, Bill 76
McKee, Des 77
McLauchlan, I 146
McLean, Paul 41
McLeod, B 147
Mcleod, Hugh 38, 55
McLoughlin, Ray 21, 57
Meads, Colin 55, 56, 123, 145, 147, 148, 159
Meredith, Bryn 55, 147
Meredith, Courtenay 147
Mexted, M 150
Mias, Lucien 77, 78, 148
Millar, Sydney 55, 59, 185
Millenium Stadium 10, 94, 180, 201
Milliken, Dick 143, 144
Milne, Iain 86, 147
Monro, Charles John 120
Montgomery, Percy 133
Moody, Lewis 193
Moon, Brendan 41
Moore, Brian 64, 143, 170
Moran, Dr Herbert 113
Mordt, Ray 47
Morgan, Cliff 33, 34, 54, 78, 145
Morkel, Gerhard 129
Morkel, Jack 129
Morrison, Mark 51
Mortlock, Stirling 198
Mourie, Graham 124, 150

Mulder, Japie 179
Mulianina, Mils 198
Mullen, Karl 53, 76
Muller, Hennie 130, 150
Mullineaux, Reverend Matthew 50
Murariu, Florica 41
Murrayfield 39, 75-87, 93, 117, 141, 174, 180
Nathan, Waka 56, 159
Nel, Philip 129, 130
Nelson, Jimmy 75
Nepia, George .122, 141, 155
Nesbeck, Edmund Van 77
Nicholls, Gwyn 73
Norster, Robert 63
Ntamack, Emile 177
Obolensky, Prince 76
O'Brien, Des 76
O'Connell, Paul 95
O'Driscoll, Brian 69
Ofahengaue, Willie 149, 175
O'Gorman, John 115
Ondartes, Pascal 175
O'Reilly, Tony 54, 55
Orpen, Gerald 128
O'Shea, John 57
Osler, Bennie 129
Oxford University 14, 23, 44, 45, 133
Oxlee, Keith 55, 130
Paparemborde, Robert .84, 147
Partridge, Lt 'Birdie' 30
Pask, Alun 56
Paul, Henry 21, 46
Paxton, Ian 86, 171
Pichot, Agustin 31
Pienaar, Francois 40, 132, 179
Pilman, Cherry 74
Plessis, Felix du 130
Plessis, M du 150
Poidevin, Simon 117, 150
Pomathios, Michel 77
Porta, Hugo 144
Poulton-Palmer, Ronnie 74, 144
Prat, Jean 77, 149
Preez, Frik du 39, 148
Price, Graham 147
Probyn, Jeff 147
Pullin, J 147
Quesada, Gonzalo 184, 185
Quinnell, Scott 20, 67, 90, 91
Randt, Os Du 146, 151, 152
Ranfurly Shield 23, 155
Rees, Gareth 177, 184
Reid, Alex 128
Reid, Paddy 77
Richards, Dean 37, 48, 64, 150
Richards, Huw 172
Richards, Maurice 80
Richmond 43, 45, 74, 98, 99
Ringer, Paul 84
Rives, Jean-Pierre .84, 85, 150
Roberts, Gareth 171
Robertson, B 144

Robertson, Ian 184
Robinson, Jason 21, 46, 50, 185
Rodber, Tim 30
Rodriguez, E 146
Rodriguez, L 150
Roff, J 142
Rogers, Mat 46, 119
Roos, Paul 128
Rouse, Dan 182
Rowell, Jack 166, 178
Rowlands, Clive 17
Rugby Football Union 12, 15, 20, 24, 36, 43-45, 50, 72,
. . . . .74, 98-105, 120, 132, 160, 186
Rugby School 10, 12, 16, 27, 44
Rugby World Cup 25, 27, 31, 32, 39-50, 62, 65, 67, 69,
. . . . .72, 78, 88, 92, 105, 106, 112, 113, 118, 119, 124,
. . . . .125, 132-137, 140-155, 170-185
Rutherford, John 86, 145, 171
Sailor, Wendell 46, 119
Saint-Andre, Philippe 88, 140
Saracens 40, 46, 98, 99, 143, 158, 164
Sauan, Cristian 33
Scott, Bob 122, 141
Seddon, Bob 50
Sella, Phillipe 73, 85, 86, 143, 158
Senekal, Heino 182
Sevens 25, 30, 42, 136, 177
Sever, Hal 76
Sharpe, Nathan 199
Shaw, M 149
Shaw, Tony 41
Shelford, Wayne .150, 172
Six Nations 22, 32-35, 38, 42, 56, 67, 72, 73, 78, 80,
. . . . .92, 93, 104, 106, 107, 158, 162
Skinner, K 146
Skinner, Mickey 174
Skrela, Jean-Claude 84, 149
Skrimshire, Reg 51
Slack, Andrew 62, 117, 165
Slattery, Fergus 57, 59, 150, 153
Small, James 133
Smith, Arthur 55
Smith, Doug 57
Smith, George 21
Smith, Ian 75, 142
Smythe, Tom 51
Snow, Rod 177
Sole, David 90
Springboks 38-40, 47, 52-58, 115, 128-134, 148,
. . . . .151, 176-179
Stanger, Tony 90
Steele-Bodger, Mickey .31
Stegmann, Antonie 128
Stephenson, G 144
Stewart, Scott 177
Stoop, Adrian 21, 74
Storer, Dennis 44
Stransky, Joel 163, 176, 178, 179
Suasua, Darryl 45
Sydney University 11, 23, 112
Tait, Alan 67
Tanner, Haydn 53, 145

Taylor, John 82, 141, 149
Taylor, Simon 68
Teague, M 149
Teichmann, Gary .40, 133
Telfer, Jim 61, 62, 67, 86, 89
Thomas, Arthur 59
Thomas, Gareth 95
Thompson, Robin 54
Thompson, Steve 185
Thorburn, Paul 87, 172
Tincu, Marius 33
Tobias, Errol 131
Tofan, Ionut 33
Toit, Piet du 130, 147
Tomes, Alan 86
Towers, Cyril 114
Tremain, Kel 55, 56, 149, 159
Tri-Nations 24, 25, 40, 67, 72, 101, 106, 125, 133, 165
Triple Crown 12, 53, 62, 76, 80, 81, 84, 87, 88, 145
Tune, Ben 184
Twickenham 23, 30, 43-47, 73-79, 84, 85, 88, 90, 91,
. . . . .98, 101, 114, 115, 118, 122, 133, 150, 158,
. . . . .162, 173, 175, 181-184
Underwood, Rory 64, 65, 74, 88, 100, 140, 175
Underwood, Tony .89, 178
Valewai, Sailosi 136
Varsity Match 14, 23, 44, 45
Veitayaki, Joeli 182
Vellat, Edmond 75
Versfeld, Charles 128
Vickery, Phil 185, 193
Villiers, Henry de 128, 129
Waddell, Herbert 75
Wakefield, Wavell 52
Walker, Sam 53
Wallace, Billy 121, 122
Ward, Tony 61
Watkins, David 33
Webb Ellis, William 40, 173
Webb, Jonathan .166, 175
Weir, Doddie 178
Westhuizen, Joost van der 133, 145, 165, 179
Wheeler, Peter 37, 62, 82, 147, 152
Whetton, A 149
Whetton, Gary 172, 174
White, R 148
Wilkinson, Jonny 12, 21, 68, 94, 104, 105, 162, 166, 185,
. . . . .192, 196-97, 199
Williams, Bleddyn 54
Williams, Chester 177
Williams, JPR 17, 35, 57, 58, 60, 141
Williams, Rhys 55
Williams, Stanley 52
Willis, Rex 78
Wilson, Jeff 118, 140, 142, 165
Winterbottom, Peter 64, 150, 175
Wood, K 147, 189
Woodman, Trevor 185
Woodward, Clive .61, 69, 91, 93, 94, 185-186, 192, 196-197, 200
Young, Dai 63, 67

BIBLIOGRAPHY

The Encyclopedia of Rugby Union - Donald Sommerville - Aurum
The Daily Telegraph Chronicle of Rugby - Norman Barrett - Guinness
A History of Rugby Union Football - Chris Rea - Hamlyn
International Rugby Yearbook - Mick Cleary and John Griffiths - CollinsWillow
Encyclopedia of New Zealand Rugby - Rod Chester, Ron Palenski and Neville McMillan - Hodder Moa Beckett
The Australian Rugby Companion - Gordon Bray - Viking
Who's Who of Welsh International Players - John M Jenkins, Duncan Pierce and Timothy Auty - Bridge Books
Springbok Rugby, an illustrated History - Chris Greyvenstein - New Holland
Welsh International Matches - Howard Evans - Mainstream
Men in Black - Rod Chester, Ron Palenski and Neville McMillan - Hodder Moa Beckett
Australian Rugby - The Game and the Players - Jack Pollard - Ironbark
History of the British and Irish Lions - Clem Thomas - Mainstream
Wallaby Gold - Peter Jenkins - Random House Pty Ltd
Life at Number 10 - Neil Jenkins with Paul Rees - Mainstream
Lions and Falcons - Jonny Wilkinson - Headline
The Five Nations Story - David Hands - Tempus
The Who, When and Where of English International Rugby - Dan Stansfield - Stansfield Publishing
The Complete Book of the Rugby World Cup 1999 - Ian Robertson - Scottish Life

The pictures in this book
were provided courtesy of the following:

GETTY IMAGES,

101 Bayham Street, London NW1 0AG.

1

COLORSPORT

The Courtyard, Lynton Road, London N8 8SL.

1

Twickenham Stadium, Rugby Road, Twickenham TW1 1DZ.

Book design and artwork by Darren Roberts.

Series Editors Jules Gammond and Tim Exell.

Written by Paul Morgan.

Edited and Proofed by Alan Pearey.

Special thanks to Jed Smith and Michael Heatley.